TURBO SUCCESS

How to Reprogram
the Human Biocomputer

By the same author:

Talk and Grow Rich
Get out of Debt and into the Money
Escape from Where I Am
The Creep (Fiction)

British Library Cataloguing in Publication Data

Holland, Ron
Turbo Success: Or How to Reprogram the Human Biocomputer
I. Title
658.85

ISBN 1 85609 051 5

While the principles discussed and the details given in this book are the product of careful study, the author and publisher cannot in any way guarantee the suitability of recommendations made in this book for individual problems, and they shall not be under any legal liability of any kind in respect of or arising out of the form or contents of this book or any error therein, or the reliance of any person thereon.

TURBO SUCCESS

How to Reprogram
the Human Biocomputer

by
Ron G. Holland

LONDON
WITHERBY & CO LTD
32-36 Aylesbury Street
London EC1R 0ET

Published 1993

MONUMENT
SERIES

ISBN 1 85609 051 5

Published and Printed by
Witherby & Co Ltd
32-36 Aylesbury Street
London EC1R 0ET
Tel No: 071 251 5341
Fax No: 071 251 1296

**THIS BOOK IS DEDICATED TO THE MEMORY
OF
HOWARD HUGHES**

'Where applicable, reference to the male gender implies
also to the female gender and vice versa.'

Forewarning

Having been an entrepreneur since the age of fourteen I have had the privilege to come under the wing of a number of mentors, various wizards who have taught me the entrepreneurial skills of selling, marketing, persistence, courage, motivation and many other things that are very obscure but give one the character to enable one to do whatever it is that one does.

The mentor that I want to talk about was an affable, grey haired Irishman by the name of Seamus O'Rourke, who taught me much of what I know. The old boy had the gift of the gab and I'm sure he'd been blessed with the Blarney Stone. He had a wonderfully colourful way in which he used the English language. He told me over and over again that we are all ordinary people, but our mission is to do extraordinary things. "Life is a do-it-yourself project, and by golly, most people are really doing it to themselves!" he'd say. He told me I could do whatever it was that I wanted to do. He told me we all had the power within us to reach incredible heights way beyond our wildest possible dreams. He'd say, "If not you, who? If not not now, when?"

I know you have been searching for a success formula, and for a number of years you've probably been doing it to yourself. I'd like to throw out a challenge to you. I have presented to you a success philosophy that is the most powerful human development program in the world today. Bar none! It can take you beyond your wildest possible dreams. However, you must start using it! Reading alone will not be enough. This is an instruction manual for your shoulder top computer! You will have to carry out the instructions to the letter, in action, as well as in spirit. Will you begin to reprogram your biocomputer for success and start to accomplish for you and yours? If not you, who? If not now, when?

Ron G. Holland
1993

A PERSONAL MESSAGE FROM THE AUTHOR

Dear Reader,

I hope that you enjoy reading this book as much as I enjoyed writing it. However, as I always strive to be the best I possibly can be, I would appreciate your feedback on the information contained in this book.

In return I will keep you in touch with news of my seminars, new books and tapes and fabulous business opportunities which pass over my desk.

You can write to me at:
    Apprentice Millionaires Club
    BCM Box 8061
    London WC1N 3XX

Positively and Profitably
Ron G. Holland

Contents

1

Two Types of Success

As a young entrepreneur I used to sit on the top of "my hill" pondering over the secrets of success. I didn't have any money, but I was desperate to make some and make myself a name and a place in the world. Over a period of many years, I did make some money and I lost some money too. I always used to come back to "my hill" where I used to ponder, reflect and meditate. I always cogitated on the same question. Why is it that some people attain success very easily and others, no matter how hard they try, never accomplish their goals? After much meditation and research, as well as being a full time businessman actually working in the entrepreneurial field, many things were revealed to me. What I wanted to know about was success. I considered that I knew everything there was to know about failure! The discoveries that I made were nothing short of phenomenal and over the next few pages I will explain them all in detail.

My first major discovery was that there are two types of success. The first type of success, is what I would call intuitive success. I have come to the conclusion that a great many people have become eminently successful, intuitively. These people include sales people, politicians, actors, actresses, entrepreneurs and many others who have attained fabulous success, wealth and recognition and are from all walks of life. They don't really know what it is that they do to become successful and sustain that success. They just carry on doing whatever it is that they do and they become more successful. They go from success to success intuitively. Everything they touch seems to turn to gold.

The second type of success is what I would call conscious success. This type of success is for people like you and me, who have seen with their own eyes the abundance the world has to offer and would very much like to participate in some of the spoils. It just so happens, that to us, all the goodies always seem just out of reach, for ourselves, at least! We know what we want and we try hard to improve. We look toward self-help books, and we try to find a success formula that will work for us and help propel us onward and upward. We search for an action plan that will work. We keep trying different approaches, we keep buying self-help books, we never give up. Sometimes we gain a little ground! This is conscious success! And hard work it is too!

After over twenty years research into the human mind, particularly the teleological aspect (goal seeking) and research into high performance human behavior, as well as being a full time businessman, one thing became very obvious to me. This became obvious to me because I was in the field of making money and attaining success. What became obvious to me, may not have become obvious to someone who may have been studying the brain with, say, some other motive in mind. Someone who has been researching the brain with a view to finding the cure to an illness, or some other research may not have come up with the same conclusions that I have come up with. My total research has been geared up to one thing. One thing only. How we can best use our minds to accomplish success, make money, achieve happiness and reach our goals in the shortest space of time. These things I wanted to know! I spent over twenty years going into every aspect of the mind that would help me understand its innermost secrets. I made some remarkable discoveries.

The common denominator of all who achieve success intuitively is that they relax and visualize the future as they desire it. If you want to attain success consciously I suggest the sooner you practice relaxing and visualizing the future as you desire it, the sooner you too will attain success.

Michelangelo thought three dimensionally before he started to chip away at a piece of marble that he would produce a beautiful sculpture out of. Edward G. Robinson bought postcards of old masters and visualized exactly where he would hang them, before he actually owned them. Charlene Tilton, who played Lucy in Dallas, visualized getting the part for the job. Conrad Hilton used to play at hotels as a young boy, years before he became a hotelier. All my heroes, who I love talking about, Getty, Howard Hughes, Onassis, Edison and Winston Churchill all used to take time out to relax and visualize the future as they desired it. I can't stress this point too heavily. This is the golden thread that runs delicately through this whole work-book.

J. Paul Getty wrote a number of books and articles on making money. Those books were down to earth guides to help executives in business. Getty always maintained that there were no secrets to success or magical incantations to be uttered. Getty puts his philosophy down to hard work and good executive decisions. What I say is many people become successful intuitively and have the faculty of being able to visualize, very clearly, the future as they desire it. Something must have prompted Getty to entitle his autobiography, "As I See It".

Many of my students, who have completed my biocomputer seminars, have actually astonished themselves with the results they have attained. By persistently visualizing the future in a relaxed mode, many of them have attained goals, they at one time, thought impossible to reach. I too am amazed by some of the things that I have attained for myself through the constant and persistent use of relaxation and visualization. Before I walked on red hot coals on the Ray Martin Midday Show (while I was on tour in Australia) I visualized myself doing it. I also saw in my imagination, Ray Martin doing the walk with me, which he did. (That was marvellous publicity, we jammed the switchboards for over three hours!) I also visualized talking in front of a massive Amway audience and getting a standing ovation for my one hour biocomputer presentation. These, among many other things have happened to me. I wouldn't dream of doing a TV or radio interview without visualizing the complete thing in advance. I always visualize business transactions, in full, in my imagination before I enter into any agreements or contracts. The results speak for themselves! I have products selling in over thirty countries around the world, and it's all come out of a vision that I've had.

By relaxing and visualizing the things that I wanted to happen in the future, I have accomplished many things. I have absolute proof of how and why the technique works. I have absolute proof that every time I fail to use the technique, failure is inevitable. I know that if I keep up with the practice of relaxing and visualizing the future as I desire it, I will accomplish a lot more. I also know that if you make the start and persist with the practice, you too, will attain your wildest possible dreams. You will literally dream yourself to riches! I know the secret of success is to relax and visualize the future as you desire it. I imagine you will take a little more convincing, before you start in earnest. The following chapters are the background and the proof of how and why it works.

Biocomputer seminars are fun. They're designed to be. During the course of the weekend we have many coffee breaks to allow our batteries to recharge. During the course of the weekend everyone gets a chance to stand up and say his or her piece. That piece is to help gel and integrate the learning process. Over the years I have learnt more from my biocomputer students than I could ever hope to teach them. I hope you pick up a few pointers too. All the time be looking to see if any of their comments apply to you. Before we start a biocomputer seminar I ask my students what they want out of the weekend. It's interesting to see how they develop over the weekend, their skepticism falls away, their confidence rises, as a whole new world unfolds!

LIVE AT THE BIOCOMPUTER SEMINAR:

USA: Darlene, "I know exactly what I want out of this weekend. All my life I only ever get so far. I keep reaching plateaus. I never get ahead. I want to live an exciting lifestyle."

USA: Frederick, "I have a business that's in trouble. A friend told me to come here, he said it would change my life."

Ireland: Geoff, "I'm in the Multi Level Marketing business. I know lots of people who have made a lot of money. I want to join them."

Australia: Helen, "I want my business to succeed, I'm hanging in there at the moment, but only just."

USA: Bud, "I go to all the seminars, I heard this was a good one, that's why I'm here."

Poland: Andrew, "I want to understand more about the mind. I read 'Talk and Grow Rich' and I wanted to hear you speak."

Singapore: Madalyn, "I'm in an industry that is very tough and competitive. I need some tools to get me ahead of the competition."

USA: Nat, "I want to be a millionaire. I've come close on a number of occasions but I've always gone bust."

USA: Jack, "I've built up so many businesses, but I must have a business destruct mode that I go into. I recognize it but I just don't seem able to do anything about it."

USA: Ron, "I've only got one goal, everything!"

USA: Ross, "I want to be a successful career woman. I'm prepared to pay the price. I've read a lot and do a lot of seminars and workshops. Nothing really works for me except hard work."

Australia: Manfred, "I want my own plane and my own business. I can fly, it's my passion, but without a plane it's not much fun."

Australia: Polly, "I just want lots of fun. I want lots of money too!"

Australia: Malcolm, "I'm in the insurance industry and I don't get enough appointments."

USA: Marion, "I want to be happily married. I was abused as a child and I think that's screwing up my relationships."

Ireland: Sam, "I run my own company but it's like I'm on a treadmill. Stop the world and let me get off!"

England: Graham, "I read your book, I wanted to hear more of the same."

England: Sue, "I'm with him!"

USA: Roger, "I've got to do something different. I've had the same goals for over ten years and I haven't accomplished any of them."

USA: Allen, "I'm already successful but I want to go even higher."

USA: Freda, "I'm stuck in my career and I want to get out and move into the big money in another career, I just don't know how. I'm hoping you can tell me."

Singapore: Ng, "If I keep doing what I keep doing I'll end up going broke. I can't get motivated."

USA: Heath, "Last week two of my colleagues came here, I have never seen such a dramatic change in two people, ever."

USA: Wes, "I have one goal, I want a friend."

USA: Erick, "I want to get my invention manufactured and into the world market place. Once I've done that I'll be a millionaire."

USA: Fred, "I wanna be a millionaire!"

USA: Max, "I have a burning desire to be a Diamond in the Amway business and live the life style of a millionaire. Then I want to be a Double Diamond."

England: Karen, "I already have my own successful business but I want more security. It doesn't feel right at the moment."

Poland: Marek, "It wouldn't make sense going through life not knowing what my real potential was."

Spain: Michael, "Your reputation preceded you. You come highly recommended. My wife and I are looking forward to the weekend immensely."

England: Patrick, "I'm a seminar junkie. I buy all the books and tapes. Nothing has ever worked, I wish it would."

ZOOM SECRETS!

1. Recognize that many of the things that you may have done successfully in the past may have been intuitive.

2. Many people who have become successful intuitively have failed and never reached great heights again, because they didn't know what they did to get there in the first place.

3. Realize that you have fantastic control over your life and your environment, because you actually and factually know the secret of conscious success.

4. It helps tremendously if we really do know what creates successful outcomes rather than use hit and miss methods.

5. You know that conscious success depends on relaxing and visualizing the future as you desire it.

2

Biocomputer Hardware

Human. That's you and me! (Sometimes, the day after the night before, I feel more like a humanoid than a human, but that doesn't count!)

Bio. (Biological) Being such biologically.

Computer. One that computes. A programmable electronic device that can store, retrieve and process data.

Human Biocomputer. This is our 'shoulder top' computer that we carry around with us in our heads. It is biological by nature. It is programmable and it can store, retrieve and process data. It can do a lot more than that, if you take pains to program it properly, that's what this work-book is all about.

Program. A set of instructions for a computer.

To Program. To devise and enter such a set of instructions into a computer.

Only recently a radio interviewer introduced me as "arguably the best motivational speaker on the international circuit." Furthermore he went on to say "that it is his ability to teach using layman's terms that has won him accolades from many quarters, including industry and the motivational speaker circuit." What more can I say other that I wholeheartedly agree with the said interviewer. My point is this, yes, I do think I can explain something that is tremendously complex. But having said that, I would ask of you one thing. The golden thread that runs through this philosophy is delicate at the best of times and in many places tends to get lost altogether. Do not get alarmed as we progress. Read this instruction manual many times over. Read it from the front to the back, then from the back to the front.

Work it, use it, carry out the instructions. Reading alone will not be enough. Reading it once will not be enough. The biocomputer simply does not work like that, at all. Recognize this material for what it is. It is an instruction manual. It tells you to do many specific things. The golden thread by the way, lest you forget. Relax and visualize the future as you desire it! Never forget the golden thread!

Computers are capable of solving a variety of complex problems with astonishing rapidity. They correlate, compile and assimilate information. They solve problems because they have an input of information that provides output for solutions. They have stored information and instructions which are known as programs.

The human biocomputer is the most powerful and complex computer in the world. It can solve problems, create, process in words, pictures and feelings as well as think in black and white and color. It has input that will give certain output under certain conditions and it has stored instructions and programs. These programs will govern your output in the way of day to day habits and when the conditions are right will provide you output in the way of hunches or Eurekas! that will take you from mediocrity to genius.

I will very carefully take you through the components of the human biocomputer, particularly the components that affect the way we succeed or fail to reach our goals. First we will look at the hardware of the human biocomputer.

Before I embarked on the biocomputer project I asked many people, including a lot of children under the age of ten, what was the difference between the brain and the mind? Many of the people I questioned could not answer even in the most simplistic of terms. Many tried, but got lost half way through their explanations. Many people did not try at all. Others tried hard but got just too complicated. The answer I liked most of all was from a wonderful nine year old girl, Abra Pickford. She told me "the brain was the real thing, you know, all blood and guts actually inside the head. The mind was something completely intangible, you know, something really hard to talk about." I would say she summed it up very well, but I would like to expand just a little.

I would say that the brain was the hardware. The actual physical organ of blood and tissue that we carry around with us in our heads. The mind is the software, the programs that have been inserted into the neurons in our biocomputer.

The average brain weighs between 45 and 50 ounces and is an over abundance of hardware. To say we use five percent of our brains is in my opinion a gross over exaggeration. We should be so lucky! We don't even scratch the surface of the true potential of what we could do with our biocomputers, as you will shortly see.

The biocomputer consists of two hemispheres that

are joined together by a very substantial band of transmission fibres called the corpus callosum. We also have a reticular activating system, RAS for short. (Don't forget I keep all my knowledge about the brain, specifically directed to the goal seeking aspects).

This is the very same hardware, that, programmed correctly has put man on the moon, invented the electric light bulb, punk rock, the pet rock, pet dragon, computer, silicon chips, fish and chips, automobile, submarine, submarine sandwich and a hundred million other useful inventions or discoveries that makes the world such an exciting place to live in. This same hardware, when inserted with incorrect programs, has caused thousands of people to fail and has caused untold misery, unhappiness, depression and in some cases premature death.

The hardware also consists of over two hundred billion cells that are called neurons. These cells are all linked together by an absolutely amazing network of transmission fibres. Some of these cells have over ten thousand connections linking them to other cells. So intricate is the network of cells and transmission fibres that there is not a single cell in the whole network that cannot communicate with another cell anywhere in the entire network. A little bit like the global telephone system. If you have a phone, you can call any number in the world, providing you have the correct number.

So it is with the two hundred billion cells in your biocomputer, they can all communicate with each other, if they want to, and they sometimes do! Those cells are filled with chemicals, including potassium and sodium and they generate tiny amounts of electricity. (The biocomputer operates very efficiently on one tenth of a volt of electricity.) Whatever information you insert into those cells would be the software programs of your own personal biocomputer. Many of those programs incidentally are inserted for you when you are young and impressionable, by your parents, by your environment and by your teachers. Only when you grow up, some of us later rather than sooner, take control of our lives and start inserting biocomputer programs of our own choice. Unfortunately many of us never exercise this control, simply because we have never been made aware that we may do so. A lucky few stumble on the facts intuitively and insert the correct programs for success.

Earlier on I mentioned that we have an over abundance of hardware. I would also say the exact opposite is true for our software programs. We don't have anything like enough software programs to take us to success. Neither do we have programs of sufficient quality or length to take us to success. In fact most of the programs we have are very inadequate or complete failure programs. We mostly have the exact opposite of what we need to attain success. Because biocomputer programs have to be inserted, carefully, and usually over a period of time, we are drastically short of good software programs in our biocomputers. In other words we have tremendous problem solving and creativity within us, but because of the massive shortage of software programs we don't put the vast biocomputer to use.

Let us look closer at the hardware we carry around with us. Many people talk about lap top computers, I prefer talking about shoulder top computers! The hardware we have consists of two very powerful computers, the left and the right hemispheres. For normal right handed people the left computer is the language center and the right computer is the creativity. For many years our educational systems have been highly geared toward programming the left computer, in language. The three R's, reading and 'riting and 'rithmetic all go straight to the left computer. Everything I am telling you here is going straight into your left computer. This powerful computer processes in words. It functions like a digital computer. It is a language center, it is analytical, sequential, rational and calculative. It has many functions and is extremely powerful. This would be the base of your will power. For those of you who are already into affirmations, this is where they would be stored after you said them over and over again.

The right computer processes in pictures and can be likened to a kaleidoscope, in the fact that it can see the whole of things, and can change its pictures, if you like, just by the blinking of your eyes. It is superior at drawing geometric figures and it perceives on a Gestalt basis. For those of you who are already into visualizations, this is where they are created. The right computer processes in pictures, it is the imagination and the workshop of the mind.

If you said the word "cabbage" over and over again, that would be happening in your left computer. However, if you were to visualize the picture of a cabbage, that would be happening in your right computer. Why don't you do that right now? Say "cabbage" over and over again. That's it. Left computer! Now visualize the picture of a big leafy cabbage. That's right. That's the right computer coming into play! Just for fun, now visualize those cabbages growing and growing to ten feet high. Enormous cabbages! Now color them red, blue, even visualize a pink one. Make fields of them. This is your right computer, the creativity coming into play. You may be one who has a hard time trying to create pictures in your imagination, let alone play around with cabbages and make them different colors and ten feet high. That's because for many years our imaginations, our right computers (right hemispheres) have become dormant through lack of use. You see, as children we have this innate ability to visualize, but unfortunately, the more we get educated, the more it gets drummed out of us.

I distinctly remember my childhood days, when I used to daydream in the classroom. The teacher, Mr Wenham, time and time again used to bounce the blackboard eraser off my head and scream at me "Holland, stop counting sheep, stop gathering wool and come back down to earth." Before I knew which way up was up, the educational system had me completely full of words. My left computer was full of reading, 'riting and 'rithmetic. Full of academic things that I would find out sooner rather than later were not too much use to me in the dog eat dog world that we live in. Unfortunately my right computer was becoming more and more atrophied. It was only by accident that I discovered by thinking in pictures I was able to solve many of the business problems that I was faced with on a day-to-day basis.

The left computer processes in words and the right computer processes in pictures. These two very powerful computers are linked together by a very substantial band of transmission fibres called the corpus callosum. Both of the computers are extremely powerful and both the computers go about their processing in totally different ways.

One of the questions that I always ask at my biocomputer seminars is "How many of you have read self-help books, that tell you, if you have a bill that you want to get paid you must visualize the bill with PAID stamped right across it. Furthermore you must 'see' yourself going into the bank and paying the bill?" Many books say if you do this you'll very quickly find a way of paying the bill! I ask my students how many have read such statements in self-help books, most of them put up their hands. I then ask them what they thought when they read such statements. Most people who I have questioned on the subject thought it was bulldust. Most of the people who I questioned passed it off as gobbledegook and in doing so failed to carry out the instruction to the letter. The few who put the instruction into practise were not disappointed, because it works one hundred percent of the time.

It's a pity the authors of such books never went to the next step and explained why such a practice should work. The reason of course is simple. The authors of so many books don't know why certain things work, and why other certain things don't work. They have probably become successful intuitively. Most people don't know how the human biocomputer works. I do! I have devoted over twenty years of my life to finding out exactly how, why and what, for both our sakes!

I'll briefly explain here, the problem solving aspect of the biocomputer in this particular instance, but because there is so much to explain, I too, stand the risk of falling into the trap of over simplification. At this moment in time I think it will suffice to reiterate that the two computers are extremely powerful. The left computer processes in words and the right computer processes in pictures. When you visualize your bill with PAID stamped right across it, the right computer comes into play. It goes about solving this problem of paying the bill for you in a visual way, it attacks the problem from an artistic viewpoint, it is creative and comes up with ideas. If you were also affirming verbally, that your bill was PAID, you had, in effect, two very powerful computers, going about their problem solving in two totally different ways. The left computer would have tried to solve the problem of paying the bill for you using logic and language in a rational and calculative way. Both computers would have been working on the same problem, but by going about it in totally different ways.

The truly amazing thing about the human biocomputer is that the two computers are joined together by that substantial band of transmission fibres we talked about earlier, the corpus callosum. In other words, the pictures and the words (the two separate computers) communicate with each other via this link using electro chemical activity at phenomenal speeds. Each computer can solve the problem on its own using totally different methods of processing or they can confer and cross reference with each other to come up with a viable solution between them. This is just one of the remarkable features of the most powerful problem solving computer in the world.

If you think I'm being repetitive, I'm not. The fact of the matter is that it has come as quite a shock to you, that you've been carrying on all these years using your biocomputer as though you only had one computer, processing in words, then all of a sudden you hear ten times in ten minutes it's not like that at all!

You are slowly, but surely, beginning to see the magic of the biocomputer. You have just had an insight of what is yet to come, the real magic of the biocomputer, the most incredible and most vastly under utilized computer in the world!

LIVE AT THE BIOCOMPUTER SEMINAR:

Australia: Gary "My first thought is one of joy and happiness. I have learnt so much this weekend. A lot of things have gelled for me. My second thought is that I should be angry. I am fifty seven years old. I had never given any thought to what could be going on in my brain. I was never told at school. I was told how to do everything except think. I am seriously considering suing the authorities for millions of dollars. My concern now is that this material is made public and taught in schools."

Australia: Daniel "I really hadn't given it much thought but when you read books about visualization you don't really think that those pictures are actually forming in the neurons in the mind. For once in my life I can understand why we have to visualize. If you can understand why you have to do a thing, bridging the gap with faith disappears completely."

England: David "I have never thought of the brain being the hardware and the mind being the software, but intuitively, I have asked people what their program is."

England: Francis "I knew I was under utilizing my biocomputer. I didn't realize by how much, nor did I realize we could program more into it."

Poland: Pawel "Just the fact that I know we have two computers is enough to turn me on."

Ireland: Jimmy "I first started mind power seminars over ten years ago. This is the best one I've ever been to. When I first got involved they started talking about the brain having ten billion cells. Then I heard a hundred billion and now you're saying with the aid of the electron microscope they say it has two hundred billion. That's an incredible amount of storage, I don't understand why we don't use it."

England: Gerald "I can certainly see that we have a vast amount of hardware, it's just having the knowledge on how to use it."

USA: Patty "I've always had this feeling inside that I should be able to do something dynamic. I just don't know how, yet!"

USA: Kilmore "I know that having a burning desire is the key to success. I know it's all in the mind. I've had a few breakthroughs, but not enough."

USA: Eddie "I can make money for other people, but I've never been able to make a lot of money for myself."

Australia: George "I keep making the same mistakes over and over again."

USA: Trevor "Most human beings are walking around with a computer bigger and more sophisticated than any IBM main frame in existence, but it's not switched on."

USA: Murphy "If we could increase the amount we use our biocomputers by just five percent that would make us all millionaires."

England: Ken "My brain hurts!"

USA: Brian "I can actually feel the words and the pictures pulling me in opposite directions."

Poland: Krystle "I actually feel as though my brain has shut down."

Spain: Frederick "I actually feel that I have made hard work of my life. There have been certain times that I've zipped through. Only seldom."

USA: Herbert "I was told that if they were to build a computer that could do all of the work a human brain can do, it would have to be the size of the Empire State Building at the very least. To think of that and all I earn is $570 a week!"

ZOOM SECRETS!

1. You have a tremendous over abundance of hardware.

2. You have a vast shortage of software programs.

3. The left computer processes information in words.

4. The right computer processes information in pictures.

5. The two computers are joined together by a band of transmission fibres called the corpus callosum.

6. The two computers use totally different methods to solve problems.

7. Many of the individual cells have over ten thousand transmission fibres connecting them to other cells.

8. Every single cell is intricately interconnected directly or indirectly with every other cell in the biocomputer, giving each and every cell, access to information that is stored in the two hundred billion other cells.

3

Biocomputer Software

The content of the two hundred billion cells account for the many software programs that we have in our biocomputers. There are many ways that we can get programs inserted into our biocomputers and I think it is necessary to explain in detail how many of these programs arrive. As far as goal achievement is concerned we are all born with a blank slate. We are born with an over abundance of hardware, just waiting for programs to come along. Any programs, not enough programs, negative programs, programs from well meaning family and friends, programs from people who just haven't got a clue about how much damage they can do, just by being around you. That's the problem. If you don't take great pains to insert correct programs, you will end up with what ever other people decide to program you with.

There is a classic story in many psychology books about a young boy who was found on a farm in France, before the second world war. The boy was thought to be about twelve years old. He was caged up with the chickens. His finger nails had grown long and curved and he used to get up at dawn and squawk with the rest of the chickens. He was filthy dirty. Of course he could not speak a single word, the only sounds he made were clucking noises like those of the other chickens. To all intents and purposes he had been programmed like a chicken. It took many years of training and teaching before this boy could walk or talk or do anything useful.

I recall years ago, a friend of mind called me in to a school in Brixton, England, to meet a five year old child who could hardly talk and because of that had great difficulty relating to her school buddies. (I used to have a bank account in Brixton. I'd be making my deposits at one counter while invariably there would be someone else making a withdrawal at another counter, with a sawn-off shotgun!) After a while I told my friend that I wanted a meeting with the child's parents. I was informed that the child was from a one parent family. In due course I met the child's mother. On questioning the child's mother I very quickly learnt that the mother had not bothered to talk to the child in it's first five years of upbringing. The mother had been waiting for the child to start talking to her! This is just a case of an ignorant woman not realizing that she had to constantly talk to her baby and implant a program into the baby's biocomputer. Once the program had been there, the baby would have started to talk.

All computers rapidly perform complex calculations, but in order to do so they must have programs. Computers all operate on an input equals output basis, the human biocomputer is no different.

I am not labouring the point when I detail out some more of the software programs that we may or may not have. Once you realize that we all have many programs and that for every function we carry out we must have an appropriate program in place. Once you take this on board, it will turn out to be one of your big breakthroughs, a real turning point in your life.

Incidentally, the output of a conventional computer will either come up on a screen (VDU) or will be printed out on paper, once the calculations or processing has been done. The output of the human biocomputer is in the form of all the habits that we have. Practically everything we do is a result of habit, and a result of what we had programmed into our biocomputers. The other output of the human biocomputer will be in the form of Eurekas! which are hunches and guidance. The more correctly you program your biocomputer the more delighted you will be with your output. Never forget, input equals output!

If you were born in France and heard French voices around you all the time, while you were growing up, you would end up speaking French. If you were born in Germany and heard German voices, everyday, day in and day out, you would end up speaking German. If you were born in the USA or Britain or Australia, and heard English voices when you were growing up, by hook or by crook, you'd have ended up speaking English. Input equals output.

One of the amazing features about the bio-computer is that it has this massive over abundance of hardware. Children who have been brought up in multi-lingual families have no problem at all learning two, three or even four languages at the same time and manage, seemingly quite easily, to separate them and use the appropriate language at the correct time.

I love to ask my biocomputer audiences, "How many of you can speak Chinese?" No one puts up their hand. "OK, How many of you think Chinese is difficult?" All the hands go up. Everyone thinks that Chinese is difficult. I always make my students laugh when I tell them, "Chinese isn't difficult, there are over a billion people in China, and all of them speak Chinese, no problem at all!"

You see it's that repetition, repetition, repetition, that puts even the most complex program into the human biocomputer. A little Chinese boy, hearing the Chinese language over and over again, day in and day out is going to get that program into his biocomputer whether he likes it or not. (Make a note of the little Chinese boy, he's a mate of mine and I'll be talking about him quite a lot!)

It is essential that you realize the neurons in the brain are just waiting for appropriate programs to be inserted. For every learning experience you go through, individual cells will link together and form a neuron chain. A neuron chain is called a ganglia. I call these ganglia biocomputer programs.

Let's take a look at how we create a ganglia, a neuron chain, a biocomputer program, for the relatively simple task of driving an auto. You have your first driving lesson and you start to implant the necessary information into the neurons in your biocomputer. You have a second lesson, maybe a week after the first lesson. You learn more of the skills of driving an auto. You have started to form a neuron chain, a ganglia, a biocomputer program. The information of learning how to drive is stored in the individual cells in the electro chemicals. The following week you have another lesson, the neuron chain is forming, the biocomputer program is taking shape. The individual neurons all join up and link together as they recognize their brothers and sisters and aunts and uncles. (Professor Roger Sperry says "neurons acquire individual identification tags, molecular in nature.") In other words neurons can recognize other neurons that have similar knowledge in them, although this may come into the biocomputer over a period of time. (When you were at school, you had weekly lessons on a number of various subjects, but the information always linked up with any other information that you had on the subject.) Next week you have yet another lesson and now the biocomputer program is really taking shape. All the individual neurons link up with one another and form a ganglia. By the time you have had, say, ten or fifteen lessons, you have sufficient knowledge in the neurons to allow you to drive competently. In other words you have a complete biocomputer program that allows you to carry out the task of driving proficiently. The more driving you do, the more practice you get, the better the biocomputer program and the better your driving will become. You are now ready to take your test. If you fail your test, it simply means that you didn't have a long enough ganglia (biocomputer program) to enable you to carry out the task proficiently. You can overcome this simply by adding to your store of knowledge, by taking more driving lessons and increasing the amount of information that you have in your biocomputer.

Another amazing fact about complete bio-computer programs is once you have impregnated those electro chemicals with a sufficient program, you never have to think about that program again. You run on that track automatically. Even the most sophisticated programs, once inserted correctly, you run on them without even thinking about them.

I have driven from one side of London to the other in peak hour traffic and suddenly arrived at my destination and found myself wondering how I got there. For a single moment I had never thought consciously about any one of the hundreds of gear changes I must have made or how hard to depress the gas or brake pedal. I never thought once of the thousand death defying maneuvers that one makes in an hours' trip across London in the rush hour. It is important for you to realize once you have programs, even very sophisticated programs, like driving or Chinese, in the biocomputer, you run on the track automatically without ever having to think about them.

When you wake up in the morning you don't have to think whether you should speak Chinese or French or German. You have a program in the biocomputer and you run on it automatically. Without any thought about what to do or how to do it, you start speaking English.

I recall, when I was a child, for many hours, I had to practice, by rote, the mathematical tables. I can now recall that ten eights are eighty and seven sevens are forty nine and six threes are eighteen without even thinking about it. The program is well and truly in the biocomputer. I have an automatic track to run on.

It's important to realize how we come to gain so many of the programs that we have inserted into our biocomputers. It is equally important to realize that once we have impregnated the electro chemicals in the neurons and formed a substantial biocomputer program, we will run on that track whether we want to or not, whether we like it or not. It is completely automatic.

Many of the programs that you have in your biocomputer will simply be there as a result of the environment where you were brought up as a child. For arguments sake, you have already seen, that your program will be English. Conversely speaking, if you were born in India the chances are that you were brought up under the Hindu faith and if you were born in Israel you were brought up under the Jewish faith. My point here is not to say which is right or wrong, but merely to point out how we get certain programs inserted into our biocomputers.

Many programs arrive in our biocomputers as a result of our parents, our environments, our educations, our religious backgrounds, our friends and later in life, if we care to exercise the control over the input into our biocomputers, ourselves.

A frightening fact is that many folk go through their entire lives with only the programs their parents and upbringing have inserted into their biocomputers. Then they try to run happy and successful lives with quite the inappropriate programs in their biocomputers and go through life being totally disappointed and unsatisfied and in many cases miserable and unhappy. In other words they have been very ill equipped for the tasks that they have set for themselves. Many people just exist on the programs they had inserted during their formative years, never adding any biocomputer programs by further self-education, reading, study, travel, seminars, goals, repetition, nothing. Many of my students wonder why they go through life struggling and barely surviving. This program that you are now getting into is the end of survival and the beginning of living! I guarantee it!

You will of course realize that not all of the programs we have in our biocomputers are good, beneficial or even true. Many of them are there due to other peoples beliefs. We quite possibly have programs that are actually counter-productive to the goals that we have set for ourselves, as we have started to observe the world around us and started to select for ourselves a few of life's goodies and luxuries that we desire. Once you have got the idea that biocomputer programs are very deep seated and that you run on these programs automatically, you will immediately see why you have had such a hard job actually attaining those goodies and luxuries that you have selected for yourself. Indeed, life may have been tough on you. You may have wondered if you really do have a self-destruct program or a subconscious death wish program or a business destruct mode. Many of us have powerful self-defeating programs that have cropped up time and time again in our lives, many times to rob us of victory and spoils just as they come into sight.

Lots of businessmen start up businesses and have them collapse after three years. Others start relationships to have these break down after five years. Some men and women are always short of money, I mean always!

If the foregoing applies to you don't worry, join the club! You're lucky to be alive. Many people have such negative programs in their biocomputers that they really do commit suicide. Subconscious suicide is far more prevalent than you realize, so is subconscious sabotage of ones own business dealings and personal relationships. So much so, I have dedicated a complete chapter to failure programs. I consider these to be just as important as success programs. At least, it is important that you recognize your failure programs. It helps to recognize them in order to be able to counteract them` and insert the appropriate success programs that will overcome the negativity and allow you to reach your goal.

Later on we will be looking at overcoming even the most negative programs, and very quickly too! In the mean time, however, we must delve deeper into programs that exist in our biocomputers.

Let's take a simple situation that happens all the time. A young lad is in his father's hobby shop and he's playing around with some saws, hammers and nails. The father enthuses the lad along and encourages him to bang nails in and saw a plank of wood. Although the young lad does not have the skill in his hands, he is encouraged, and the next time in the hobby shop he does a little more. Over a period of years, with his father's constant encouragement, he turns into a self-reliant young man who goes out into the big wide world full of confidence and courage and brimming over with self-esteem. The program inserted into this lad's biocomputer was one of self-reliance, confidence, a go-for-it attitude, encouraged by his father. Input equals output.

Let's take a similar scenario, again in the father's hobby shop, a young boy is playing around with some tools and some nails. This time the father clips the youngster around the ear and screams at the top of his angry voice "Stop messing around and getting under my feet, you'll never be any good at anything." You can easily see the negative program being inserted into this child's biocomputer. This young lad will go through life with an inferiority complex. Once again the input will express itself in output.

Here I want you to take a few notes. The first one we have already mentioned, but no harm will come by hammering the point home, in actual fact that is the exact way in which the biocomputer takes on board a program. So the first point: Input equals output. The second point, is that we should all reflect on our upbringings, our environments, our teachings and our backgrounds to see what negative programs have been inserted into our biocomputers during our formative years. The third point, and I'll go into much greater detail at a later stage, is the case where the youngster was chastised. Don't be misled into thinking that if his father only did this once, the child would not get a permanent program in his biocomputer. I deliberately pointed out that the father screamed at the child. If the father was emotional and angry and the child was emotional at the same time, it is highly likely that the child took this program on board, hearing it just once! More on this later, but make a note right now, that the way to reprogram the biocomputer very quickly is not just through repetition but by adding emotion. Emotion is the key to reprogramming the biocomputer quickly!

It is extremely important for you to realize just how deeply ingrained these programs are. Once the program is in the electro chemicals in the neurons you will run on that track whether you like it or not.

Probe now and over a period of time. Who programmed you and with what? Were you ever a recipient of any of the following negative programs? Perhaps you can recall, what was inserted into your own biocomputer. "You'll never be as good as your sister/brother" or "You'll never amount to anything" or "You never start anything you finish" or what about this one, "You'll end up in jail!" maybe you had the "You're a brat" or the "You're useless!" treatment. Have a look at your programs right now and as we develop, take more and more notes. Probe deeply because what has been holding you back, is still a very part of you, deeply imbedded in electro chemicals of the neurons that make up your biocomputer programs.

Some programs can be very complicated and disturbing as L. Kubie discovered in a patient's biocomputer, "Mother has abandoned baby, run to Daddy; Daddy beats me and leaves; Mommy comforts me and leaves; Daddy loves me and hurts me and leaves; Run to Mommy. Mommy has my sister, loves her, abandons me: run to Daddy; Daddy hurts. Daddy leaves. Run to Mommy. Mommy has my sister, loves her, abandons me: run to Daddy; Daddy hurts. Daddy leaves. Run to Mommy. Mommy leaves... Mother has abandoned baby", etc etc etc. This was a program the patient carried into adulthood.

By now you should be seeing a clear pattern emerge. You should see, by now, that for everything that we do, we must have an appropriate program in our biocomputer. You will realize that if you can drive it's because you have an 'I can drive' program in your biocomputer. If you can speak French, it's only because you created that 'I can speak French' neuron chain, slowly but surely, until it formed into a complete ganglia, which is a program in your biocomputer. If you can't drive or can't speak French it is solely because you don't have the appropriate programs in your biocomputer.

If you can weld or sew or repair auto engines it is solely because you have those programs in your biocomputer. You have seen there are many ways we can get programs inserted into our biocomputers. Many have been inserted by our parents, our teachers and our friends. As we were growing up the culture and environment automatically inserted programs into our biocomputers. These are extremely powerful programs that have impregnated the electro chemicals in the neurons and are tracks we run on automatically.

Whether the programs that you have had inserted into your biocomputer are desirable or even compatible with the goals you have set yourself remains to be seen. If you have had difficulty reaching your goals and I suspect that you have, maybe the programs that you have in your biocomputer are working in direct opposition to yourself.

You can probe deeper and deeper and have a look at some more of the programs that may have been unwittingly inserted into your biocomputer.

Did your parents tell you, "Don't make money your God!" did they often say, "we haven't got two pennies to rub together" or, "I don't know how we're going to make ends meet!" maybe they said, "I can't cope" or, "I wish I was dead!" yes, you'd be surprised what parents say over and over again in front of their children.

You may have witnessed your parents argue all the time. You may have seen your parents relationship break down. You may have (and more likely have, than have not) witnessed all sorts of things that have become part of your own biocomputer programs. Now is the time to become aware. Look inward. Look to the past. Look at your programs.

The programs that you have in your biocomputer control everything that you do. Ninety nine point nine percent of what you do is governed by habit, which is the end result of your biocomputer input.

As a child were you encouraged to be punctual, successful, pleasant, respectful, industrious, creative, useful, a fighter, a winner, or were you brought up in an environment where loosing, tardiness, laziness, scrimping and scraping was just a way of life? Any old input will begat any old output. Maybe now you are beginning to realize why you may have experienced difficulties in accomplishing even the simplest goals.

The problem that we face is because our biocomputer output is habit, we very rarely give any serious thought to the power that controls us. Very rarely when we fail to close a deal do we put it down to a biocomputer program, but it is. Many times you have gone to ask that special girl out for a date but changed your mind at the last moment, that too, was due to being controlled by a biocomputer program. How many times have you put off things until tomorrow, that should have been done last week? And just how many times do we need to fail in business before we become a success? These things are governed by one thing and one thing only, our biocomputer programs, that produce habits that have become so subtle and insidious, we never even notice them.

One of the things that I have noticed as I have travelled across the world is that there is a vast difference in individuals' biocomputer programs. That's what makes us all different. You are, literally, what you have in your biocomputer programs. Although there are vast differences in our personal programs, on the whole I noticed that there was a huge amount of negativity around that was ending up as programs in various biocomputers. That's perhaps why historically, there are more failures than successes. All this has to change, we really do live in a high-tech society where we know that input equals output.

The time has come for us to insert programs into our biocomputers that will take us to the goals we have set for ourselves regardless of the programming that we may or may not have received during our formative years.

We will insert programs that will take you to the pinnacle of success, to the top of the highest mountain, or whatever you have set your sights on. But even more important, we will insert programs that will give you sustained success, programs that will keep you moving onward and upward for ever!

LIVE AT THE BIOCOMPUTER SEMINAR:

USA: Barry, "One thing that I've come to grips with this weekend is the vast range of programs that I have been trying to run on are just no good at all for the job that I'm trying to do. No wonder I feel as though everything I do is hard work. At times I feel as though I'm hitting my head against a brick wall. I can quite easily see that by inserting the correct programs for the job I will literally be pulled toward my goal."

USA: Patricia, "I have to confess that I'd never considered all our knowledge to be software. Now I have come to grips with it I can see the implications are vast. I shall be making sure I analyze myself to see what negative programs have been inserted into me since childhood and I shall be taking great pains to insert programs of my choice, starting from tomorrow. I consider that I have made a quantum leap this weekend, I forget when I was last so excited about something!"

USA: Marvin, "I'm almost ashamed to admit it, but I have not inserted any new programs into my biocomputer since I passed my driving test about fifteen years ago. I have been running on the same old programs. I didn't know that you could change them."

Australia: Pat, "I have really got the message that everything I do is a habit. I smoke as a result of habit. I'm always late as a result of habit. I only earn enough money as a result of habit. I go for a drink every Friday night as a matter of habit. What I didn't realize is those habits are programs in my biocomputer and that they can be changed. That throws a whole new light on things. I think I'll get me a wife!"

Singapore: Nelson, "It never dawned on me that your habits are completely governed by your programs. Just a simple one I remember was, 'wash your hands after going to the bathroom.' My parents must have told me that hundreds of times. Now I do it automatically, I even tell my children the same thing. The potential for telling yourself to do various things is huge."

USA: Jenny, "To see that people from different countries speak different languages is a beautiful way to explain to people input equals output, I wonder why no one has ever thought of it before!"

USA: Rose, "I joined my company last spring and there was a trip to Canada for top sales persons. I programmed and I got the trip. That was the first time I have ever really wanted something and actually got it."

USA: Harry, "I have never taken the trouble to look at my programs in the past. For all I know I may have been walking around like an automaton with someone else's programs in."

England: Chris, "You're either a success or a failure all according to the programs you insert in your biocomputer."

England: Richard, "I never equated learning with installing biocomputer programs."

USA: Marty, "I must have told myself I'm fat a million times.. No more."

Poland: Michael, "You are what you are because of your biocomputer programs."

USA: Neil, "I didn't know that once you have a program in the biocomputer you run on it automatically."

USA: Boyd, "It comes as a shock to the system that everything we do is just a habit. And that those habits are biocomputer programs that can be changed."

USA: Dudley, "I didn't realize that the words we use over and over again in our heads could have such a strong influence over our lives."

USA: Scott, "Because I have an inferiority complex I always sell myself short. I always end up with fat women and no money."

England: Dez, "All my programs are working against each other."

England: Graham, "I've been telling myself for years that I can't speak French. Now I know it's just a program, I'm going to start learning it immediately."

USA: Allen, "The thing that has frightened me is that I haven't bothered to put any new programs in."

USA: Alex, "I've been telling myself I can't travel for years. Now I know I can."

USA: Bill, "Most of my programming has been negative self-talk from within."

ZOOM SECRETS!

1. The individual neurons contain electro chemicals that contain the information in your biocomputer programs.

2. Many of the programs that we have were inadvertently inserted by our parents, our environment and our teachers.

3. Many of the programs we have work in exact opposition to the goals we have set ourselves.

4. Whatever you program into your biocomputer will become output.

5. Many people try to run happy and successful lives with the programs they had inserted in their formative years, although these may have no bearing whatsoever on the goals that they are trying to accomplish.

6. The output of the human biocomputer comes in the form of our habits.

7. Properly programmed we will also receive output in the way of hunches and inspiration, Eurekas!

8. With the proper programs in place, we will also be able to go beyond the point where we usually fail.

4

The Secret of Success

You probably realize that I have taken great pains to explain things in great detail to give you a good background into biocomputers and their programs. The reason why I have done so is simple. What I am about to reveal to you is what I would call the 'secret of success'. However it would have been no good to you knowing the 'secret of success' if you didn't know how the biocomputer works.

The greatest 'secret of success' is this: **The human biocomputer cannot tell the difference between a real experience and a vividly imagined experience!!!**

The implications of that statement are vast. The implications are awesome! This one secret, if you use it, will take you to your goals in the shortest space of time. This was the turning point of my life. Let it be the turning point of yours!

What in effect it means, in simple terms, is that we can insert any programs we like into our biocomputers, simply by vividly imagining whatever it is that we want to achieve, or what we want to become. Not only can we reprogram our biocomputers like this, but it is absolutely essential that we do.

It is relatively easy to see that a downhill skier or racing car driver has to have the program in his biocomputer before the event takes place. The downhill skier will learn gradually on practice runs before he goes in for a major event. When he does go in for a major event he does not think about what he has to do in order to win. He just ski's! In actual fact if he starts to think consciously about what he is doing, that is just about the time when he's most likely to have an accident and break a leg. The racing car driver is the same. He learns the skills of the sport in slower autos and on slower tracks. Only when he has a complete program in his biocomputer does he take on the fast autos and the fast tracks. Again, he has the program deeply imbedded in the electro chemicals of his biocomputer program. He runs on that track automatically on race day. If he slips into thinking mode, that is just about the time he is likely to have an accident, spin off, kill himself, or worse, kill someone else.

From the foregoing I hope to illustrate how important it is for the salesman or businessman to have a complete program in his biocomputer before the event, sale or deal takes place.

It took me many years to realize just how important it was to visualize being a millionaire, closing deals, making money, 'seeing' myself as a success. Of course I had read about visualization in all the books and even in the bible it says "Through lack of vision my people perish," however no one took the time out to explain why we must visualize our goals before they happen.

Napoleon visualized battle fields and battles before he ever saw a battlefield in real life. By visualizing, he put a program into his biocomputer and that became the track that he ran on in his real life. Aristotle Onassis, one of my heroes, before he used to enter into any business deal, he used to play what he would call 'war games'. He used to have all his functionaries sit around a table. He used to set the scene as though these were the people he would be doing a real deal with. He then used to go over the deal in great detail, over all the objections and why the deal couldn't be done this way or that. What the price would be, what would be the best scenario and what would be the worst scenario. He would go over every aspect of the deal, sometimes playing his "war games" for twelve hours at a stretch. Then he would reverse the roles of the functionaries and get them to act out different parts to see if different objections may come up. Of course what Onassis was doing was putting programs into his biocomputer and this would be the track that he would run on when the real deal was taking place.

The human biocomputer cannot tell the difference between a real experience and a vividly imagined experience. Therefore you must vividly imagine the future as you desire it in order to insert the program into your biocomputer. The way to do this is by visualizing intently the things you want to happen for yourself. If role playing and war games help you create the correct programs in your biocomputer and give you a correct track to run upon, use them for all you're worth.

I recall back in 1980 when the Americans were taken hostage in Iran. Many of them were captive for a number of months and quite a few of those captives taught themselves how to type by making up a cardboard mock up of a typewriter keyboard. I taught myself to type by sitting in a chair and visualizing over and over again that I could type. I put a program into my biocomputer, that was the track that I ran on.

Earlier on I was talking about intuitively successful people, they put success programs into their biocomputers without even realizing what they were doing. They always have a good picture of where they are going in life. They relax and visualize the future as they desire it. They do that intuitively and by doing it they put programs into their biocomputers that become tracks that they run on, automatically.

History is full of people who reached wonderful heights of achievement and then for one reason or another have failed. A lot of these people have never been able to get to the top again because they didn't realize what they were doing in the first place to accomplish the successes that they found so readily. These people really had lost their vision!

The most important thing, is that we do know, what it is, that will take you to success beyond your wildest possible dreams. We know that before the reality takes place you have to have the program in your biocomputer to allow the reality to happen.

We can put any programs we need into our biocomputers to achieve the goals we have set for ourselves. We can insert any program we desire into our biocomputer in many ways other than doing the real thing. All have the same result in the fact they give us a permanent and automatic track to run on. The input will provide the output. We can visualize ourselves being successful salesmen, or being millionaires, or owning Rolls Royces. We can role play various success scenarios that we would like to happen, thereby creating a program in our biocomputers which will give us a permanent track to run on. Not only can we do these things but it is imperative that we do so. I would go one step further. Until you do visualize the things you want to happen you are doomed to fail. You are doomed to mediocrity. You are doomed to poverty.

Many people think that the most important thing that Neil Armstrong said when he landed on the moon was "A giant step for mankind" I think the most important thing he said when he landed on the moon, was "Just like it was in practice!" You see a lot of people don't realize he practised that maneuver right here, down on the ground, thousands of times, before he ever did it on the surface of the moon. What he was doing of course was implanting the program into his biocomputer before the event actually took place.

Before I do a seminar I always visualize the complete scenario before the real performance. I put the biocomputer program in before the event takes place. Before I travel off to a foreign country, I visualize it before I even leave my own living room. I insert a program into my biocomputer before the plane takes off. Before I enter into a business deal I visualize it, in advance. I give myself a permanent track to run on. The outcome is what I want it to be, because of the way I programmed my biocomputer. Input equals output, lest you forget!

At my biocomputer seminars I have my audience in fits of laughter. I say "Do you think they send 747 pilots up into the skies learning how to fly. Do you think they send them up with learner plates on?" The answer is "Of course they don't!" 747 pilots are trained down on the ground, in massive simulators. The pilots play pretend flying in these simulators for hundreds of hours, practising all the things that can go wrong. He practises take-offs and landings, over and over again. He builds up a permanent program in his biocomputer and that provides a track for him to run on. Only when he has a complete program in his biocomputer is he allowed to take a real 747 up into the sky, without learner plates on!

I personally have a vast amount of skills that I like to use. Skills like public speaking, firewalking, welding, driving fast, typing, writing and many other skills that I have taught myself through the art and practise of visualization. By putting those programs into my biocomputer, just by visualizing the fact that I could do it, enabled me to carry out those tasks in reality.

It's important for you to make a note of the formula. The human biocomputer cannot tell the difference between a real experience and a vividly imagined experience. By visualizing over and over again, that you are a success, that you are a millionaire, a super salesperson or a successful public speaker, (Before I ever became a public speaker I used to practice in my living room, in front of thirty empty chairs, over and over again, I gave those chairs the complete works, jokes and all!) you put the programs into the biocomputer, that in your real life, you will run on automatically.

Alfred Hitchcock was once asked if he enjoyed making movies. He replied that he hated it. The reason why he hated it was simple. It was because he had already run the film over and over again in his imagination before he made the actual film. Steven Speilberg does the same thing for his epic films. He has a card in front of him for every stage of the film. He knows what each part of the movie looks like before the filming actually begins.

Irvin Feld who was in charge of Ringling Bros and Barnum and Bailey Circus once commented, "You know the most amazing thing about my dreams is that they all came totally true!"

You should begin to see a pattern unfold. You should be 'seeing' yourself over and over again, as a millionaire or as an Amway Diamond or as a Direct Distributor or as a first-class salesperson or as whatever it is you personally want to be or want out of life.

The idea behind visualization is simple. You create a ganglia, which is a chain of neurons that have linked together. These are full of electro chemicals. When you have sufficient information in the neurons that is a complete program for your biocomputer, which in turn, is a permanent track for you to run on. The input will equal the output. Once you have a complete program in your biocomputer you will start getting beneficial output. That output will first appear in the form of correct habits. The second type of output will appear in the form of Eurekas! and hunches and guidance. The third type of output will be described in detail in a subsequent chapter, this is the output that will get you beyond the point where you usually fail.

The high achiever will use his imaginative faculty to take him to the top. Once he's discovered it, he will never stop using it because it is such a tremendous tool. The underachiever will use the same faculty to create three dimensional excuses.

I want to make a profound statement: I have occasionally met the odd editor who comes across my work and says it's too repetitive. Once in a blue moon I come across a reader who says it's too repetitive. However, I never come across a single one of my biocomputer students who says my material is too repetitive.

I'll tell you why. Most people have read self-help books that go heavily into visualization in one form or another. Most readers of these books have failed to take it on board and go away failing to actually put visualization into practise. The reason why they failed to do it was the author failed to bring the point home strongly enough about why visualization was so important and what it actually accomplished. If you think what you have learnt so far is repetitive you are making a grave mistake. This is exactly how the biocomputer operates and you won't be surprised when I tell you this instruction manual has to be read many many times, possibly hundreds of times before a program will be inserted into your biocomputer. Reading it once will have no effect whatsoever. Let's come back to the little Chinese boy learning Chinese. If he had heard that language just once, would that have created a program in his biocomputer? It most certainly would not! So not only am I going to ask you to read this instruction manual over and over again and not stop, but I am also going to instruct you to read it aloud onto an audio cassette tape and play the whole thing over and over and over again while you are driving your auto. Further I am going to instruct you to actually take time out, at least twice a day, to vividly imagine the things that you want to happen in your life. Once you have taken all this on board you can tell me you know a little about the subject of repetition. Until then, you're just going through the motions!

LIVE AT THE BIOCOMPUTER SEMINAR:

USA: John, "I live over at Huntington Beach and I want to share a story with you about Howard Hughes. After the war Hughes had a massive aircraft factory that was laying idle. The overheads were colossal and all of his aides advised him to close the place up and sell it out. Hughes ignored them and he eventually won a multi million dollar contract to build civilian airplanes. Now coming to the second part of the story, he built the Spruce Goose, the largest airplane in the world. But it never flew. In actual fact it flew only one mile and that was with Howard Hughes at the controls himself. He 'saw' the contract for the planes coming in, but he couldn't 'see' the Spruce Goose ever flying. It's still at Long Beach now, you should check it out!"

England: Gary, "Before I bought my house I used to go every night and sit outside in my car, looking at it. One night I was visualizing what improvements I'd make and I 'saw' in my imagination a way of adding an additional two bedrooms and giving the property the look of a hacienda. This I did when I bought the house, and I have increased it's value by over thirty grand. I have now started to look around for other properties."

Australia: Marcia, "I used to stand for hours on end looking at the red Porsches in the showroom in Melbourne, where I come from. One day a voice popped into my head and showed me the way I could afford to buy one."

England: Martin, "Years ago well before I could afford a brand new car I decided to build a garage at home for it. I didn't have the money for the car, but I built the garage anyway. All the time I was building the garage I could 'see' the new car in my imagination. The day I finished the garage I had enough money to buy the car with. I paid cash for it. A brand new Volkswagen. I didn't even realize what I was doing."

Singapore: Sing, "I know what you mean about thinking in pictures. If you had a television set with just the words playing it wouldn't be operating at fifty percent efficiency it would only be operating at maybe one percent. However when you switch the pictures on as well, that's when things really begin to happen."

USA: Kathy, "I lost over thirty pounds in weight and didn't put it back on either. I cut out the picture of a model and stuck my face over hers so I could actually 'see' what I looked like. I placed this on the refrigerator door. It worked for me."

Ireland: Joel, "I had heard before that the mind cannot tell the difference between a real experience and a vividly imagined experience but it never registered. You have explained it in such detail that only a fool would miss the vast potential you have just handed him on a plate. That's the difference between a good public speaker and a brilliant one!"

Singapore: Peter, "I can see why so many people have had to rely on faith, faith in God, faith in things unseen, faith in a higher power, it's because they never understood the principles. If you can understand why it's so important to visualize things before they happen, faith doesn't come into it."

USA: Helen, "What you have shown us are some very powerful living skills, I wish they had been taught to us when we were children."

ZOOM SECRETS!

1. The greatest secret of success is that the human biocomputer cannot tell the difference between a real experience and a vividly imagined experience.

2. We can insert any programs we want into our biocomputer simply by visualizing whatever it is that we want to achieve.

3. We know that to achieve success we must have the program in the biocomputer before the event.

4. Successful people visualize things happening in their biocomputers, before they happen in real life.

5. You can insert programs into your biocomputer in three different ways. You practice the actual thing you want to accomplish. You can role play or simulate the event, or you can vividly imagine it happening.

6. If the racing car driver or down hill skier slips into 'thinking mode' he crashes. On race day he runs on his biocomputer automatically and without thinking. Business people should program in advance as well.

5

How to Visualize

For a start I'm not going to tell you how to visualize. I want to go a little further into the detail of visualization and why we should visualize.

Imagine a plank of wood, six inches wide and ten feet long, has been placed on the ground in front of you. Your verbal affirmation (left computer) is "Walk across the plank of wood" So you do it. No problem at all. What I do at my biocomputer seminars is hold in my left hand a dictionary to signify the left computer processing in words, and in my right hand I hold a dozen picture postcards to signify the right computer processing in pictures. Next, imagine the plank of wood being raised on two oil drums six feet off the ground. Again the verbal affirmation is, "Walk across the plank of wood, you know you can do it, you've just done it once." This time I have a little incongruity between the two computers. I 'see' myself maybe falling off the plank of wood and hurting my ankle. This time I walk across very cautiously. Now imagine the same plank of wood, six inches wide, ten feet long, being placed between two buildings three hundred feet in the air. The verbal affirmation is the same, left computer, again I hold my left hand up in the air to show the dictionary. "Walk across the plank of wood, you know you can do it, you've just done it twice!"

However, when I actually try to walk the plank, I thrust up my right hand into the air to signify the right computer, the pictures have taken over. In my imagination I have 'seen' myself splattered out on the sidewalk three hundred feet below. I ask my audience "Can I walk across the plank of wood three hundred feet up in the air if all the time I'm 'seeing' myself as strawberry jam down on the sidewalk?" The answer is of course I can't! Splat! Strawberry Jam! Nasty! For a laugh I always ask my audience if there is anyone at all who thinks they could walk the plank three hundred feet up in the air. Before they have time to answer I tell them we have the experiment set up outside. I've never had any takers!

All the time I'm talking to my audience I hold up the dictionary and the picture postcards to signify the left computer processing in words and the right computer processing in pictures. This tends to bring it home to a lot of my students and I suggest that before you read any further, that you hold a dictionary in your left hand and some picture postcards in your right hand and go over the plank of wood exercise for yourself. (The only people who can walk across the plank of wood three hundred feet up in the air, are the tightrope walkers, who don't have an incongruity between their two computers).

The whole point is that for years you have been verbally telling yourself (left computer, words) that you are going to be a success, going to own your own business, going to be a millionaire, going to be a winner, going to be top salesperson, going to own a Rolls Royce or Porsche but have been 'seeing' for yourself (right computer, pictures) the exact opposite.

In other words most people have an absolute total incongruity between what their left computers 'say' in words, and what their right computers 'see' in pictures.

You are also beginning to see that the pictures are a thousand times more powerful than the words. A wonderful little formula you should remember: When the words and the pictures are in conflict it is ALWAYS the pictures that win, without exception. Of course the other half of the formula is equally powerful and just as true: When the words and the pictures match and are harmoniously pulling in the same direction an irresistible force is the result.

If you have been doing affirmations over a period of years and not been getting anywhere quickly you would be wise to look inwardly at the pictures (right computer) that you have been holding about yourself. Most people in their affirmations (left computer, words) say that they earn $10,000 a week. However, what they 'see' (right computer, pictures) for themselves is that they are earning $500 a week. Don't forget the pictures win every time, without exception. What most people say as their affirmation (words, left computer) is that they own a Rolls Royce, or a Porsche. However, what they 'see' for themselves, what they visualize (pictures, right computer) is of course the auto they have right now. It's a Ford or a pick-up truck, right! The only time you can and will accomplish the goals that you have set for yourself is when you get the words and the pictures to match. As I've told you before, you have two very powerful computers, one thinking in words and the other thinking in pictures. Most people have absolute total incongruity between the words and the pictures. In other words what they have is two very powerful computers pulling in opposite directions. Now you will realize why so many people fail to accomplish their goals and why others suffer from unhappiness and depression.

It really is all in the mind! Input really does equal output! What I have just shown you is the secret of happiness. Many folk try to live happy and successful lives, but all the time, unbeknown to them, they have two computers working against each other. You start matching your verbal goals up with your visual goals and immediately the cloud will lift, the weight of the world will be removed from your shoulders and you will begin to feel happy again. Thousands go to the doctors suffering from depression and usually get prescribed an anti-depressant, that many patients stay on for two or three years. People come to me suffering from depression and I usually cure them in about ten minutes flat. I get them to match their words up with their pictures. Most people go through life, feeling, literally torn apart, (you must have heard the expressions, I have a splitting headache, I'm in two minds, I feel torn apart, I don't know whether I'm coming or going, I've only got half the picture, these are the words people use to describe what is quite literally the feelings going on inside their heads) because they have one powerful computer pulling them in one direction and another powerful computer pulling them in the opposite direction.

Many would-be-entrepreneurs find it very difficult to be self-starters, to get self-motivated. What I have just shown you is the secret of motivation, both for yourself and people you are trying to motivate. Most people set themselves verbal goals (left computer) that have absolutely no relationship to the pictures (right computer) that they are 'seeing' for themselves. Once you actually start visualizing the goals that you have set for yourself a lot of things begin to happen automatically. Depression lifts, motivation begins. The goal gets clearer and the goal gets nearer. The more you actually visualize the goal the clearer it will become and the nearer it will become, until you actually achieve it.

I've been to a lot of seminars about creative visualization and I've also read a lot of books that have endeavored to show people how to visualize and at the end of it all the students learnt how to do everything except visualize. The first point to make is that some people can already create pictures in their biocomputers without any problem at all. However, there are thousands of people, no matter how hard they try, up to now, have not been able to create any pictures at all. I always get a chuckle at my biocomputer seminars when people who can visualize clearly in color, 3D moving pictures, are amazed to discover, that just about two thirds of the people in the class have great difficulty seeing any pictures in their imaginations (right computer) at all. Don't forget as children we all have this innate ability to visualize but the educational system is so antiquated that you probably never got any input into your right computer whatsoever, therefore the faculty has become dormant. However, like all muscles, the brain can be revitalized and stimulated into productive activity by use.

Imagine for the last twenty or thirty or forty years your right arm had been tied down to your side with lashings of rope. I came along and explained to you that there had to be a better way. Surely, I tell you, that it would be easier if you used both hands to do your daily chores. The driving, housework, typing, washing dishes and hanging out the clothes, or whatever it is you do, on a daily basis. You agreed with me because it's pretty obvious, so I cut the rope that's been binding your right arm for so many years. Do you think that just because I cut the rope, you would have the instant use of your right arm. No, of course not! You would need physiotherapy and have to start building the strength of your right arm by lifting weights, little ones at first, getting heavier and heavier as your strength built up. So it is with your right computer. It has been shut down for twenty, thirty or forty years. It has atrophied. It has dried up. (I often wonder if those pickled walnuts aren't right computers some one's getting hold of and selling to make a few bucks!) It has stopped working. It has become impotent. The most powerful tool that you have in your possession, your billion dollar biocomputer, is switched off! Now is the time to do something about it!

I have turned a lot of people on and changed many peoples lives for the better. I have had feedback from people who have read my books and attended my seminars. I get great joy out of helping people, especially if they have read all the books, listened to all the tapes and done all the seminars, and they tell me my program actually works! I know what works and what doesn't work. The following exercise should be done by everyone, even if you can visualize already.

At my biocomputer seminars I get my students to close their eyes and try to imagine they are walking along a beach they are familiar with. I get them to imagine that their toes are squelching through the sand and every now and then a gentle wave comes in and baths their feet. Everyone knows what that sounds and feels like. Marvellous! I get them to feel the hot sun on their soft skin and hear the sounds of the sea gulls. I get them to place their hands in the hands of a lover or spouse and have a pleasant conversation. I get them to listen to the waves and again to feel those waves washing the sand out from between their toes. I get them to access the sounds, the feelings, the emotions, the smell of the salt air and the fresh ocean and ALL OF A SUDDEN THEY'RE VISUALIZING. Yes ! Thinking in pictures after so many years inactivity. It hadn't gone away. The faculty had just become lazy. Time to celebrate, because this is a tool, you will now use for the rest of your days, or perish!

When I know my students are actually visualizing I then say "Now go around the next corner of the beach, and there you will see your dream house, or your dream auto. Walk around your dream house as though you own it, see the flowers in the vase, admire the soft furnishings, walk out into the grounds, pick a few roses, swim in the pool, have a barbecue and entertain your friends, play pool in the games room, cook a meal for two in the kitchen. Get in your dream auto and drive it away, change up and down the gears, go for a spin down the coast highway, feel the air conditioning on your face. See the look on friends faces as you pull into their driveways in your new Mercedes". They don't have any problem at all slipping from the beach into their dream auto or dream home. You can expand the exercise. You can take people around the next corner of the beach and get them to move into a business scenario, where they are closing a deal or selling something or paying a huge check into the bank. The technique works for thousands of people and it may be one that works for you.

The reason why this technique works so brilliantly is that you are accessing many parts of the biocomputer that you don't normally have any difficulty using. Also it takes you from a reference point that you are already familiar with (the golden beach, the lovers hand, the squelching of the sand between the toes) to a point that is not so familiar, the dream house or the dream auto or you closing a particularly large deal.

Another simple exercise that I use. If you are a predominantly auditory person (you have no problem talking internally and spend most of your internal time processing information in words) what you should do to start off your visualization is to start talking internally about the deal that you want to come off. For argument's sake let's say you are trying to visualize your dream house. You could create a situation in your minds eye whereby you are talking to the real estate agent. You could then get him to drive you over to your dream home. All the time you could be discussing with him verbally all the things that you require your mansion to have. Then as you drive up the front driveway, feel and hear the gravel hitting the underside of the auto. Slam the auto's doors so you can hear them shut. All the time you are doing this you can get emotional about the dream house as well as increasing the verbal description of the house and deal you are about to enter. As you are going through this process keep trying to access the pictures. It will only be a matter of time and practice before you are able to create pictures in your minds eye (right computer).

The most important fact that you must know is that you really do have to create pictures in the electro chemicals in the biocomputer. Many biocomputer students create foggy messes and wonder why they don't get any useful output from their biocomputer. It's easy to explain about the left computer, the one that processes in words. You know that if you programmed the computer with English or Chinese or Russian you would sooner or later get the equivalent output. Say if you programmed your right computer with very clear pictures of your dream house, or your dream auto, or of you doing a very big deal. Sooner or later your biocomputer would give you the output you needed to attain that goal. Input equals output. The output will come in the form of correct habits and Eurekas!

Let's say you programmed your left computer with word salad, gobbledegook, a language that doesn't even exist. That would be the output of your biocomputer. If you programmed a mishmash of words that didn't even exist, the output of your biocomputer would be useless. Garbage in equals Garbage out. Input equals output.

Let's say you programmed your right computer with a foggy mess of unclear pictures. What would be the output? Nothing. You are now dealing with the most powerful computer in the world. The billion dollar biocomputer. It demands having concise and clear pictures and words for its programs. Nothing less will do. However, if you take the trouble to insert the proper pictures in the right computer and match them up with the equivalent and appropriate words for the left computer you will find you are getting output that can only be described as genius. Don't forget I only drink to genius!

If you're having difficulty visualizing because you can't get the image right, the following technique may help you. For argument's sake let's say that you are trying to visualize yourself looking slim (which of course is imperative for those seeking to lose weight). Every time you bring a picture of yourself into your bio-computer you 'see' yourself as you are or worse, fatter. What you should do is to create a screen in your imagination with a smaller screen in the bottom left hand corner. In the large screen let the 'fat picture' appear but in the small screen 'see' yourself looking the way you want to look, slim, tight muscles and the Adonis or Venus look. When you have both the large and the small screens very clearly focused very quickly switch the two pictures around. Like all visualization techniques, especially when it's difficult for you to visualize, it takes a little practice and concentrated effort.

Another tip to help you get visualizing properly is to cast your eyes upwards when you are trying to visualize. The eye movements are connected to the neural patterns in the biocomputer. When you look upwards you will be in the visualizing mode. To check this out for yourself ask some friends "What is the top color of traffic lights?" or "Describe to me what your bedroom looks like?" Their eyes will immediately go upwards as they start to search for the information that is of a visual nature.

Have you ever noticed down-and-outs in the street, or people who have failed, they always shuffle around with their heads down, looking towards the ground. They are talking internally, negatively, about the past. On the other hand if you take notice of successful individuals you will soon see that they look straight ahead or upwards, they are in the visual mode and they are thinking positively in pictures about a successful and happy future.

It concerns me a little, that the businessmen who buy self-help books are the same people that buy all the self-help books. Don't get me wrong, there's nothing at all wrong with self-improvement, but there is a folly to that way. Reading is a left computer activity, (If reading maketh a full man, you're over-flowing!) and many entrepreneurs get stuck into reading and reading and reading, trying desperately hard to find the secret that they are looking for, they are seeking motivation, a way of getting their biocomputers to fire on all eight cylinders (I like the expression 'Getting your biocomputer firing on all cylinders.' In actual fact the neurons do fire. The range of frequency of the neuron cells firing is divided into four brain rhythms, delta, theta, alpha and beta.) and they are looking for the one tip that will take them to the top. This is the folly, this is the error. You can read all day everyday, you still won't click, until you learn to put the books down, close your eyes, (if necessary) and start thinking in pictures about the future. It's a totally different computer that you haven't used for twenty, thirty or forty years, yet it's the right computer that controls everything you do, with regard to your goals.

It's also important for you to realize people visualize in many different ways. Some see clear pictures. Others see foggy messes, (no good at all for reprogramming the human biocomputer.) Others see themselves in each picture. Others visualize themselves being part of the picture, therefore can't actually see themselves in the pictures. Many see pictures in full color. Others see pictures in black and white only. A lot of people see everything they visualize much bigger than it is in real life. And a vast majority of people find it very difficult to visualize at all.

Once you have realized how imperative it is to actually create the images in the individual neurons in the electrochemicals of the biocomputer you will of course realize how vitally important it is to use concentrated effort, if necessary, to make those images.

The biocomputer can be compared to battery. It only has so much energy that it can dissipate before it needs recharging. Once the battery runs down the performance of the battery is affected and it will not carry out its duties in a reliable manner. When reprogramming your biocomputer you will find that it only has a certain amount of energy, in particular, electrical energy. (One tenth of a volt gets used up pretty quickly especially if you are worrying about petty trivia!) If you fritter away your energy on useless activities and then try to reprogram your biocomputer you will find that you are wasting your time. Because of the concentrated effort involved in creating pictures in one's right computer you should only try when your energy levels are high. I suggest when you rise in the morning, take your shower or bath, then start your visualizing. Have your breakfast after you have reprogrammed your biocomputer. Have you ever noticed that after eating you feel tired? Well, if this happens to you, you'd be wasting your time trying to reprogram your biocomputer in that state. In the evening don't try to practice visualization just before you go to bed. Have a shower early in the evening when you still feel fresh and full of vitality, after you have fully recovered from a days work. Only practise visualization when your energy level is high.

I have helped a lot of biocomputer students get back into the visual mode by introducing them to white noise, which is heterogeneous mixture of sound waves covering a very wide range of frequencies. White noise will blank out any other noises that may be distracting you from your visualization. You can buy white noise machines very cheaply or you can do what I do at times which is leave a fan running at a continuous speed. You can even make a tape recording of a fan or freezer or similar noise and take that wherever you go, as an aid to concentration.

If you are one of the many unfortunates that find it very difficult to visualize, you must persist. You must keep doing various exercises and find a way for yourself to get back the faculty that has become dormant. You may like to do the tea-pot exercise. Just leave a tea-pot on the table in front of you and concentrate on it. Then close your eyes and try to recreate a picture of the tea-pot in your biocomputer. You can do the same exercise by turning your head away and casting your eyes upwards into the visual mode, this works better on some occasions. You can practice exercises like this all the time and you should, until you have brought back the potency of the right computer.

You can expand the exercise by trying to visualize how the dinner table is set when you get home or trying to visualize which way the auto is parked in the drive-way. All these exercises will pay off handsomely in the long run because the biocomputer really can take you to the moon, once you have it firing on all eight cylinders.

The biocomputer fires on different computers at different times. I once read that it fires alternatively in ninety minute cycles, I really don't know if that's right. I would think the properly tuned biocomputer would be able to fire from left to right at just the appropriate time for it to function really efficiently. What I do know is, from my own experience and from talking to many biocomputer students, that it definitely does fire on different computers at different times. Obviously if you want to visualize you should make sure that your biocomputer is firing on the right computer. You can work out relatively easily which computer is firing and you do it fairly quickly. If you are being very analytical and talking a lot internally, I would suggest you are firing on your left computer. However, if you are feeling creative then you are firing on your right computer and this is when you should start visualizing.

I think that one of the problems of the past has been that the authors of so many self-help books have grossly underestimated the difficulty that some people actually have creating pictures in their biocomputers. For all we know, the books may have even been written by visuals, who have absolutely no problem with visualizing themselves! I would like to assure you that I haven't underestimated the difficulty and frustration some people go though trying to create those pictures. I have done everything in my power to show you ways of visualizing. If my techniques don't work for you, you should not stop there and give it up as a bad job. All it means is that my techniques don't work for you. You can correct that by working out some techniques of your own or doing some research into other material about visualization. There are many books about visualization and one I would recommend is 'Creative Visualization' by Shakti Gawain.

Many would-be achievers have been in a rut for years. A rut is nothing more than a grave with both ends missing. What I am showing you here is the end of survival and the beginning of life. This is more than just a book to be read just once and then placed on the shelf, it is a work-book, an instruction manual. It needs to be studied as though your very future depended on it. Believe me it does!

If you care to reprogram your biocomputer, by vividly imaging the future as you desire it, you are in for some very pleasant surprises. Don't wait for as long as it took me to find out some very elementary truths!

You should get used to planning things out in pictures before the event takes place. You can start by visualizing what you are going to do at the weekend. See the whole scenario take place in your imagination. You can practice like this on everyday events of your life. Then start visualizing scenarios with your bank manager. 'See' the proposition you are going to make him about that business loan in great detail. Use your imagination more and more everyday. Bring that faculty back into use. Take time out everyday to plan out your day in pictures before the day takes place. By 'seeing' things happen in your minds eye you will very often come up with ideas that will allow you to literally glide through life.

Of course about an estimated one third of the population can already visualize very clearly. I would suggest that people who come into this category would discover the secrets of success and do the right things intuitively more easily than the rest of us. However, many of the people that have come to biocomputer seminars said, although they could visualize easily and clearly, they had never put the faculty to use, because they had been told so many times, to stop fantasizing at school!

LIVE AT THE BIOCOMPUTER SEMINAR:

USA: Joe, "One thing I've learned this weekend is that I'm not the only one who finds it hard to visualize. Of course I've read all the books and done all the seminars. I thought I was missing something. Now I realize it's a universal problem and Ron has gone to great pains to actually show me how to visualize. Before I never appreciated that with concentrated effort you can actually 'see' pictures in the mind. I know I have a long way to go but now I feel I have the right tools to work with. I know that I shall move forward because for years I have been reading that this is the secret of success. Now I know why, and I also know how!"

USA: Sarah, "After hearing so many people say they can't visualize I have to confess I'm rather baffled. I always thought every one could and it comes as a bit of shock to hear they can't."

England: Mary, "The major highlight for me this weekend was actually being taken though a visualization exercise. When someone else takes you through it you can spend your time concentrating on the pictures. That's the first time I've experienced it. It was very good. A lot of things are getting clearer for me."

Australia: Clare, "I'm in a business where they talk

about dream building all the time. It never dawned on me what it really was or what it really does, until today. I shall start building my own dream because now I have a very clear picture of how I can accomplish it. I think too many times in the past I've lost my vision and gone off with someone else's dream."

England: Ivan, "I have made many things happen for myself by actually buying part of whatever it is that I wanted. For example I wanted a new set of golf clubs so I actually went out and bought a caddy to put them in. The golf clubs arrived about eight weeks later. I wanted to go to Thailand so I bought a tour book all about Bangkok. I flew there first class because I actually 'saw' myself flying first class. I've done a lot of this stuff without even realizing what I've been doing. Now I actually understand the principles there will be no stopping me."

England: Lee, "When I was doing the visualization exercise I couldn't help laughing. I was driving a green Lamborghini and I swung it into my driveway at home and I crashed into my old Ford Escort that was parked in the drive. So if you see a redheaded girl going over Chelsea bridge in the morning in a green Lambo you'll know I got it!"

USA: Peter, "My sales manager has been taking me out to look at new BMW's to get me excited, to get me goal oriented. The trouble is that I haven't been getting excited. Today I know what I've got to go and look at. I've got to go and look at those Winnebagos. That's what I want! Karl has been trying to get me excited about something he likes."

Australia: Terry, "For the first time in my life I have really understood what the two hemispheres are all about. No one ever put it over in such simple terms before. I don't know why, but I really think you're onto something!"

Australia: Guy, "My pictures have always been in conflict with my words. As Ron was talking I went through every one of my goals and I hold the exact opposite in my pictures to what I keep telling myself. That's an astonishing revelation."

Australia: Gerry, "During the coffee break, four of us were discussing eye movements. It's fascinating to watch people's eyes move in accordance to the type of thought they are thinking. I'd never noticed it before but when it's pointed out to you, it's obvious."

Poland: Carolinka, "For many years I have tried to affirm things to myself but I have never been repetitive enough and I certainly haven't visualized those affirmations!"

Ireland: Kerry, "I find when I relax in the bath, I can visualize easily."

USA: Keith, "I didn't know we could bring the faculty back to use with practice and exercise."

USA: Melvin, "I just didn't know how much concentrated effort was required, but it was worth while. Ron convinced me that I should not give up. In the end I succeeded in creating pictures."

England: Clive, "Ron taught me to think in pictures over a year ago, since then I have become World Fishing Champion and won a gold medal. Thanks to Ron Holland."

USA: Rod, "In the bible it says 'Through lack of vision my people perish' only it doesn't say why."

USA: Curley, "Visualization can increase anyone's skills. If you 'see' yourself as a better carpenter, auto technician, paint sprayer, lawyer or accountant, you will automatically become better. Visualization helps gel the learning process. It will turn laymen into skilled workers and skilled workers into masters!"

USA: Darrall, "For many years I've been an avid gardener. At the end of every year I always visualize what the next years garden will look like, then I plant it accordingly, I always have the best garden in the neighborhood. It's never dawned on me to use that practice for my business."

ZOOM SECRETS!

1. The most important thing to remember is that you must actually create the picture that you are visualizing in the electrochemicals in the neurons.

2. Remember that the pictures dominate everything we do in our lives.

3. It helps to look upwards when visualizing so you can access the visual mode.

4. By imagining that you are walking along a beach that you know intimately, you can slip into the visual mode very easily.

5. It is imperative to visualize subjectively as opposed to objectively.

6. The most important faculty that you possess may well have become atrophied through lack of use. Start using every visualization technique now, to find one that works for you.

7. People create pictures in their biocomputers in very different ways, find the way that works for you.

8. Once you have discovered visualization, use it on a daily basis. Try to use it at every opportunity that you can.

6

Failure Programs

Many of the programs that we have in our biocomputers were placed there by well meaning parents or teachers or are there as a result of our environments. Many of these programs will work in direct opposition to the goals that we have set for ourselves. We have already touched on self-defeating behavior, subconscious death wishes and self-destruct programs, that time and time again, rob us of victory just when the spoils come into view.

In talking about success, I have to talk about failure so you can really tap into the power that will take you to the top and beyond!

Many years ago I had a big deal coming together. To close this deal I would have to go to the United States. I'd never been there before, but I had a good idea of what it looked like from all the films that I'd seen and everything that I'd read. I didn't have the money to get myself to America and at the time such a trip seemed daunting to say the least. I'd never even flown before!

Every night I drove out to London Airport and looked at the Jumbo jets. I could 'see' myself getting on a Jumbo jet and flying to America. I could 'see' myself land in New York, I 'saw' myself, in my imagination, go up the eighty seven floors, at the address I had, go through the doors and the man offered me the money for my deal. I have to tell you the full story. Next night, what did I do? I drove out to London Airport again, I 'saw' myself get on the Jumbo jet, fly to New York, I could see myself in New York, I had on a white suit, crocodile shoes and I went up the eighty seven floors in the skyscraper, through the doors and the man offered me the money for the deal. The imagination is truly the workshop of the mind. Don't laugh, but the next night I did the same thing. I drove out to London Airport. I 'saw' myself fly to America. I 'saw' myself land in New York. I had on a white suit, crocodile shoes and I was carrying a brand new brief case. (My visualization was getting clearer!) I went up the eighty seven floors in the elevator, through the doors and the man offered me the money for the deal. Then all of a sudden one day, Wham! Bingo! Eureka! I came up with a way of getting the money to get me to America, I bought my ticket, I was finally on my way. Not only did I have the air fare, but I was motivated into action! The visualizing had ended, the dreaming had ended, the reality had begun!

This is a true story! I found myself on a Jumbo jet flying to America. This was the real thing. No more role playing. No more visualizing. It was very exciting. I landed in New York, what do you think I was wearing? (This is where my seminar audiences shout out "pyjamas" because they think I'm still daydreaming) I had on a white suit, crocodile shoes and a brand new brief case. I went up those eighty seven floors, just like I had visualized so many times, I went through the doors and the man offered me the money for the deal.

I'll tell you exactly what he told me, it was sheer magic! He said "We love your product so much we'll give you $125,000 up front for signing a contract with us. We love your product so much we'll give you a $200,000 advertising budget and here is a complete list of all the things that we will do for you." I couldn't believe my own ears! What do you think I did next? Yes! You got it in one! I BLEW IT! My biocomputer found so many reasons why I should not sign that deal. I made up all sorts of feeble and lame excuses. I made up some other excuses that were not so feeble and were not so lame, but they still had the same end result, I BLEW THE DEAL! I walked out of that office with my tail between my legs and it took me a long time to get over the loss of the money and the loss of my self-confidence and self-esteem.

After a lot of soul searching I came up with the answer why I blew the deal. Since then I have recouped my losses many times over and I have helped thousands of people all over the world with my biocomputer seminars.

Let's examine in detail the program that I carefully impregnated into the electrochemicals that made up my biocomputer program. I drove to London Airport every night. That part happened! I 'saw' myself flying to America. That part happened! I 'saw' myself land in New York. That part happened! I 'saw' myself in the white suit, crocodile shoes and a brand new brief case. That part happened! (I wish that part had never happened, when I saw some of the looks I was getting, and those stretch limo's kept pulling up next to me and the guys inside were asking me the weirdest questions! You just don't wear a white suit and crocodile shoes in New York!) I 'saw' myself go up the eighty seven floors, in the elevator. That part happened! I 'saw' myself go through the doors and the man offered me the money for my deal. That part happened! In actual fact everything happened exactly how I had visualized it! So what went wrong?

What was wrong, was the fact that I did not visualize signing the contract or getting the check. I had come to the end of the program in my biocomputer. There was no track for me to run on. When the man offered me the money I could hardly believe my own ears! I was lost for words. I did what I always did, which was, in many cases, not move ahead in life, keep myself at a level where I felt comfortable at, not do the best thing for myself, self-destruct, self-defeating behavior. I did all that automatically because that was my program. That was the track that I had been running on for years.

My biocomputer never let me down. My biocomputer has never let me down. Neither has yours! Your biocomputer will take you to exactly where you program it for. When the program ends, the journey ends, simple as that. No ifs or buts about it. If you come to the end of a program that is in your biocomputer, whether it was inserted by yourself or some other person, that is the point in your life when you come to a GRINDING HALT!

Many times life appears to be like a game of snakes and ladders. You go up the ladders when things are going well. You slide down the snakes when things are going badly. (You may know this game as chutes and ladders but the principle is just the same) I have done enough work now, both on my own biocomputer programs and the programs of literally thousands of other people who have attended my biocomputer seminars to know that all the time you are relaxing and visualizing the future exactly as you want it, you will be going up the ladders. The minute you stop relaxing and stop visualizing the future as you desire, you slide down the snakes. Have you ever noticed in your own life, you're either moving toward your goals very quickly or sliding away from them very quickly. That is the effect I'm talking about.

How many times in your life have you got so far with a project then quit? You quit at the point where you 'saw' yourself with that particular project. How many businessmen have started a business, many times without capital, against the wishes of the family, overcome all the objections and financial problems, only to fail two or three years down the road? I guarantee you failed at the exact point where your dream ran out. You came to the end of the program in your biocomputer and you came to a GRINDING HALT. How many people have had relationships that run for two or three years? Many men and women have lots of relationships that run for two or three years. Many couples have relationships that run for five years or seven years. That is their pattern. That is the program they have in their biocomputers. As soon as the program ends, the relationship ends. If you want to have long term relationships, what you must do of course, is visualize over and over again the future with your partner. Visualize over and over again all the things you will do together, the building of a home and a family, the vacations, the schools your children will be attending. Everything, in detail. Fail to do this and you'll go down one of the snakes. Practice visualization and you'll keep moving onward and upward, up those ladders!

While we are on the subject of relationships I want to point out another aspect of the biocomputer. Because the biocomputer is extremely powerful it really will take you to your goal, providing you have programmed it correctly. If you and your partner have different dreams and aspirations you will have two very powerful computers pulling in two different directions and the break up of the relationship will be inevitable. By far the best way is to constantly talk and communicate about your dreams and aspirations and goals and plans to one another. Even if you don't agree on everything all of the time, at least you will have the information in the biocomputer, which in turn will process it, and assimilate it and come up with viable options that make for a happy and harmonious future together.

The same would go for business partnerships. If you keep swapping ideas and keep your partner informed of the way you 'see' forward for the business, and what it is that you 'see' accomplishing with the business you will both end up with the same programs in your biocomputer, you will end up working with each other, not against each other, which happens in so many partnerships.

Back to my unfortunate and expensive New York experience. What I do now is to visualize that not only I am getting the offer for my deal, but I also visualize that I am signing the contract, getting the check, paying the check into my bank, cashing the check, and going out and buying a Rolls Royce. (Which is exactly what I did with the money I made on my last deal.)

I have also learnt that to overcome the snakes and ladder effect, what you must do, to keep moving onward and upward, is to keep setting new goals all the time. The biocomputer is teleological. It is goal seeking. If you fail to keep programming it with new goals you will keep sliding down the snakes.

Just out of interest, so you have a chance to compare yourself with others. At the end of my biocomputer seminars I am always deluged with people who want to get autographs, ask questions and give thanks. I am constantly thanked for showing people the New York deal, obviously many people have got so far with a deal or a project only to have it collapse on them at the crucial moment. See if these stories apply to things that have happened (or are happening) in your own life and see if you can get yourself beyond the point of collapse by visualizing the outcome that you desire.

Many people visualize getting a dream house or a dream auto. Many students of success go to the automobile show rooms and test drive the auto of their dreams. Others get the real estate agents to take them around the mansions with the landscaped gardens and the indoor and outdoor pools. They put the appropriate input into the biocomputer and in due course the output comes. They end up with the dream house or dream auto very quickly. Many people are equally shocked, when they get evicted from the dream house or the dream auto gets repossessed, just as quickly, because they had been unable to keep up the monthly payments. I have interviewed many such people and they told me "I knew it couldn't last" or better still, "I saw it coming!" If you don't visualize things properly you are doomed to get only what you have programmed into the biocomputer. Remember once the biocomputer has completed YOUR INSTRUCTIONS it says to itself MISSION ACCOMPLISHED.

What you should do, when visualizing the dream house or dream auto is also visualize a way of creating an income to pay for the monthly installment. Or better still put a program into your biocomputer that 'sees' you paying for the house or auto with one cash payment, so there are no monthly installments.

What people do when their businesses start to fail, is they start visualizing checks bouncing and the bailiff coming in the front door and themselves going out the back door. They 'see' their businesses going from bad to worse, they 'see' their cash flow drying up, they 'see' themselves standing in the bankruptcy court and they 'see' themselves having to sell off all their assets. In actual fact they put such a clear and powerful program into their biocomputers it becomes a track to run on, a self-fulfilling prophecy. In actual fact the only antidote to failure is to visualize very clearly and concisely exactly what you want to happen in the future. You have to 'see' orders coming in. You actually have to 'see' cash in your hip pocket and in your bank account. You have to 'see' products walking out of the store. You have to 'see' your cash flow improving. You have to put the program into your biocomputer, success too, can be a self-fulfilling prophecy. Please learn it, sooner rather than later. Input equals output!

How many books are available on diet and losing weight? Thousands! How many people would just love to lose weight, they've bought all the books, they've tried every diet. But what happens? Nothing, or worse still, you lose weight only to rapidly gain more than you lost! You have to understand a little about the biocomputer to lose weight. It's simple.

As a busy entrepreneur I don't get a lot of time to watch a lot of videos, but when I do, I enjoy it. I like Clint Eastwood. I've got all the videos. I like escapism. Let me give you a scenario of me trying to lose weight!

I have a goal 'I have lost twenty pounds', I start watching Clint Eastwood. Every time I see him, his gun gets bigger and bigger. He's saying the same old stuff, "Make my day, punk." Don't you love it? In my imagination I begin to wonder if my housekeeper has got in my favorite cheeses. Clint Eastwood chases the guy down the road, I'd swear his gun gets bigger during the course of the actual movie. My imagination is 'seeing' pictures of my favorite crackers. Clint Eastwood is kicking the door open. He's got this enormous cannon in his hand. I'm wondering to myself, "I wonder if there are any prawns in the refrigerator." In my imagination I've created a gourmet snack! Before I know where I am I've forgotten all about Clint Eastwood. I've lurched myself out of the comfy chair, I've practically ripped the door off the refrigerator. I've got out the prawns and the cheeses and I've got down the crackers. I pick up a Budweiser for good measure. (I lied about that, I pick up a six pack for good measure!) I go back to my hero, but alas, the video has just come to an end. My imagination has just got me again. The pictures win every time. If you really want to lose weight, the only way to do it, is to program in words and pictures that match! You actually have to 'see' yourself eating the correct food, 'see' yourself doing the correct exercising and 'see' yourself being the right weight! You have to control your right computer otherwise it will control you! Comprendé?

How many thousands of people would be public speakers, actors or actresses or singers or public performers but they can't possibly, because they suffer from 'stage fright'. They can't 'see' themselves standing up in front of an audience and performing. It doesn't matter if the world needs to hear what you have to say, it doesn't matter if your message is timely and topical. If you can't 'see' yourself up on stage because your imagination (right computer) is controlling you, then you have little or no hope of becoming a public performer until such time as you care to control your pictures.

Smokers try to quit smoking every day of the week. Lots of companies are making big bucks teaching people how to stop smoking. The real key of course lies in the imagination, in the biocomputer. Most people say to themselves that they'll quit. They go right on smoking and they can't understand why. What they do is simple. They keep affirming (verbal, left computer) they'll quit smoking. They go into a room full of people and they'll keep telling themselves verbally that they don't smoke, they're non-smokers and they've quit. However at the same time they're doing this they are imagining what a cigarette tastes like. They can 'see' themselves smoking. They may not have brought any cigarettes with them but they can 'see' themselves going up to someone and saying "I don't suppose I could bum a cigarette off you, I've quit really but these meetings give me bad nerves?" The next moment has them puffing away merrily. The pictures win every time. If you really want to quit smoking you have to get your right computer under control. If you don't control it, it'll control you, like it's been doing for years!

Many people from all walks of life, come to a plateau in their lives. They have simply come to the end of the programs in their biocomputers. They have accomplished all the things that they have 'seen' themselves doing. If this applies to you, and you want to move onward and upward, all you have to do is start relaxing and visualizing the future as you desire it. Start impregnating the electrochemicals with visions of what you want for the future. Create a program for your biocomputer to run on. You will be taken there, automatically and furthermore you'll travel first class, if that's what you visualize!

There are two main programs that affect the way we either survive or surthrive. (Surthrivers not only survive tough economic climates but they thrive in them!) The two programs are 'guns' and 'butter'. 'Guns', because they are solid and are around for a long time and 'butter' because it melts and dissipates into nothingness.

The survivors by virtue of their biocomputer programs waste all their money on 'butter' items. They splurge their money on things that dissipate. Things like holidays, cheap cars, clothing, rent, cheap jewelry, dinners out, entertainment, lotto tickets. In other words they never have anything to show for their money, it's just frittered away, it melts, just like butter. 'Butter' items are things that depreciate in value!

The surthrivers invest their money on totally different things. They are programmed differently. They invest their money on 'guns' items. They invest their money in homes, mortgages, antique paintings, books, coin collections, gold, antique jewelry, businesses, further education, plant, equipment, machinery, Rolls Royces, things that don't dissipate, things that are going to be around for a long time. 'Guns' items, are things that appreciate in value!

If you have ever wondered why some people make it and why others don't. What you have just seen here is a major difference between success and failure. The most amazing thing about it is that the real difference comes back down to deeply rooted biocomputer programs, that can be changed!

LIVE AT THE BIOCOMPUTER SEMINAR:

Australia: Susan, "For the first time in my life I can see why I keep failing. Every time I reach a goal I just stop and rest on my laurels. As you say I keep sliding down snakes. When I get to the bottom, I get bored and start looking for new things to do. I always get to the top very quickly, no matter who's branch I join, I'm always the top sales person. What I've learned more than anything is the reason why I come to grinding halts. And that it's my own fault not anyone else's."

Singapore: Kishore, "Even when things have been going well for me I tend to start visualizing the bad times that I've known. What I realize I have to do is use my concentration and my will power to stop me bringing back those bad things to mind. I can see that I have been very lackadaisical in my approach to reprogramming my biocomputer. I haven't been consistent. I always get serious about putting programs in when I'm at rock bottom, when I have nowhere to turn. As soon as I progress upwards I ease up on the programming. In future I will make an all out effort to keep visualizing more and more when I begin to succeed. All out massive effort for all out massive profit."

USA: Max, "For years I've hung out with Hells Angels and I've never had a bike. If you like I've allowed myself to be the village idiot, I've even told myself I'm an idiot at times. I have affirmed it over and over, I've even felt like an idiot. Today I've come to realize I'm not an idiot and I want to thank Ron Holland for that. In future I will be taking on various seminars and classes to start improving myself. As Ron says input equals output. I've got that one Ron! The output that I've been getting has been nobody's fault but mine, but I intend to change it, Ron Holland thank you once again."

USA: Connie, "I have tried in the past to be positive and insert proper programs. What I've got out of today is simple. I can see that if my negative program is made up of ten million neurons and that's what I'm running on, I have to put in a positive program of maybe twenty million neurons, or even thirty million neurons, to overcome the negativity. In the past I've given up on my affirmations without giving them a chance."

England: Maxwell, "I've seen Ron Holland speak three times now and every time he gets better and better and I learn something new each time. Incredible stuff! I had a thought come to me today about one of my programs about losing weight. I've been trying to lose weight for ages now and I've finally found yet another part of my negative programming. Where I work there are always free candies, cookies and pastries that are left over from various clients. We are allowed to help ourselves to these. I have come to realize my program has nothing to do with food or with hunger. It has to do with the food being FREE. When I was a child we were very poor and I was programmed to think in terms of getting things for FREE. I can actually feel myself salivate when I know those FREE goodies are around. That one program has taught me that we have other programs in us that cause self-defeating behavior that aren't at all obvious."

USA: Tommy, "I can relate to your description of going out of business because that's what's happening to me right at this moment. It has happened before and you're right I actually 'saw' my company go bust before it did. This time around the same thing is happening, it seems to be the story of my life. I hope I have caught it in time. I will definitely visualize myself out of the situation. That's how I got myself into it."

USA: Marie, "Like many other kids, when I was a child, I was badly abused. I must have had some terrible programs inserted into me because I've been married three times now, always to a drunk and I always get beaten. I'm sure it must be my fault but what I've got out of this weekend is that I don't need to understand those programs, what they are, or who inserted them, as long I visualize programs that are more powerful, of what I really want. In the past I've just gone along with whatever felt right at the time and all I've ever had is problems. The time has arrived for me to take control and start getting out of life exactly what I want."

Australia: Mark, "I am already a millionaire and you're right, it took me a lot longer than the anticipated five years, however that's not why I'm here today. I heard that your seminar was the best and I'm not disappointed. I'll tell you a story. I've been married three times and I have three separate families. Not one of those women did I love, but everytime someone came into my life I'd marry them. In my business life I have always set goals and accomplished most of them by using your techniques, as you say, intuitively. What I intend to do now is program for the person of my choice, someone who really likes the things that I like doing so we have something in common."

USA: Sid, "The description of guns and butter you gave was good. I have always spent everything on butter and I've got nothing to show for it. But I also have a lot of friends who have made it and you're absolutely right. I can visualize their homes and life styles right now, very easily, and in my imagination I can see all their guns."

USA: Joe, "I've come to a grinding halt man so many times it's not funny. I have come to realize that when you program your mind, sorry, I mean biocomputer, you have to be very careful to tell it what you really want not just what you think you want, because it can't tell the difference. I can see hundreds of cases of people getting autos or homes or yachts and businesses and not keeping them. You have to program your biocomputer not just to get you the thing but to keep you the thing, man, it's crazy, but I like it!"

Australia: Don, "When I was really down and out and bust my mate offered me the use of his four wheel drive, which was a really nice thing for him to do. I told him where to shove it. Fair Dinkum! I was running such a negative program the words just came out automatically."

USA: Ron, "I have read hundreds of books about motivation and visualizing, but not one of them brought it home to me that you actually have to create the pictures in the chemicals. I think that's where I've been going wrong."

USA: Charlie, "All this time I've been telling myself that I want to be rich and I haven't been visualizing it. I've been very unhappy for twenty years because I can see I have two computers pulling in totally different directions. What I really want is a little cottage in the country where I can write songs and play my recorder and now I know I can get them easily."

USA: Reg, "As of today I have really stopped smoking because I can actually 'see' what it looks like to be a non-smoker. I'm using you as a role model."

England: Bruce, "I can visualize very clearly but I've never really put the faculty to use because I didn't know how. It wasn't obvious to me that you could think into the future about what would happen and that would put a program into your biocomputer."

England: Jill, "I have never visualized because I was told it was evil and one must not play around with the mind. Obviously that's wrong. I wonder how many other people have been told the same thing."

USA: Cynthia, "If I had a dollar for every time I had come to a grinding halt I would be a millionaire right now. I've started lots of projects and came to a grinding halt on all of them. I wish I'd known this before. I guarantee the next project will make me a million because this time I'll program to see it through until the end."

USA: Jay, "I must be a classic case for you. I have accomplished many things, luxury house at Newport Beach, condo in Miami, two Ferrari's, various businesses. I always get what I've programmed for very quickly. Like Ron says, some times so quickly it frightens you. Then all of a sudden you lose it and have to start from scratch. Now I know you have to keep programming and never stop!"

USA: Henry, "Knowing what I know now I can see that I have talked myself out of hundreds of deals and opportunities."

USA: Randy, "I can see my big mistake has always been blaming other people for my mistakes, when really and truly my own biocomputer programs have been out of control."

Australia: Carl, "Everything I have ever done has been with an inappropriate program. Where have you been all my life?"

ZOOM SECRETS!

1. Many of the failure programs we have were inserted by well meaning parents and teachers, but have absolutely no correlation to the goals that we have set ourselves.

2. If you have a failure program in your biocomputer you will run on that program automatically, until you replace it with a more powerful program.

3. When your program comes to an end, you will come to a GRINDING HALT!

4. When your biocomputer reaches the end of its program it says " Mission Accomplished."

5. We must keep programming new goals all the time, we must not become complacent or we will slide down the snakes.

6. Take a look at your programs in detail. Do you have 'butter' programs or 'guns' programs?

7. Failures lose their vision and slide down the snakes!

8. Successful people hone up their visions and go up the ladders!

7

Biocomputer Language

You're beginning to see how much the mind is really like a computer, incredibly like a computer. Except that it has tens of thousands of times more capacity than any other computer in existence, for it's size. In actual fact we have already mentioned that we have a tremendous over-abundance of hardware and a vast shortage of positive software programs that will actually help us to accomplish our goals.

Like a conventional computer you have to program into the computer in order to get output. Input equals output. Garbage in equals garbage out.

Imagine that you have a little robot in front of you that can serve drinks to your guests, answer the telephone and open the door. Imagine that it has little arms and legs and it sweeps around gracefully on your living room floor. Your job is to program the little robot and you're in the process of writing the software. You're writing a software program that will allow the robot to play a simple game of ball with your children. What you do is put a rubber ball in the robots hand. Let's give the robot a program. Let's say the program says, "I will drop the rubber ball." You are convinced that you have started to create a good program. Let's take a closer look. "I will drop the rubber ball." Really and truly what the robot's saying is that he will drop the rubber ball, will sometime, but not now. Will means in the future. The robot in effect will be saying, "standing by, standing by, standing by, waiting for instructions."

Let's insert another program into the robot. This time you write, "I can drop the rubber ball." Again the little robot won't drop the rubber ball. Can means the future, I can do it, but I'm not going to now. The robot stands there saying, "standing by, standing by, waiting for instructions." The next program you write for the little robot says, "I HAVE dropped the rubber ball." Immediately the robot drops the rubber ball. That was the command the little robot was waiting for!

Recently I picked up a book in a Los Angeles bookstore and started browsing. The book was about Cybernetics and Semantics, it looked quite good until I got to nearly the last chapter where there were various individuals goal contracts. I couldn't believe my eyes! Practically every single goal started with I will, "I will earn $50,000 a year," or "I will be a successful teacher of psychology," or "I will be punctual for all my meetings.". Every single one of these goals would have the effect of putting the biocomputer on standby. The guy who had written the book had missed the whole point himself.

Semantics, the meaning of words! All the books that you have ever read on the subject of goal accomplishment have told you to word your goals in the present tense, now you know why. The biocomputer relies on concise instructions. The biocomputer has a language of it's own.

Your mind is just like a computer, it is teleological (goal seeking). It understands the program only in the way that you have inserted it. Let me give you a few examples. Ron hits Jim is a very different program to Jim hits Ron. Only three words but all according to how you insert them into the biocomputer would give two totally different outcomes. The biocomputer carries out instructions to the letter. I cannot emphasize strongly enough that your biocomputer is very much like a conventional computer and will respond to specific instructions. It really does operate like a computer. You have to think about that.

To all intents and purposes conventional computers are all basically alike. It is the programs that determine the value of the computer and so it is with the human biocomputer: I recall a guy I used to know, who would say, "I see for myself a pink Cadillac." Do you know what? That guy used to see pink Cadillacs everywhere he went. The biocomputer is teleological, his biocomputer pointed out all the pink Cadillacs to him, I doubt he ever missed one! He never owned a pink Caddy, but he certainly saw lots of them!

Many people make the mistake of programming their biocomputers with, "The money they make," or "I make $10,000 a week." In actual fact we don't make money at all. Only governments and counterfeiters make money. The rest of us have to earn money. I suggest you program your biocomputer with "I earn $10,000 a week." Or "I earn $1,000 a week." That is how to reprogram the human biocomputer with information that is semantically correct.

I have a lot to say on biocomputer language because I think in the past too many books about success and goal accomplishment have been written by people who haven't actually done it. They've dabbled in the theory of it, and in doing so, have lead many people astray.

It will pay you dividends to carefully study and observe your biocomputer language. The biocomputer understands only and exactly what you have programmed into it. For example, say if your biocomputer language is, 'Open up a corner grocery store.' Your biocomputer will give you the output that you have programmed into it. (I'm assuming now, in all the following instances you will be visualizing as well!) Your biocomputer will find a way for you to 'open a corner grocery store.' The moment it's accomplished that for you, it will stand idly by, staring right through you, with a stupid grin on its face saying, "MISSION ACCOMPLISHED!" and it will do nothing further for you until you give it specific instructions in the form of a program. In the mean time you'll be getting frustrated because the shop's losing you money, draining all your time and resources and you will slowly but surely begin to slide down one of the many snakes. (In many cases it won't be slowly, but it'll always be surely!)

Your program 'Open a corner grocery store' has a meaning that is precisely defined. It said absolutely nothing about making the business continue to trade, making it profitable, making it a viable business that you could sell, that it would give you a good salary or that it would allow you to work flexible hours. That's why so many corner store owners find themselves losing money, working all the hours God sent and paying employees wages before they pay themselves.

The biocomputer knows nothing about whether you have made a wise decision or made the right choice, nor can it tell whether you should be doing more or should be doing less or for that matter nothing at all. It cannot tell whether your overheads are too high or whether you should be marketing in a different way. What it will do for you is carry out instructions to the letter very quickly and efficiently. However, once it reaches your goal for you, it will STOP PERFORMING IMMEDIATELY, until you insert the next program. Most of us watch idly by as our businesses disappear down the gurgler, not having the savvy to summon up the power that got us the business in the first place.

Let's have a look at some more biocomputer language and see what other troubles people openly invite into their lives. 'I must start a relationship or I must get a lover or I must get married.' This is a common enough program that causes untold misery and unhappiness. The biocomputer can lead you into a relationship very quickly. It can, it does and it will, all the time! However, what you have unwittingly programmed into your biocomputer is not what you really want or desire. By hook or by crook you will end up in a relationship but the chances are it will be with someone you don't really fancy and the chances are that because that new person in your life may very well fill a few of your needs, you may be with that person for a very long time indeed. Many times the girl may even fall pregnant and the couple end up marrying each other. They may even go through many years of married life together, being very frustrated, unhappy and unfulfilled. Believe me it happens far more often than you could possibly imagine. (To add insult to injury the biocomputer pats itself on the back, puts its feet up and takes it easy, thinking what a marvellous job it's done for you, lining you up with a Pet Dragon or an Ozone Friendly Trout!)

With a little more care and a little more understanding of the human biocomputer, you could just have easily put a program in, along of the lines of, 'I am dating a wonderful girl who is between 30 and 35 years old. She loves dancing and jogging and politics. She has a university education and we date each other for at least six months before we start living together, we compliment one another and she satisfies me in every way imaginable.'

Most of the time we short change ourselves by giving the biocomputer only short messages that are very open ended and ambiguous. The biocomputer will bring to fruition exactly and only what you intentionally or unwittingly instruct it to.

Why do you think people who are left inheritances or win lotteries, spend, spend, spend and very quickly end up where they were before they won the lottery? They do it because they are running on old computer programs. This is something you must look out for, it's an easy trap to slip into.

When you set yourself a goal and you haven't visualized far enough into the future, what happens is that you start to run on old programs and take the least line of resistance. For arguments sake, say if you program that you will leave New York and go to Boston to start a new life. You only put in half a program because you've never been there, don't have friends there and just don't know what to expect. In other words you don't bother to stretch your imagination.

You arrive in Boston and you start running on the half program that you've inserted. You get a job, a place to live and try to make new friends. However things don't work out too well and you start imagining what it's like back home in New York. You start running on old programs. You become homesick. You miss the old ways, your favorite haunts, old friends. You start visualizing that you're back home and before you know where you are, you arrive back in New York, only a year or two after you left there in the first place. Your program ran out and as soon as it did you started running on the old programs. (With a little care you could have put a complete program in your biocomputer while you were still living in New York about how you would excel at your job, all the things that you would be doing to create a social life for yourself. That's what the right computer is for!)

Let's say you half program for a business. You actually get the business, let's imagine it's a drycleaners that you've bought. You start running on the program and you begin to operate this dry-cleaning business. Unfortunately things don't go too well, the cash flow begins to dry up, customers are few and far between. Instead of visualizing business picking up and the money coming in, what do you do? You run on the old programs. You go back to thinking about the days when you were a carpenter or a cab driver or a house painter. Very quickly the business folds or you sell out at a loss and you find yourself back on the building site or driving a cab.

When you have set yourself a goal and have only half visualized it and only inserted a very incomplete program into your biocomputer, you're drawn like a very powerful magnet to run on old programs. You really do feel pulled towards the line of least resistance and sense that irresistible force that tells you to go back to where you belong and start doing again, doing what you've always done. Go back to your comfort zones! Slide down a few snakes!

Of course what you have to do, is use your will power and more than anything, your imagination. You have to nail the devil's ass to the wall and come out fighting! You may have to fight very hard, remember where there's no pain there's no gain and where there's no guts there's no glory! You're fighting for your very future and you may not get too many bites at the cherry. Use all of your will power and all of your imagination to keep your biocomputer off of what you don't want to happen and concentrate fully on what you do want to happen. When you feel powerfully drawn to go back to your old ways and start running on the old programs there is some good to be discovered out of the situation. Namely, you will realize the power of biocomputer programs! You have to take pains to harness this extremely powerful force.

What you have to do is vividly imagine exactly what you do want to happen. Create in your imagination a track for yourself to run on. Once you have impregnated those electrochemicals with the correct program, that same magnetism, that same irresistible force, will literally pull you toward your goals. It's exactly the same chemistry involved. (The chemistry is wrapped up in the sodium, potassium and electricity in those tiny neurons that contain the words and the pictures, the biocomputer programs!)

I remember very clearly that I programmed my biocomputer with 'I have built a chain of seven motorcycle shops.' In actual fact I couldn't believe how quickly I accomplished the mission. I bought shop after shop, I did some magical takeovers, my biocomputer performed faultlessly. I used to employ mechanics and salesmen without any problem. (In the industry at the time, skilled mechanics were as rare as rocking horse, you said it for me!) I had a very clear vision of where I was going. Everything came together like a cosmic jigsaw puzzle. I went toward my goal like an arrow leaving a bow. Unwittingly that was the last program I gave my biocomputer for a long long time. (The day I moved into the seventh shop it was down hill all the way. Again my biocomputer had cups of coffee and jelly donuts, took it easy, took a vacation, and watched with amusement as I started sliding down the snakes! It didn't raise a finger to help me!)

Only when the last shop was cleaned out and I nearly went bankrupt did I start visualizing that the shops were full of motorcycles once again, I very quickly, (with the aid of my biocomputer I hasten to add, who by this time had put down his cup of coffee and got into high gear within the space of about three days!) got the shops stocked and up and running again.

Every time I insert programs into my biocomputer I

become more astounded every time by the rapidity the goal is achieved. Every time I forget how I got there in the first place I slide down a snake. Every time I remember how I got there I start programming away at a specific goal and again the biocomputer takes me there, many times first class and often at the speed of Concorde. The secret of course is to keep visualizing into the future about what one really wants and all the time keep programming the biocomputer for future successes.

I have come to the conclusion that the bio-computer is a wonderful piece of apparatus, if only we could remember to use it all the time. The reward for using it constantly is moving onward and upward, up all the ladders. The price you pay for not using it every single day is sliding down the snakes!

Many of my students have reported to me that they have attained their dream autos and dream house and become Amway Directs or Amway Diamonds or attained certain other stations in life only to be deserted by their biocomputers at the crucial moment when they need to make a payment or move forward. The moment you reach your goal the biocomputer says MISSION ACCOMPLISHED. At that very moment it goes for a game of golf or a drink at the club house and leaves you in the lurch. The only antidote is to hand over more goals. The biocomputer is a faithful and loyal servant. It will never desert you providing you program it. The moment you fail to program it, it will go on vacation, for all you know, a trip to the moon! However, it will return immediately you have some work for it to do.

Countless contenders for the millionaire stakes have programmed that their book is published or their product is being manufactured. Very quickly these same contenders find that their book is being published (even if they publish it themselves) or indeed their product is being manufactured. I know countless people, all over the world who have basements full of books, the complete first print run of three thousand copies, less the twenty copies they gave to friends, who never read them and less a further hundred copies that were sent to potential distributors, of which not one responded. (Well in actual fact one did, but he was trying to sell you something, right!)

Unfortunately not one of these contenders put in a program of sufficient length about distribution, financing, marketing, P.R., advertising, rights sales, or what to do once the product is actually in existence. The biocomputer thinks it's accomplished the goal. With a goal like 'Get the book in print or get the product manufactured.' What does the biocomputer do? It immediately goes into? Yes! You've got it! MISSION ACCOMPLISHED MODE. It will stay there with its dark glasses on, solar beanie, stupid grin on its face, as it watches you sit on a pile of three thousand books or five thousand board games or seven thousand posters or twenty thousand tooth brushes or fifteen thousand clips that you've just collected from the plastic injection moulding factory. The biocomputer will sit on its heinie sipping strawberry Daiquiris, with one of those stupid little umbrella things, laughing its head off, feeling ever so pleased with itself, actually congratulating itself that it accomplished your goal for you in record time. (Look back on it. Once you decided that you wanted those books printed or those widgets manufactured it didn't take long to get them, did it? Despite the fact that you didn't have the money in the first place!) The biocomputer will stay in MISSION ACCOMPLISHED MODE until you give the magic command. NEXT GOAL!

Once you program into the biocomputer that you need distribution, finance, P.R., agents, advertising and a whole range of other things that you will need for success, the biocomputer will immediately come back on board and start performing miracles at the speed of light. (Probably really is the speed of light as well, that's the speed the electrochemicals can whizz around the biocomputer from cell to cell as it goes on its problem solving mission, but only if you tell it to!)

If you had properly visualized the goal: "My book is a bestseller" you would have spent a lot of energy creating mental images of you signing a deal with a literary agent. You would have vividly imagined the agent selling the manuscript to a publisher. You would actually see yourself receiving an advance, in your imagination. You would see yourself doing promotional seminars all over the country, maybe even all over the world. You would see yourself making numerous TV and radio appearances. You would see yourself being interviewed by the newspapers. You would actually be able to see, in your imagination, the book in stores all over America. You would not stop there, not unless you like sliding down snakes. You'd keep going. You'd see that six monthly royalty checks were coming in and then you'd see the book on the bestseller list, all in your imagination, you'd create a very strong program in the electrochemicals of your biocomputer and that is the track you would run on.

You would then see yourself writing the next book, because that's the way to sustain success. You have to keep on programming for the future, never stopping!

Do an exercise right now. Write down a brief description of the following six items on a sheet of paper: Your livelihood, auto, living accommodation, money in pocket, relationship and assets. Once you have done that you should then write down next to those items the biocomputer language that you used to attract those things to you. Go back to the day when you decided that you wanted those specific things for yourself. I can assure you that you have got exactly what you programmed for, six cases out of six. The next part of the exercise, is of course, honing the goals up in any other areas of your life where you think you may like improvement.

Why are you reading this paragraph when you haven't done the exercise? I suppose the next thing you'll do is rush out and buy a pile of self-help books hoping to find the secret of success. I suppose the thing you'll do after that is go through another ten years of poverty, misery and not accomplishing your goals and sliding down all those snakes. Hey, this is me you're talking to. I can't be fooled. If you really want to do yourself a favor and start going up ladders, FOR A CHANGE, carry out the instructions, get a sheet of paper and write down those six items before you forget. Have a close look at some of the biocomputer language that you have inserted unwittingly into your billion dollar biocomputer. Do it now! I'll still be here when you get back!

Before a conventional computer can solve any problem it first has to define the problem. When you reprogram your biocomputer, in future, you must take great pains to define your problems and goals and give specific instructions for the accomplishment of the same, taking particular regard for going further into the future than you would do normally. Don't forget, from here on in, you want to go way beyond the point where you would normally self-destruct.

The first major point about understanding the biocomputer is that it does what it is told, no more and no less. The second thing to understand is that instructions to the biocomputer must be very simple and straight forward.

I have read the same books that you have. Many say give a time limit to your goals and give a detailed description of your goals. I agree with most of it, but I think you can go too far and I think if you are not careful you can cut yourself off from many things that could come into your life and be very beneficial to you. I think it pays to work with various programs for your own biocomputer and see what works and what doesn't work. Let me give you some examples. Let me tell you about how I got my first Rolls Royce.

Of course I read that you have to know the color of the auto, the year of the auto, the model, all the details, but that had never worked for me. But nevertheless I decided I wanted a Rolls Royce. Right there and then, I wanted it! As I drove my little Ford around London, I used to visualize the Rolls Royce emblem, the Spirit of Ecstasy on the hood. I imagined this little Ford was a two ton auto and twenty feet long. If a gap came up that was not large enough to park a Rolls Royce, I'd drive around until I found a gap big enough for a Rolls, only then would I park. When I used to go home at night, I'd get out of the imaginary Rolls Royce and make an inspection for envy lines. (If you own a Rolls Royce in London the kids scratch the length of the auto with pennies, these scratches are known as envy lines!) I used to make my inspection, usually with my next door neighbor leaning over the fence, trying to puzzle out what on earth was going on. After the inspection I used to polish the imaginary Rolls Royce grill and the imaginary Spirit of Ecstasy on the hood. I put the program into my biocomputer that I owned a Rolls Royce, right now. I didn't put in the color, or the year, who, where, when, how or what. I did 'see' that I owned a Rolls Royce right then and there, I even went as far as washing my imaginary Rolls Royce every weekend. I distinctly remember that I was flexible about the year, the model and the color. In a very short space of time, about two months, that input became output and my biocomputer yielded to me the way I could get a Rolls Royce. Eurekas! I love 'em!

I guess you could say I'm from the old school. I was fourteen when I left school and there certainly weren't any computers around. The greatest thing was a transistor radio and we used to marvel at them crackling away, kidding ourselves how good they were.

Now although I've been a writer for a good number of years that doesn't mean to say I can use a word processor. The first book I ever wrote was in long hand and I got my favorite secretary to type it up for me. After that I progressed from manual typewriters to various electric models. I have to confess I liked the old IBM Selectrics. I tried later models with daisy wheels and memories but they never seemed to work too good for me. I always went back to the heavy old IBM's. I was building up quite a negative program towards modern word processors.

Quite recently one of my partners sat me down in a chair in front of a desk top computer and thrust a 'mouse' in my hand and tried to get me to move the cursor around on the screen and try to get the feel of it. I really couldn't understand what I was meant to be accomplishing. I knew this wasn't for me and after a few moments I got up and walked off.

Over the next few months I bumped into a number of colleagues and on each occasion the conversation got round to word processing. Each of them told me how simple it was and how I could type up my manuscripts and edit them all so simply. For some unknown reason I started to visualize myself at a word processor (that's exactly how I taught myself how to type) typing up a manuscript. Very shortly that input became output and I found myself merrily working away on a word processor. I had about seven minutes of lessons, and away I went. I called my colleague from time to time to get me unstuck on a few minor points, but nothing dramatic. Let me tell you, I'm hooked. I love it. What a device. I cut and paste and edit and do headings in bold. When I'm feeling really flash I do some paragraphs in italics and some in another script. I print out on the laser printer when I want to see what it all looks like. The spell check is amazing, with spelling like mine it's an absolute necessity. Magic! Double Magic!!

But let's have a look at my biocomputer program. When those transistor radios came out they didn't work too good. They were very tinny to say the least. Always problems with the printed circuits and dry joints. When I got the typewriter with the memory, always problems, didn't work too good, always printed out the wrong paragraph at the wrong time. I know I was building up a negative program about word processors. I knew they wouldn't work too good. Why put myself through all that when I had a good old Selectric? It's easy to see, anyone can get a program and just because it's a very strong program doesn't make it right.

That little example opened up my eyes. What else do I have programs about that I defend, that I just know I'm right about, but really and truly I'm totally wrong? Is there a simple program in your biocomputer that is holding you back. You just know you're right, but really you're wrong? Stop! Think! Look!

How many people have cut themselves off from goals by putting time limits on them? I know in all the books it tells you to put a time frame to each goal. Many people I've talked to say the most common goal they were going for was to be a millionaire in five years. Not one of the people I talked to made the million in five years. Don't forget I come from a very privileged position, being able to talk to so many people at my biocomputer seminars.

Let's look at the biocomputer language involved in

someone trying to make a million in five years time. Most people write down the following. 'I will be a millionaire in five years time, and for this I will sell such and such or so and so, or I will deliver goods and service to such a value.'

Before we get into earning a million dollars in five years, let's take a look at a conventional computer. Let's say you have two mailing lists with ten thousand names and addresses on each list. Quite a few of those names will be duplicated on each list so you decide to do a 'merge and purge'. That is to say you will combine the two lists together and you will kick out any duplicates. This operation will take quite a period of time, so you decide to run the program overnight while the computer is doing its work. The program may take five hours or ten hours or fifteen hours to run before the task is complete. It may only take an hour depending on how complex or simple the task is. The point is, that it will only take a fixed amount of time. Everything takes the time it takes. If you were to have added in one more instruction to the merge and purge operation, an instruction like, IT WILL TAKE FIVE YEARS TO COMPLETE THIS OPERATION the computer would not have done the task in hours, it would have taken five years.

So many would-be-millionaires have cut them-selves off from the target by allowing too long a time period for the accomplishment of a goal. The biocomputer in effect would be saying, 'standing by, standing by, standing by, ready when you are, five years time, but not now.' If you think about it, the biocomputer can only take a certain amount of time to assimilate the material you have programmed into it. If you have been careful in the way that you have inserted your program there is no reason in the world that the biocomputer should take five years to process the information and come up with a brilliant solution to your problem, a plan or a Eureka! to make you a million dollars in six months or one year or three years.

There is every reason in the world, if you have programmed for something to happen in five years time, why it won't happen at all. I have come to the conclusion, not lightly, but only after working for many years with many biocomputer students, the way to accomplish a goal is to set specific goals, but be flexible enough to allow options to come in. Develop a burning desire about a specific project and set a short time frame. If it's a million dollars that you desire, break down the project into smaller goals and attack the first part of the project with all the gusto and stamina that you can muster. Also read and learn and continually add to the material you are programming into your biocomputer with regards to the specific project in hand.

The bottom line is certainly not the time frame. If anything, the majority of contenders allow far too long a period of time to accomplish their goals. The bottom line is a number of factors, namely, that you have set a specific goal, but allow flexibility and most importantly, that you are actually visualizing (creating proper mental pictures for the right computer) and that your words and pictures match. Get a burning desire for your short term goal, just out of sight, but not a million miles away. These are the things that will take you to your goal in the shortest space of time, guaranteed!

You are beginning to learn the secrets of sustained success. If you look back over your past you'll realize that in all probability you haven't done so bad. You would have done a lot better though if you hadn't kept slipping backwards, (sliding down the snakes) if only you had managed to keep the ground, once you had attained it, you may very well be telling a different story right now. When making up goals it pays handsomely to look at them very carefully to ensure that you know exactly what you are going to do when you arrive.

Don't be afraid to experiment with the biocomputer. If you have been doing affirmations and visualizations for a number of years and are not getting appreciable results, (these results will be in the form of output from your biocomputer, namely correct habits and additionally hunches, inspirations and Eurekas!) you are doing something wrong. Do a little inner searching. Are you really visualizing or are you just paying lip service to it? Do you really want the goals you have set yourself? Have you set such a long time frame, that your biocomputer is on permanent stand-by? Are you using the completely wrong biocomputer language?

LIVE AT THE BIOCOMPUTER SEMINAR:

Singapore: Chew, "I can see where my frustrations stem from. I keep programming that I will be top salesman every month and I always achieve the goal. However what I really want to do is make a lot of money. I have never programmed to make a lot of money. I have never 'seen' myself make a lot of money in my imagination. I always accomplish my goals. I thought they would lead me to making a lot of money. I am obviously wrong. I can now see if you want to make a lot of money you actually have to put that into your biocomputer. It has nothing to do with being top salesman. They are two separate things."

Australia: Paul, "When I did the exercise of writing out my biocomputer language for my six items I was mortified. I realize what I have been doing and I'll share it with you. In every case I've short-changed myself. Because of my negative program of just getting by and that will do and she'll be right, in every case, I got what I had programmed, not what I really desired. No wonder I am so frustrated in my life. The auto, the women, the home, are exactly what I programmed, but not what I want, they're all just gap fillers. I can't believe that my biocomputer took the language and got me the things that I programmed for, but not the things I truly want. I thought I was in control, but now I realize it is."

USA: Claudia, "I come from a very wealthy background and for years I've been telling myself I don't want to be like that. Over and over again. Not for any particular reason, rebellion I guess. Today I've realized I do want to be like that. I hate doing what I've been doing. As of today I'm going to go for it, with some proper programs. I wanna be a millionaire!"

USA: Marcus, "What I'm amazed about is your description of the billion dollar biocomputer standing idly by with a stupid grin on it's face. I can't believe the amount of times I have programmed myself to get something, got it very quickly and then all my power deserts me. I have done it hundreds of times and it has never dawned on me that I stopped using my biocomputer. That has made my weekend!"

USA: Damion, "I can't believe the small amount of positive programming I've been doing compared with the vast amount of negative programming. I've been eating, drinking and breathing negative thoughts for the last five years, ever since I went bust. I can't believe I have sat on my tuchus for five years and done nothing. My biocomputer has literally been switched off. As of today I am going to start a major pro-gramming campaign."

USA: Davson, "I have always had the goal of being a millionaire in five years. To me that sounded quite logical. However what is even more logical is that if you put all the input into your biocomputer that it could possibly need, why on earth should the goal take five years? In todays world, money is switched from one account to another by selling shares or dealing on the money market. At last I see a dozen ways how to make a million very quickly. It has nothing at all to do with time, it has to do with getting the right idea from the biocomputer and implementing that idea. The idea is the main thing, you let capitalistic America do the rest! My thoughts have been clarified."

USA: Carl, "I have a story to tell, about five years ago I wanted this huge house on Long Island. I put the program in and very quickly I bought it. I couldn't believe the financial maneuvers my biocomputer showed me to do, in order to get the house, but I got it, all quite legally. Once I got the house I stopped programming. My biocomputer obviously told me I had arrived. That was the program. I could never figure out a way of getting the place furnished and I never moved in. In the end I ended up losing money on the deal because of all the fees involved. I now know that I could have enlisted the aid of the biocomputer to furnish the place and keep the place. If I'd met you five years ago I'd still have it."

USA: Grant, "I want to thank Ron Holland for what he's done for me. No one has ever told me I'm not a failure. No one has ever told me people don't really hate me. Last night, when I walked out of here, my balls were glowing, I felt that good. I've had lots of failures and I've been walking around telling myself over and over again that I'm a failure. I've convinced myself everyone hates me. I can see that I've made things come true by my self-talk. Last night I began to put some new programs in. Thank you Ron Holland."

USA: John, "Not all that long ago I reluctantly got involved in a business with two other guys. I kept telling myself I'd do it, and all I wanted out of it was a laser printer. We all went through hell together and in the end we never got the business off the ground. It cost me a year of my life, a lot of debts and aggravation. All I got out of it was a laser printer. I understand exactly what you mean by programming for what you really want. In actual fact you have to think things through."

England: Geoff, "I am beginning to see how complicated biocomputer language is. You have to program in what you really want, don't short-change yourself. You have to program way beyond where you think you want to go and you have to make sure that you keep programming in once you attain your goal, otherwise the biocomputer will stop working. I can see why my life has been a series of ups and downs like a yo-yo. I can also see my way clear to my own success."

USA: Nolan, "Looking at it now I always thought I was doing my biocomputer a favour by giving a good length of time for it to solve a problem or accomplish a goal. The exact reverse is true."

USA: Pat, "I wonder how many people are doing their affirmations with the wrong words and are getting frustrated because they think they're doing it right?"

USA: Marion, "My biocomputer has been on standby because I let my intellect tell me five years was realistic for making a million dollars."

England: David, "Ron Holland, I am lost for words. I have heard you speak four times now. Marvellous. Please come back to our branch soon!"

USA: Vincent, "I can quite easily see the brain operating like a computer would be able to solve problems very quickly."

USA: Martin, "I can see that every time I have programmed a goal I accidently program in the place for my biocomputer to stop working."

USA: Tina, "I have always talked to myself about my lack of self-worth. I keep telling myself I doubt I can do it."

USA: Barbie, "The biocomputer really does have a language of its own. The buzz words to watch for are Mission Accomplished Signals. Standing By, Waiting for the Next Program and Self Destruct. You really do cause your own demise. I have done so on many occasions."

Singapore: Yati, "I have always gone up the ladders at the speed of sound and come down the snakes at the speed of light!"

USA: Hazel, "You have a wicked sense of humor and a merry twinkle in your eyes. I like it!"

ZOOM SECRETS!

1. The biocomputer understands the exact meaning of words.

2. The biocomputer will act exactly on the words that you have programmed into it.

3. Don't confuse the biocomputer with programs that have not been worded semantically correct. You must word programs in the present tense.

4. If you program 'I will make a million in five years' you will immediately put the biocomputer on standby.

5. Certain flexibility is essential to allow unknown variables to come into the equation.

6. When the biocomputer arrives at your goal it will say to itself, MISSION ACCOMPLISHED and immediately stop performing, until you give it another program!

7. Don't make the mistake of programming just to reach your goal. Make sure you program way beyond the goal so you actually keep it, once you have accomplished it!

8

Feedback

Everyone wants to increase their performance. One of the ways of increasing performance is through the use of feedback. The human biocomputer operates continually through the use of feedback and once you understand how the mechanism works there are many things you can do to increase your efficiency.

If your biocomputer has been getting too little feedback or on the other hand too much feedback the consequences can be disastrous.

Feedback is a method of controlling a system by reinserting into it the results of your past performance. You will increase your performance by correctly using feedback. Let me give you some examples.

During the second world war, the statistics have it, for every six torpedoes that were fired there was only one hit. The submarine commander would shout "Fire One" and off went the torpedo toward the battleship. Invariably it would miss, but he was able to increase his performance because he now had some feedback. He would make some adjustments and fire the second torpedo, which, again would miss its target. The submarine commander would keep firing the torpedoes, making adjustments each time, and with every shot he was able to increase his performance, using feedback, by reinserting the results of his past performance. Nowadays torpedoes are one hundred percent accurate because they are wire guided. A wire is connected to a computer on board the submarine and it is also connected to the torpedo. As the torpedo rushes towards its target, feedback is sent down the wire from the computer on the submarine that enables corrections to be made until it finally hits its' target.

Let's look at another situation, one most of us are familiar with. Let's say you're throwing darts at a dart board. You say internally, "I'm going to hit the double twenty." With the first dart you miss, but you saw the dart go a little to the left. When you throw the next dart, you say internally, "OK, this time I have to throw the dart a little harder and over to the right." This time you get a little nearer your target. You have increased your performance by using feedback. The third dart goes straight into the double twenty, and as you threw it you said, "OK, this time not so hard and just a little more to the right" Bingo! Double twenty! You kept increasing your performance through the use of feedback. If you were blindfolded you would not be able to increase your performance through the use of feedback, not unless there was a friend of your's watching out for you and shouting instructions. However, if you were blindfolded and had too many friends shouting instructions you'd be no better off, you'd just be confused. Too much feedback is just as bad as too little feedback.

In the Navy when a Captain shouts an order to a subordinate he must immediately repeat it back to the Captain to show that he has heard and understood. It's this kind of feedback that prevents mistakes from happening.

Another interesting example would be how we tend to drive an auto on an icy road. Our entire performance depends on the feedback we get from road surfaces. If you go out for a drive one day and suspect ice on the roads you would be foolhardy indeed if you waited until you hit a patch of ice. What experienced drivers do every now and then, is deliberately hit the brake pedal, not sufficiently hard to put the auto out of control, but certainly enough to skid slightly. By doing this you get feedback to see just how slippery the road is and you can also see how the auto responds in a skid. Should you then accidentally hit a patch of ice you already know how to correct skidding and you can also regulate your steering and driving in accordance to the conditions.

We can all benefit by setting up 'think tanks' or 'master mind' groups or having 'skull sessions' with friends to help us get feedback. Many times a close friend will be able to give you valuable feedback about your programs that you can't see, because you are too close to them.

How can feedback help the salesperson or the entrepreneur? Let me give you an example of how most people run their biocomputers. Most people run on a negative feedback loop. We have already seen how many of our failure programs are inserted by other people. However, many of our failure programs are inserted by ourselves and then, constantly reinforced through the practice of negative feedback. When people fail, and many do, ranging from minor hiccups to major financial disasters, what most people tend to do is play those failures over and over again. I had a student at one of my biocomputer seminars who got jilted by a girl. He played that over and over in his mind. He said he couldn't think of anything else. That was ten years ago. He hadn't had a single relationship in ten years because he was jilted once. I had another guy who had failed in business; he went to work for someone else because he played his failure over and over again in his biocomputer. I have had salesmen who have been rejected so many times they quit the industry altogether because they couldn't stop playing a negative loop. This is what people do, they run on negative feedback loops and consequently they get more of the same.

I remember a personal situation from way back. I nearly went bankrupt. I had lost all my money, all my assets and my self-confidence and my self-esteem. I rented a small office. I did a lot of mail shots and a lot of classified advertising. I'm good at it, too, the phone rang constantly. Potential customers would call up and say, "I saw your advert, send me over a hundred of those." I'd jump down the phone, "You must be joking, only a hundred, we're wholesalers!" with that I'd slam down the phone. I'd do more mail shots and more advertising. If there's one thing I know about business it's being able to make the phone ring. I discovered if you're in business and you don't know how to make the phone ring, forget it. The phone would ring constantly. Again, another potential customer, "Send me over five hundred of those widgets!" again I'd jump down the phone, "You gotta be kidding feller, we're wholesalers!" again I'd slam down the phone. I'd do more mail shots and more classified's and this went on for three months. The phone rang non stop and I blew out nearly every deal. I wasn't making any money and yet I was desperate to get back to the top. One day I sat down and thought: This is ridiculous. I thought I would analyze what I was doing. I was making the phone ring, I had the enquires flooding in, yet each time I had someone on the line I blew it.

I racked by brains for many hours, then it suddenly hit me. I knew what I was doing wrong.

For three months I had been sitting in that office stewing.

I was running a negative feedback loop about myself. I was sitting there waiting for the phone to ring and all I kept thinking about was my crashes, all the money I had lost, all the people who had ripped me off, all the possessions I had lost, all the people who I thought had wronged me. Of course when the phone went, I was in the 'negative mode', all I could possibly do was put out more of the same. I had put a perfect negative feedback loop into my biocomputer and of course the output had to match.

As soon as I realized what I had done, I made up a list of all the things that I felt good about. I listed down the deals that I had made in the past, I listed down all the properties that I had successfully purchased and sold. I listed down each deal that I had closed. I listed down all my successes. There were many of them. I listed down all my friends. I then went about making up a film in my biocomputer about all these successes. I made up a complete film in my imagination and I played it over and over again. All the time I was sitting in the chair waiting for the phone to ring, I ran my positive film of my past successes. I did my mail shots and continued with my classified advertising campaign. The phone would go. "Send me over a hundred widgets you're advertising in todays paper!" I'd reply, "Certainly sir, I'll get those off to you today, but I would like to say one thing. We're wholesalers and I'd like the opportunity to get together with you over coffee so I can explain our complete product line to you, how about Friday 10am?"

I never failed to make an appointment and I started to make serious money as a wholesaler. I put down the phone and the next customer would phone in. I'd do the same thing again, I closed deal after deal and the only thing I had done was change the film that I was running in my biocomputer. I used to run a negative feedback loop and all I got was more of the same. I changed to positive feedback loop and put myself in 'success mode' and got more of the same. I stopped stewing and I started doing!

You will either be in the 'success mode' or 'failure mode' all depending on the film you play inside your biocomputer.

Now the marvellous thing about the human biocomputer is that it cannot tell the difference between a real experience and vividly imagined experience. So, even if you haven't had any successes, it doesn't matter, all you have to do is visualize that you have had some successes, over and over again and impregnate the electrochemicals in the biocomputer to create for yourself a positive program on which to run.

I have helped numerous insurance salespersons and door to door salespeople, simply by getting them to visualize that their last six calls were 'yeses' not 'noes.' Most salespeople don't do that at all. They keep playing a film over and over again of all the rejections that they've had and when they knock on the next door they actually elicit a negative response from their prospect. Once the sales person is used to playing a success program over and over again in their biocomputers they find they actually elicit business from their prospects.

Successful people are invariably successful all the time. They run a positive tape loop in their biocomputers continually and therefore elicit the desired responses from customers. People who are failures run negative films in their biocomputers and they too, get more of the same.

LIVE AT THE BIOCOMPUTER SEMINAR:

Ireland: Mitch, "When you first started talking about feedback I thought you were mad. Suddenly it hit me, what you were saying was directed at me. I play my failures over and over again. I know I've been getting more of the same. I'd say the life assurance industry is tough at the best of times, but with the wrong programs in, it's been diabolical!"

USA: Martha, "To run a film in the imagination is such a simple thing to do, but no one does it, because they've never been told."

USA: Robin, "Thank you for the feedback you've given us!"

USA: Marlene, "I never realized what damage I was doing by just running a negative loop. I've been running it for years. All I was doing was feeling sorry for myself, but I never realized it kept me at that level."

England: Tops, "I have been talking to myself positively for a very long time now and I haven't been getting anywhere. I've just realized I have to add pictures as well."

USA: Chico, "That which we vividly imagine will be attracted to us!"

England: Leon, "I have come to appreciate the cause of my headaches is because I am being pulled in two different directions by two separate computers."

Poland: Stanley, "We have to replay our past successes and preplay our future successes and then we'll be successful all the time."

Australia: Basil, "I have had lots of times that I have been eminently successful but I've never thought of playing those successes in my imagination. I play the failures over and over again."

Poland: Dineli, "All the time I'm tense I never get any ideas. As soon as I loosen up they begin to flow."

USA: Guistina, "I liken the program in the right computer to a piece of celluloid film. If the pictures were blurred the sound track would not make any sense."

USA: Kimberley, "I think it is vital to get feedback from people who know you well, about your programs. Often the negative programs that hold us back, are difficult to acknowledge and painful for us to look at. We need help from a friend, who is impartial and unbiased, to help us see ourselves as we really are."

ZOOM SECRETS!

1. Feedback is a way of increasing your performance.

2. The biocomputer operates on feedback all the time.

3. Too much feedback is just as bad as too little feedback.

4. Feedback is a method of controlling a system by reinserting into it, the results of its past performance.

5. You can insert a positive feedback loop by visualizing past successes. By doing so you will get more of the same.

6. Most people have a habit of playing their failures over and over again. They too get more of the same!

7. Even if you haven't had any successes visualize some successes and you'll get more of the same.

9

No Razz Ma Tazz. Just the Ras!

Before I divulge what I consider one of the most important discoveries of the twentieth century, I would like to reiterate one or two points. We have so far discovered that to perform certain tasks, successfully, in our own lives, whether the task be selling, or earning money, or closing a certain deal, or carpentry, or welding, or to accomplish the task of being a success, we must have certain knowledge in the individual neurons, in the electrochemicals that make up our biocomputer programs. We can get that information into our biocomputers in a variety of ways. We can actually practice the thing that we wish to achieve, we can simulate or role play the event as though it is really happening or we can relax and visualize whatever it is we would like to happen in the future. All these methods accomplish the same thing, namely, they impregnate the electrochemicals in the neurons, the neurons link together to form a ganglia, which is a program for your biocomputer, a track for you to run on.

I never want you to forget that the biocomputer cannot tell the difference between a real experience and a vividly imagined experience. So by vividly imagining that you are a millionaire or a pop star or a successful entrepreneur, you put that program into the biocomputer and that becomes a permanent track for you to run on. I'm determined that you never lose sight of the golden thread that runs throughout this complete philosophy! (By the time you finish this book I am determined that you will start visualizing and programming, not rush out to the store to buy yet another self-help book that will further gum up your already overloaded left computer!)

Just to cover a few more major points before we get heavily involved in the reticular activating system, RAS for short. Let's talk about the hardware that we have already discussed in detail so far. We've discussed the two hemispheres, the left and the right computers. The left computer processes in words and the right computer processes in pictures. We've talked in detail about the corpus callosum that is the substantial band of transmission fibres that joins the two computers together. We've talked about the neurons, which are the cells full of electrochemicals that link together to form a ganglia, which is a biocomputer program. We have talked about visualizing, in detail and how that puts programs into the individual cells, because the human biocomputer cannot tell the difference between a real experience and a vividly imagined experience. We have talked about the necessity of having this information (biocomputer programs) if we are going to attain the objectives we have set ourselves. We know we must have these programs in place before the actual event, to enable us to have a track to run on. Good! (For a moment I thought I was talking to myself!)

The part of the biocomputer that I am now going to discuss with you is what I would call the most 'significant' discovery of the twentieth century. The Reticular Activating System, as I said before, RAS for short. The RAS is a bundle of densely packed cells located in the central core of the brain. It is about the size of your little finger and it contains approximately one hundred and forty billion cells. That's an incredible seventy percent of the total two hundred billion cells that make up your complete biocomputer. It runs from the top of the spinal cord to the middle of the brain. The RAS is a very important component of the human biocomputer. Very important! It is the coup-de-grace, the crowning glory, the apex of the complete philosophy! (Incidentally the RAS was discovered by Messrs H. W. Magaun and G. Moruzzi, I personally wouldn't call them messers, I'd say Doctor was more in line!)

One of the functions of the RAS is that it acts as the filter of the mind. Let me give you an example. Suppose you are driving your auto in heavy traffic. As an auto comes toward you, at that moment in time it is the most important thing in your life. However, the split second the auto has gone past and is out of your field of vision, it is no longer a threat and it is no longer necessary for you to remember that vehicle. The RAS filters that information out. It allows certain information to come in and it filters out what is not necessary. If you were to remember every auto that came toward you, you would go mad in a very short space of time. Only information that is really needed is allowed through to your biocomputer.

If you live out by an airport, I doubt you ever notice the sounds of the jets flying in and out, your RAS has filtered out the noise, it is not important for you to hear. Friends come over in the evening for drinks, and the first thing they say is, "How can you put up with this noise, it would drive me nuts?" They don't believe you when you tell them you never hear a thing, but it's true. Your RAS is doing a good job.

If you live out in the country, the local lads get out their motorcycles on Sunday afternoon. The first time you hear them it's bothersome, there is no second time because the RAS acts as a filter and no longer lets in information that is not important to you.

Of course the RAS works the other way around as well. Anyone who has ever done research knows they can 'skim' hundreds of newspapers and articles and the RAS will always allow what is important to come into the field of vision. This is sometimes known as 'mind set', but all it is, is the RAS operating efficiently. If you develop a burning desire for a project the RAS will allow everything to come to your attention that is needed for you to complete the project successfully.

The RAS has a number of other very important functions. It takes note of your environment. It knows everything about where you're at in your life. It takes notice of your surroundings, who you are, where you are, and what it is that you are trying to accomplish.

The RAS has other functions which are equally important. Don't forget this tiny mechanism accounts for a whopping seventy percent of the total neurons in your biocomputer. The RAS is responsible for activating the mechanism of the words, (left computer, words, affirmations, I will, willpower) and it is also responsible for activating your imagination (right computer, pictures, visualizations, imagining the future). We have talked many times about the secret of success but I very much doubt that you have picked it up. I don't mean to insult your intelligence either, there is no reason in the world why you would have picked it up unless you were already conversant with the functions of the RAS.

I have emphasized the secret over and over again, relax and visualize the future as you desire. There's no way that you haven't picked up the bit about visualizing, I know you have, (nobody in the entire universe could have failed to have picked up that I think visualizing the future as you desire it is the most important function for human beings in the entire gamut of human behavior. I consider that I have one of the toughest jobs in the world to accomplish. You see, you have read in ALL the motivational self-help books that you must visualize and you still don't, I will stop at nothing, short of actually being rude, to get through to you, that you do actually have to visualize!!!) the bit we're talking about now is the word RELAX. This is going to turn out to be one of your greatest keys and I'm pretty well convinced that it's something that you haven't been doing in conjunction with your visualizations.

I emphasized that all my heroes, Walt Disney, Howard Hughes, Winston Churchill, Aristotle Onassis, would take time out every day to RELAX and visualize the future as they desired it. It's this word relax that I want to talk to you about in great detail.

The RAS is the mechanism that the stage hypnotist relaxes when he's doing some hypnosis with someone up on the stage. You don't usually see what he does, but the procedure is usually the same. He selects some people from the audience before the show begins. He takes these people back stage and establishes a rapport with them. He then gives them a five or a ten minute relaxation induction. He tells them they are relaxed and that they feel comfortable and their legs and arms and eyes are getting very heavy. He may carry on like that for quite a while. (I nearly went into an altered state just proof reading that last sentence!)

The hypnotherapist will use an identical technique. He will have a client come into his office and he will establish a rapport with them. He will then proceed to relax them using the same five or ten or fifteen minute relaxation method the stage hypnotist uses.

By relaxing someone for a short induction period you deactivate the RAS. Once the RAS is deactivated you can insert new programs into peoples' bio-computers very quickly by getting below the threshold of consciousness, WITHOUT THE RESISTANCE OF THE INTELLECT.

The stage hypnotist deactivates a person's RAS then he tells them they can't pick up a magic marker, or they can't remember their name, or they won't be able to move from this position or that position. He gets his subjects to hallucinate a bunny rabbit or a parakeet. All sorts of weird and wonderful things the stage hypnotist can do, but only after he's deactivated his subject's RAS by using a ten or fifteen minute relaxation induction. Don't forget that a person has had his name for thirty or forty years, yet the stage hypnotist can overcome that program very quickly by deactivating the RAS and inserting a new program.

The hypnotherapist does the same thing. He inserts new programs into his patients biocomputer very quickly, he cures them of smoking, helps them lose weight, cures them of stuttering and stammering all sorts of wonderful things, but always, before the new program goes into the biocomputer, there is always a period of relaxation that deactivates the RAS.

There is a high probability that you have been unsuccessful with your affirmations and visualizations because you never took time out to relax and deactivate the RAS first. No one told you to! I'm telling you, in no uncertain terms, failing to comply with this instruction is to court disaster!

You have probably tried to insert programs into your biocomputer, "I'm a millionaire, I own a Rolls Royce, I earn $10,000 a week," and immediately your intellect says "That's ridiculous, you can't do that! Why should you be able to with your humble background? You can't do that, you don't have two pennies to rub together, you can't do that you're only a carpenter or dentist or accountant," or whatever it is that your intellect tries to tell you!

With the RAS deactivated things are totally different. The programs go directly into your bio-computer, like I said, below the threshold of consciousness and without the resistance of the intellect.

It's this mechanism that all my heros used to deactivate without even realizing what it was they were doing. Make no mistake about it though, they all did it. As an avid reader of biographies and autobiographies I made the discovery that many of the rich and famous did the same thing, they relaxed and visualized the future as they desired it, intuitively.

I don't want to make too much of a fuss about the RAS, because it's so simple to use and so simple to deactivate. Like I said all my heroe's used it intuitively. The only reason why I'm giving a little background, from the scientific and medical angle is that I want you to know it is a real part of the brain and when you deactivate the RAS you really are doing something physiological.

When you relax, the RAS gets deactivated and that allows you to put programs directly into your biocomputer, by by-passing your intellect. Once the RAS is deactivated there is no resistance to any programs going into the biocomputer. For this very same reason many books say the best time to do your visualizations is just when you awake in the morning and just before you go to bed at night. They are quite correct in one respect, at these periods the RAS is automatically deactivated. I made the point before, that you should reprogram your biocomputer when your energy level is at its highest. I have noticed that many people try to visualize just before they go to sleep, but end up actually falling asleep instead.

Many esoteric books talk about meditation and

say that when you are in a state of meditation you have to be very careful that evil spirits and evil suggestions of other people do not enter your biocomputer. This would be quite correct because once your RAS is deactivated you would indeed be very susceptible to the negative suggestions and influence of other people.

While talking about the subject of meditation I just want to mention a couple of thoughts I have on the subject. I have come to realize that it is beneficial to meditate on a daily basis. (In 'Talk and Grow Rich', I go into great detail about meditation and the S.S.S. formula, Silence, Stillness and Solitude which has helped thousands of people, worldwide, stop their internal dialogue) By relaxing you allow the two computers to be able to communicate with each other. I have found it beneficial to get my students to link their meditations with some kind of input, their affirmations and visualizations. (Although the input should not be done at the same time as the meditation, it should be done at a separate time, albeit in a relaxed state) I have discovered that students who only meditate, without doing affirmations and visualizations don't get sufficient or correct output from their biocomputer. They may be able to sustain happiness, peace of mind and be able to live a stress free life, but that isn't getting rich. Most people who meditate don't bother to snap themselves out of the meditative state. In other words when they finish meditating they do not bother to reactivate the RAS. This is not to be recommended. I discovered this on a personal level. Many years back when I first got into mind stuff, I messed around with everything. I did lots of experiments. I was the original space cadet! (I'm surprised I never got beamed up!) I got into meditation. For about two years I meditated every day, religiously!

When I finished I just got up and went about my work. For two complete years I felt really lethargic, tired, the life had drained out of me. I walked around like a zombie. I really did. I thought I had attained peace of mind. (I thought I had attained a tranquil state) In actual fact I'm not sure what I thought, I was out of it. I was out to lunch! as they say. Little did I realize I was continually walking around with my RAS in the deactivated mode. Knowing what I know now, I can only assume that I was susceptible to all the negative input you can imagine. I am only thankful that I wasn't exposed to too much negativity.

When I first stumbled across the RAS I decided to do an experiment. I did my daily meditation and when I had finished I deliberately snapped myself out of the altered state. I shook my head, splashed water on my face, jumped up, ran around, shook my head and really snapped myself out of it. I couldn't believe that I became almost human again. After walking around for almost two years like a humanoid, I began to feel like my old self again. I started to take an interest in life, I was motivated, I was happy, I was alert, I was raring to go. I felt good. (This last tip would probably help those guys in the saffron robes at Los Angeles airport!)

My next experiment was when I actually started adding some input into my biocomputer when I was in a relaxed state. That's when I started to get the real breakthroughs!

When I first came across the RAS I realized it was such a powerful mechanism, I wanted to explore further and find out everything there was to know. I set myself up in business, in the State of Massachusetts, as a hypnotherapist to prove to myself I could really insert programs into people's biocomputers and create permanent change in people and overcome maybe ten or twenty or thirty years of negative programming very

very quickly. I cured many patients of all sorts of problems, nicotine addiction, weight problems, phobias (including snakes, height, elevators and flying) I helped many people with depression and relationship problems. (You noticed how I linked those two together!) I always used the same routine. I used to get clients into my office. I would establish a rapport with my clients very quickly, (I suggest that if you are in sales or deal with people, establishing a rapport is the first step in the art of selling oneself. I suggest you get hold of a copy of my book, Talk and Grow Rich, which has been written up as the most definitive book on reading people that's ever been written. Plug, plug, plug!) then I would proceed to give them a five or ten or fifteen minute relaxation induction. Everyone is different, you don't want the subject asleep, you do want them relaxed enough to deactivate the RAS. I would then proceed to insert new programs into their biocomputer. In the period where I was establishing a rapport with my client I would of course be finding out all about them and what their particular problem was. When I had finished inserting the new program into my clients biocomputer, I would then make sure I really snapped them out of the altered state so they didn't walk around with their RAS in the deactivated mode.

The RAS is a very important mechanism, everything you have learned so far, about reprogramming the human biocomputer, the left computer processing in words, the right computer processing in pictures, the automatic feedback loop, the corpus callosum, all of this is a waste of time unless we insert our new programs with the RAS in the deactivated state. You must relax before you start visualizing the future as you desire it.

In a moment I'll give you a five or ten minute relaxation induction. This is a similar induction that would be used by stage hypnotists and hypnotherapists all over the world. It is the same induction that I used as a hypnotherapist and it is the same one I use in my biocomputer seminars and it's the same one I use on myself on a twice daily basis. It is important to realize the state of consciousness you are trying to attain. You want to attain, what I would call, ultra-consciousness. You will be totally relaxed but you will still be awake and aware of your surroundings. You don't want to fall asleep. If you do you won't be able to visualize and that defeats the object of the whole exercise. With your RAS deactivated there is no resistance to new programs going into your biocomputer. I suggest that the induction that I give you is read aloud in your own voice onto an audio cassette tape. You can then play this tape to yourself on a twice daily basis. You can also add your own specific goals to the tape and listen to them, with your RAS deactivated, on a twice daily basis. More on that aspect a little later.

This is the relaxation induction. Just relax in an armchair and read it gently to yourself. Read it in a gentle monotone voice. As one of my biocomputer students exclaimed one day, "No Razz Ma Tazz, just the RAS!" and Oh! how I agree with him! Remember, what I am showing you is the end of survival, the beginning of living! Putting the induction onto an audio cassette saves you having to read out the words, once in the morning and once in the evening.

RELAXATION INDUCTION:

I am thinking of my legs and I am allowing my legs to relax. I am thinking of my arms and I am allowing my arms to relax. The more I think of my arms and legs the more pleasantly relaxed I become. I am now breathing deeper and deeper. The deeper I breathe the more pleasantly relaxed I become. As I relax I slip into a deeper and deeper state of relaxation. My arms are getting heavy and my legs are getting heavy and the deeper I breathe the more pleasantly relaxed I become. My facial muscles are fully relaxed and so are the muscles around my eyes. The more I relax these muscles the more pleasantly relaxed I become. I notice my breathing getting heavier and my eyes getting heavier, I am now completely and utterly relaxed. My head is getting heavy, my arms are getting heavy and my breathing is getting deeper and deeper. I notice that I am very comfortable and very relaxed. My legs are now very heavy. My eyes are now very heavy. I have slipped into a very deep state of relaxation that covers the whole of my body. I feel very relaxed and very comfortable. All the parts of my body are in a deep state of relaxation.

This is an induction that you can experiment with. You can read this out over and over again onto an audio cassette tape. You may find that you need a five minute induction to completely relax you. Others may need fifteen or twenty minutes. Find out what works for you. Remember you don't want to be asleep, just relaxed.

Edison, one of the world's greatest inventors, used to sit in his armchair on a regular basis and hold a bunch of keys in his hand. He would then relax (deactivate his RAS) then start visualizing his inventions. If the bunch of keys fell from his hand the noise would wake him up and he'd start again. He knew he didn't want to be asleep, just relaxed. Edison came up with thousands of useful patents and inventions and in doing so made himself a multi-millionaire.

Winston Churchill used to lay out twice a day on his hard oak office desk. He found that if he lay on the bed he tended to fall asleep. Churchill (We are all worms, but I'm a glow worm!) was a prolific writer and artist as well as being probably one of the most successful and revered Prime Ministers of Great Britain, of all time. He was and still is a great inspiration to many people including myself.

Aristotle Onassis used to rent his room out at night but during the day he used it himself. He used the hard floor to rest on, he too found that he would fall asleep on the bed. He used to lay on the hard floor and relax. Then he used to visualize the future as he desired it. If it's good enough for Thomas Edison, Winston Churchill, Howard Hughes and Ron G. Holland it should be good enough for you! The method works!

It hasn't escaped my attention that over the years I have noticed many times, both from my own experience and observing other people who are striving for the top, human beings hate to take time out to relax. They fight and struggle and make hard work of it, they go against the flow. On the other hand every time I let go (I love the expression, let go and let God!), I start to move forward again, I go with the flow.

Jungle creatures live with all sorts of predators around them but they don't live in a constant state of stress, only in emergency, at the very last moment their backs arch, ears stand on end and concentration comes into their eyes. It's only humans that live in constant state of stress and worry all the time.

Relaxation is a key to high performance human behavior. Relaxation is the key to success. Relaxation is the key to making the biocomputer operate efficiently and it is also the key to controlling the RAS.

One of the main functions of the RAS is to activate the mechanism of the words (left computer) and to activate the mechanism of the pictures (right computer). We have mentioned this before, but it's only becoming apparent now, why this is so crucial.

When you try to solve problems consciously you

can usually only come up with say ten or fifteen options, variations of the theme, of how you may solve your particular crisis. Many of those options aren't even viable, but because you're pressed, you consider them anyway. When you enlist the aid of the biocomputer to do your problem solving, you have at your disposal two computers functioning in totally different manners, tapping into two hundred billion bits of information in the form of neurons.

Imagine if you had a Rolodex full of words and a Rolodex full of pictures. These Rolodex's were not full of telephone numbers and addresses but they were full of one thing only. The left Rolodex has in it a complete description of your dream house and of course it has your complete language in it. Everything you've ever heard or said or thought in words is in that Rolodex. In the Rolodex on the right is a picture of your dream house and of course millions upon millions of other pictures, of all the things that you have ever done, all the things you have ever seen and all the things that you have even thought of in pictures. These Rolodex's are next to one another and would you believe they are both joined together by a connecting link and the two Rolodex's can communicate with one another. As they communicate with one another they swap words and pictures and sort out all the different permutations of how to get you your dream house by matching various words with various pictures; the whole idea is to come up with a workable solution for you. That may be a way you can get a handle on what we are talking about.

Let's look at it another way. Say you have two IBM computers, one programmed with hundreds of millions of words and the other one programmed with hundreds of millions of pictures and these two computers were joined together by a band of transmission fibres to allow them to communicate with each other, to sort through a myriad of possible combinations of words and pictures that would give you a viable solution to your problem.

To all intents and purposes that's exactly what you have in the human biocomputer. Absolutely staggering amounts of storage both in individual words and combinations of words and individual pictures and combinations of pictures.

In your biocomputer you have a vast bank of millions upon millions upon millions of words and pictures. In your biocomputer is all the stored knowledge of everything that you've done since you were born. That filing cabinet of knowledge is there for you to draw upon at any time you need. The only trouble is, when you draw upon it consciously, you can only access maybe ten or fifteen various 'bits of information.' All the other 'bits of information' are deeply hidden in the vast resource of the biocomputer.

This is where the RAS comes into play. If you are properly operating your RAS, by deactivating it and inserting proper programs in words and pictures that match (in other words you have totally ironed out any incongruities between the two computers) then you reactivated the RAS and go about your work in the proper state of consciousness, you will be switching on the mechanism that will activate the biocomputer to its full potential. On top of this you have to have periods of relaxation in order to allow the two computers to communicate with one another.

Once you have done that, you will have finally turned on the massive computer that is at your disposal. What will happen is that as you feed the biocomputer various problems, the two computers will literally sift and sort through those two hundred billion 'bits of information' that are stored in the two computers. It will diligently try to match words with pictures to see if it can come up with viable solutions to problems, all the time taking into consideration, what you have programmed into it as the preferred outcome and what it already has in storage in the two hundred billion cells.

The permutation of two hundred billion bits of information is absolutely staggering. The figures are literally astronomical. There is just no way that you could consciously try to match the vast number of words up with the vast number of pictures in order to find a healthy combination that will actually solve your problem. The only way you can do it is to hand the problem over to the biocomputer and let it get on with its computerized labour, flashing information back and forth between the two computers with the aid of its electrochemicals. By using this procedure the bio-computer can literally try and test millions or even tens of millions of possible options to your problems until it finds one that cross-references perfectly, is totally viable, within your means of activating and is the right solution for you. Only then will it kick it full force into your stream of consciousness, and you'll shout Eureka! (Eurekas! I love 'em!)

This is how the RAS plays such an important role in motivation. When you enlist the biocomputer to help you solve problems you literally have a massive resource at your disposal. The ideas it comes up with to propel you forward are so obviously right because of all the cross-referencing and the checking out of millions of other possible permutations, combinations and possible options. When you finally get the output from the biocomputer it is doubtful that there are any other solutions left that would suit you better. All the work has been done for you. Because the answer you receive is so obviously right, you will feel MOTIVATED INTO ACTION.

So you see, when you employ the RAS and properly program the biocomputer not only do you get the idea or solution to the problem but you will also get the amazing feeling that you have to activate it immediately if not sooner.

If you have had ideas in the past but haven't had the motivation come with them, it's probably because the idea was not a result of computerized labour from the biocomputer. You had this little niggling suspicion in the back of your biocomputer that something was not quite right and you are probably right! If the biocomputer never got to do its work properly and never checked literally millions upon millions of various combinations, permutations and options for you, I doubt very much if you could have done a proper job of cross referencing all your billions of possible words and pictures on a conscious level.

You feel de-motivated all the time you have niggling suspicions things are not quite right and you feel de-motivated when you have an incongruity between the two computers. You feel de-motivated when you don't know what to do next. MOTIVATION comes from doing something that is so obviously right!

Employ the RAS properly and you will find that you activate the key to motivation! The RAS is literally the Jewel in the Crown!

LIVE AT THE BIOCOMPUTER SEMINAR:

USA: Ed, "When Ron took us down into that altered state, that was the first time in my life that I have ever relaxed. Although there are sixty other people in the room I was totally unaware of them. I could actually 'see' my dream house for the first time ever. I didn't know you were meant to put yourself in the picture and walk around and be part of it."

USA: Joseph, "Before Ron told me to relax and deactivate the RAS I really could hear my intellect telling me I couldn't be a success. It actually told me I couldn't be a success because I don't have a college education. It was great to hear Ron say that he left school at the age of fourteen, with hardly any education and that he has no formal qualifications at all. I think the University of Hard Knocks is a good proving ground."

USA: Mundy, "I didn't know what it was before but I knew the best time for me to visualize is when I am watching television. I don't actually watch it, I stare right through it, if you know what I mean. I must be dropping my RAS and 'seeing' what I want to happen in the future. If people come into the room they know I'm out of it."

England: Ian, "I had read that you must relax before you visualized, but because they never explained why, I never did."

England: Sue, "I think the key words to the whole workshop are 'below the threshold of consciousness and without the resistance of the intellect' because for years I know my conscious mind has been telling me I can't do things, I can also hear my mother's voice telling me I can't do things."

Australia: Howard, "This weekend I have become aware of the fact that I just don't know how to relax. I'm up tight all the time. Someone else told me that's why I'm overweight. I'd never put it all together before. I can now see that relaxation is a very powerful key. That's why you always see rich people relaxing and enjoying themselves. That's why they say work hard, play hard. Ron brought that home to me."

Australia: Sean, "I had heard about the RAS before but it was so complicated I didn't understand it or how important it was. I didn't realize that the brain ran on electricity, now I understand people when they say they have to recharge their batteries. It all makes sense."

Australia: Bruce, "I went to a hypnotherapist once for shyness and it really worked. I didn't know we could use the exact same method on ourselves for any programs we like. He never told me that."

USA: Calvin, "I have noticed that every time I let go and relax that things happen. But until now I'd never put it all together. I can certainly see that by following a proper formula I will advance quicker than by using hit and miss methods."

USA: Justin, "I can see why Ron is so excited about the RAS. For one thing he really knows how to explain it. I'd heard of it before but it's importance was not stressed. What is obvious to me is that wealthy people and successful people must do something different to the rest of us. This is it!"

USA: Will, "I never realized that the RAS activated the mechanisms of both computers, thereby getting them to communicate with one another."

Poland: Chris, "I know my induction period is about twenty minutes, shorter than that and I just don't relax. Sometimes it may even be longer, but I do recognize when my RAS is down."

USA: Herman, "I've noticed a few people at various seminars of yours not closing their eyes and dropping the RAS, when it comes to do the exercises, they're only fooling themselves."

USA: Hartley, "I didn't realize the biocomputer had so many components and that you've got to get them working as one."

England: Christopher, "I can visualize my failures very easily. I always have done, they torment me. I guess I've got to start visualizing successes now."

USA: Sly, "The RAS is really the switch of the mind. If you're not using it properly, you're switched off!"

Spain: Cortessa, "I have never relaxed when doing affirmations or visualizations and you're absolutely right, my intellect has rejected them out of hand."

USA: Tyrone, "No RAS, no Jazz!"

USA: Martha, "I have noticed when I am half asleep in the morning I am nice and relaxed and I can visualize very easily."

USA: Zap, "For simply ages I have been meditating and not reactivating the RAS, I just know it."

Australia: Roland, "I had heard of the RAS before, but I had not grasped its significance. I'm a doctor and I think you've done a brilliant job of explaining it!"

ZOOM SECRETS!

1. The RAS is an extremely important mechanism in the biocomputer.

2. It accounts for 140 billion neurons, which is a massive seventy percent of the total two hundred billion cells in the biocomputer.

3. The RAS acts as the filter of the mind. It will keep the bad things out and let the good things in!

4. The RAS activates the mechanism of the words (left computer).

5. The RAS activates the mechanism of the imagination (right computer).

6. The RAS deactivates when you relax.

7. By deliberately deactivating the RAS you can insert programs into the biocomputer below the threshold of consciousness and without the resistance of the intellect.

8. It is absolutely essential to reactivate the RAS after a visualization session.

10

Reprogramming the Right Computer

This is a major and most crucial aspect of reprogramming the human biocomputer, simply because it is the hardest to do and requires concentrated effort. Only now will you realize why I have taken such great pains to emphasize and reiterate certain points.

By far the simplest way to reprogram the human biocomputer is to put certain information on an audio cassette tape and play it back to yourself at various times during the day.

The first audio cassette you will make up will be to reprogram your right computer only. (The left computer processes in words and needs to be reprogrammed in a totally different manner).

You will need a new, high quality, thirty minute cassette tape and a tape recorder. Using this method to reprogram the biocomputer will save you a lot of effort and will prove to be the shortest route to achieving your goals. You will accomplish your goals once and for all. You really will move onward and upward, (ladders only!) like a rocket! You begin to make your audio tape by recording a five or ten or fifteen minute relaxation induction that was given to you in the previous chapter. You need a long enough induction to relax you, but not put you to sleep. You will need to experiment. If you find yourself falling asleep, shorten the induction period, if you find yourself not becoming fully relaxed, lengthen the induction period.

After you have read the induction onto the beginning of the tape you will be ready to put a few selected goals on the tape. I would suggest between four and ten goals initially, depending on your ability to concentrate and visualize.

Let's say that your first goal is that you own a dream home. You would read onto the tape the following: **"I own my dream home. I have paid $200,000 cash deposit and I can easily afford the mortgage repayments. It has six bedrooms and an indoor swimming pool."** Then you would leave forty-five seconds blank on the tape where you will be visualizing the goal. The words are just a cue for the pictures. Your success will be in direct proportion to how much mental energy you spend creating subjective images for your right computer. You would vividly imagine the following:

You would visualize walking through your dream house, taking note of the pictures on the walls, the flowers in the vases and the pile of the carpets on the floor. Actually take a dip in the pool, splash around with some of your friends. See the smiles on their faces, hear the laughter in their voices. Have a barbecue on the lawn, smell the roast chicken and kebabs. Go back in the house and take some fresh roses that you have picked in the garden, actually see yourself picking the roses. Display them in a vase, add some sprigs of lilac, smell them. See yourself entertaining guests in the living room. Dance with your spouse, hear the Moonlight Serenade playing on the stereo. Hear the voices of family and friends talking merrily in the background. Cook up a meal in the kitchen, open a bottle of pink Champagne and pour it into tall crystal glasses full of strawberries. Admire the patterns on the soft furnishings. Put yourself in the picture. Go into the study and check your bank statements, take your glass of pink Champagne with you. See the mortgage payments are right up to date. Have a look at the bank balance, make sure there is plenty of money in the account to sustain the upkeep of your dream home. Vividly imagine that there is snow on the front drive, shovel the snow out of the way and park your Porsche. Now imagine raking up leaves in the fall, see yourself planting bulbs in the spring, see yourself having a garden party in the summertime. Visualize the scenario through your own eyes and then visualize the same thing, seeing yourself in your dream home but through someone else's eyes. Use both types of subjective visualization. Imagine that you are in your dream home through the various seasons. (Make sure you see yourself paying for the property either in cash or actually paying the monthly mortgage payments. Don't forget, seeing yourself keep the dream home is probably more important than getting it in the first place! Never forget, our failures come about, because we fail to visualize far enough into the future.)

Your next goal is that you own a corner grocery store. On the cassette tape you will say the following. **"I own a corner grocery store. This is a very profitable business. It has a tremendous cash flow that allows me to expand into other business areas that I choose."** Then you would leave a forty-five second blank on the tape where you will vividly imagine the following. Again you only use the words as a cue to start you visualizing.

You would vividly imagine that you are signing the lease for your corner store. See the lease in your imagination in great detail. Look it over carefully in your minds eye. Has it got weasel clauses so you can get out of it if you can't afford to keep paying the rent? Is the lease long enough to make it valuable to someone should you decide to sell the business after you have built it up? Does the lease allow you to sell the business? Visualize intently, all the prerequisites that you want to happen. Vividly imagine moving into the store. See who is helping you, make sure you can actually see reliable and trustworthy help. See the shelves full of groceries and produce. Vividly imagine unloading new lots of stock from pickup trucks and delivery wagons. See the girls at the cash registers, actually see the money they are taking from satisfied customers. Imagine collecting the cash from the cashiers at the end of the day and paying it into the bank. See yourself paying all your bills on time, see the business expand. Actually see yourself in the bank discussing your business with your bank manager. Imagine in detail the overdraft coming down and that you are trading in the black. See yourself reading sales figures whereby you know you can sell the business for a good profit. Or see yourself taking money out of the business to parlay into some other venture. See yourself embark on another venture because this one was so successful. You know from past failure programs that the reason why we fail is because we don't visualize far enough into the future to give us permanent tracks to run on. Don't make that mistake this time round! You've been there, done that! It is far better to expend mental energy at the beginning of a project, rather than try to sort out the problems when the project begins to fail, because you are coming to the end of your biocomputer program.

Your next goal that you list on your tape may be a dream auto. You would word the goal like this:

"I own a brand new Mercedes. It is fully loaded with every optional extra. I have paid $20,000 deposit and I am easily able to keep up the monthly payments." You would then leave a forty-five second gap on the tape where you would vividly imagine the following.

Imagine that you are picking up the auto at the showroom. The salesman is handing you the keys and you drive off. Vividly imagine the look on your girl friend's face, when you pick her up at work. Go for a drive in the country or along the coast highway. Feel the pride when you pull in for gas, and the attendant smiles at you because he can feel your pride. Vividly imagine the next morning when you drive off to work. Going to work has become a joy once again! You can smell the new upholstery. Feel the air conditioning on your face. Actually see the grins on your colleagues faces when you arrive at work. In the evening go to the tennis club, offer to take your tennis partner for a drive. Vividly imagine the weekend at home cleaning the auto. You have just come back from the car wash, now you are just putting the finishing touches to it. This is your pride and joy! (I spent a lot of time visualizing that I was washing and cleaning my first Rolls Royce and that's exactly what I did, because I couldn't afford to run it, it spent most of its time in my front drive, as a tourist attraction! So spend most of your time visualizing that you are driving and enjoying the auto, not cleaning and repairing it.)

It is very important to vividly imagine the financial aspects of owning your dream auto. Actually see yourself paying the monthly instalments or paying off the balance in full. Vividly imagine that you are looking at your bank statements and you can actually see that there are funds to pay the running expenses. Visualize into the future and see yourself getting top dollar as you part exchange the Mercedes for a Rolls Royce or next years BMW. (Again, a crucial part of the programming is that you actually visualize beyond just accomplishing the goal of getting a dream auto. The key to sustained success is reaching goals, keeping them and then going beyond them, without slipping down any snakes!)

Maybe the next goal you want to put on your right computer tape is that you are in a wonderful relationship. You would word the goal like this. **"I am dating a beautiful girl who is between twenty and twenty five years old. We date each other for six months before we live together. We get married in a lovely little church in the country and have a marvellous white wedding. We begin a family in our second year of marriage."** You would then leave forty-five seconds blank on the tape. You would then vividly imagine the following.

You would see yourself with the lady of your dreams. Actually see yourself cruising down the highway with her in your dream auto. (When you get used to using your imagination you can put many goals together in the same picture.) Vividly see what clothes she is wearing, also see what clothes you are wearing, put both of you in the picture. See what you look like through someone else's eyes. Also be actually there in the picture yourself. See yourself dating and having fun. Vividly imagine that you are talking away merrily with each other and discussing all sorts of interesting topics. See that you have a lot in common with each other. Visualize going out on various trips. Imagine that you are going to parties together. See yourself going away for weekends. Vividly imagine that you are proposing marriage to her at your favorite restaurant and she is saying, "Yes!" See yourself giving her a diamond ring. See the sparkle in her eyes. See the sparkle in the Diamond! See your bride in her white wedding gown and see the church. See how happy you both look at the reception. (At the moment I am doing the work for you. You actually have to be creating these images, and many more, in your own mind's eye, in the electrochemicals of your biocomputer if you are going to attain success!)

Your next goal may be that you have successfully relocated both your home and your job. This is how you would word the goal. **"I have successfully completed the transition from Boston to San Francisco The move was successful and I am happy in my new job."** Don't forget the forty-five seconds blank on the tape. You would then intently visualize the following.

Vividly imagine that the removals firm carefully crates and stores all your possessions. Actually visualize the furniture van departing from your house in Boston and see it arrive in San Francisco. Watch the removal men carefully put all your belongings in your new home. Vividly imagine that you are driving around your new neighborhood familiarizing yourself with the area. See yourself going into the stores, bank and the local school.

See yourself in your new job. See yourself being particularly successful because some of the skills you bring with you are a tremendous asset to the company that you are now working for. See the look on your employer's face, as they wonder how they got on without you, before you arrived.

See yourself earning more money than you are currently. See the appreciation from your new boss. Imagine that you are driving to work in San Francisco and it's very enjoyable, new and completely different. You love it. You love being there, in the Californian sun.

Let's say that the next goal is to earn $1,000 a week. You would read that goal onto the tape in its present tense, **"I earn $1,000 a week"** then you leave a gap of forty-five seconds with no words on it. During the blank period on the tape you visualize yourself earning $1,000 a week. You use the words as a cue for the pictures. When you are visualizing the fact that you are earning $1,000 a week you must actually 'see' yourself selling autos or real estate or computers or whatever it is that you do in order to earn money. You can 'see' yourself go to the bank and pay a check in. You can 'see' yourself delivering the product or service that you intend to give in return for the money. As well as 'seeing' you should add the appropriate sounds, feelings, tastes, smells, in as rich sensory detail as you possibly can to make the visualized experience as close to the real thing. Subjective visualization is the key to success!

Let's take another goal. **"I have paid all my debts."** Again leave a blank on the tape where you are going to spend some time visualizing. The words are just cues for the pictures. Don't forget programming the right computer is something that most of us have never taken great pains to do. Remember also the pictures are far more important than the words. The real key to your success will be in direct relationship to how much concentrated effort you are prepared to spend on creating mental pictures for your right computer. When you visualize your debts being paid, don't forget to 'see' the bills with PAID stamped right across them. Also 'see' yourself going into the bank or store and getting bills receipted. Use your imagination, put in detail, hear the clerk "thank you" for the money, 'see' the money coming into your possession that allows you to pay the bills, actually feel the immense relief that all your bills are paid, live out the whole scenario of you paying all your bills.

Visualize in detail that funds are coming in to you, and that you are paying off your debts.

We talked earlier about each computer going about its problem-solving in totally different ways. The left computer will be processing the problem "I have paid all my bills" in words and the right computer will be processing the problem, "I have paid all my bills" in pictures. The more input you can give to your biocomputer the more material it will have to work with. The more realistic you can make your pictures the quicker the biocomputer will solve your problems for you.

Let's have a look at the goal that's on the tip on everyone's tongue. **"I am a millionaire."** (Be time specific at your own peril!) You would leave the customary forty-five seconds blank on the tape. Then you would visualize the following.

You would see in your minds eye, that you were actually selling a lot of products. Obviously the bigger and more complicated the goal the more you must stretch your imagination. You would see yourself selling a thousand electrical gadgets with a thousand dollars profit in each. You might try vividly imagining that you were selling five hundred blocks of land with two thousand dollars profit in each. You may see yourself selling a million items with a dollar profit in each, you may see yourself getting royalties on a bestselling book or hit song or some other item that pays you a royalty. These things happen to people like you and me every day of the week! You may envisage a mail order business with thousands of checks coming through the mail, all made out, with your name on!

Use your creativity! You know the kind of things that you like doing and that hold interest for you.

Vividly imagine that you are in your warehouse and the orders are coming in rapidly over the fax. Make the pictures life-like. Catch a glimpse of the future. Place in the workshop of the mind that you own your own factory and it produces products twenty-four hours a day, in three eight-hour shifts. Visualize your own product in someone else's factory and they are sending you a royalty check. Go beyond the point you would normally go. Actually see the check in your imagination and see yourself handing it over to the cashier as you pay it into your bank account.

Imagine that your goal is to earn $100,000 in a single year selling life insurance. You would word your goal on the tape, **'I have earned $100,00 selling life insurance, in a single year'** (In this instance a time and date is essential) You would leave forty-five seconds blank on the tape where you will be vividly imagining that you are on the telephone making appointments to see prospects. You would then 'see' yourself in your imagination in great detail at either your prospects' home or place of business actually closing the transaction. You may even want to run through a number of meetings with him, all in your biocomputer, first you establish rapport, then you get him quotes and finally you close the deal. Vividly imagine that you are talking with him, 'see' what you are wearing, 'see' how he is dressed. Go over the proposal and go over any objections that he may have, live the complete scenario out as though it is really happening.

'See' in your imagination the commission checks coming through your letter box. 'See' yourself actually pay them into the bank. Visualize your bank, and what it looks like to 'see' those commission checks being paid in. Also visualize what it looks like to live the life-style of someone who earns $100,000 a year.

Try to model yourself on someone in the industry who you know for sure is making that kind of money.

Intently imagine the kind of people you will be dealing with. You may have to deal with individuals of a certain net worth. Imagine that you are dealing with these people right now. See and hear yourself qualify prospects over the telephone. Remember the more money you are going to earn selling financial products means that you will have to work smarter, not harder.

Vividly imagine that your clients readily give you referrals. They do this because you give them that little bit extra in the way of service.

So you're getting the idea. You must word your goals in the present tense, the words are just a cue for the pictures, then you leave a blank of forty-five seconds on the tape, then you put on the next verbal goal.

I suggested that initially you only put about six goals on the tape for the right computer, because subjective visualization really does take concentrated effort, especially if you are not used to it. Once you get into the swing of things and are really adept in the use of visualization, there is no reason at all why you can't increase the number of goals on your tape and the amount of time that you actually spend visualizing them. The whole idea of spending just forty-five seconds visualizing is to get you used to practicing and creating mental images every day. The sooner you can spend longer periods visualizing the better!

At the end of your goals you should place one last verbal message. This is to give yourself a positive feedback loop. You can use the words **"Now I will visualize these six successes from my past"** Don't forget to leave the customary forty-five seconds blank on the tape. Here you visualize six things that you feel were your greatest successes, relive them every day.

Imagine vividly the day you passed your driving test. See how happy you were. Vividly imagine the day you got married. Actually see yourself when you won your first sports trophy. Or perhaps you can visualize the six best sales that you made. Or visualize the six most lucrative deals that you have closed. You must vividly imagine the successes from the past as though it were happening right now.

Don't forget that most people play their failures over and over again and get more of the same. Their biocomputer programs keep them there, at failure level! Input equals output!

Last but not least, at the end of this tape, you must take great pains to actually snap yourself out of the state of 'ultra-consciousness.' **You do that by raising your voice and saying, "On the count of four I'm going to snap right out of this state and I'm going to come round. One, two, three, four!"** Make sure you shake your head and feel lively and alert. The most important point is for you to realize that you have been in an altered state of consciousness and that you must snap yourself out of it. The state of consciousness that you will have been in will not be the one that is conducive to everyday living. (Not unless you intend getting a saffron robe and start working the Los Angeles Airport!)

The tape that you have just made up should be listened to every single day, once in the morning and once in the evening when your batteries are fully charged. Because of the amount of energy required to make mental images it is a waste of time trying to do so unless your energy level is high.

LIVE AT THE BIOCOMPUTER SEMINAR:

England: Margaret, "I can't believe how simple you've made it. I can see that I have never put anything into my right computer before. I have been ignoring it completely. I've got a lot of catching up to do."

USA: Seymour, "We've come a long way since we thought we did our everyday living in one hemisphere and our serious thinking in the other!"

USA: Wally, "I know that when Einstein came up with $E=MC^2$ he saw it all in pictures in his imagination. He visualized that he was riding on a beam of light at 186,000 miles per second."

Poland: Borshenka, "I had heard that we must visualize before, but I had never equated it to putting a program into our biocomputer, so that we would know what the future looks like for us, so we would know what to do when we get there."

USA: Donald, "I know of a guy who visualized having a million dollars in his bank account and his wife got injured in an auto accident. He ended up with $1.8 million. I think you have to program exactly how you want the money to come to you."

England: Muffy, "I have been telling myself for ages that I'll lose weight, but my imagination is not yet under control. I keep buying Twinkies and Snickers when I think no one's looking. I have a program that says, 'if no one sees me, it doesn't count'!"

USA: Corry, "By regular use of visualization I literally doubled my income the first week I started using it. I haven't looked back since."

USA: Christine, "You have to keep practising with your own biocomputer to find out what works for you. I have to confess loud pop music puts me in the right mode for visualization."

Ireland: Isabelle, "Every now and then I pull the car over to the side of the road and start to visualize. It's like a zoo at home and at the office, it's just too noisy."

USA: Ollie, "At times I've used visualization accidentally and got fabulous results. What I've got to do now is get the faculty under control."

USA: MaryLynn, "I have found it's best if my friend takes me down and then takes me through my visualization. Then I do the same for her."

USA: Homer, "I'm a builder and often when I get stuck, I visualize the project finished, then very quickly, I come up with an idea. I don't understand why I have never used it in other areas of my life."

Australia: Bert, "By visualizing, some of the Eurekas! that you get are outstanding. It pays to put the idea into practice as soon as practically possible because that's what kicks the biocomputer into work quicker next time."

Poland: Eva, "You're the first seminar leader to tell us just how hard it is to visualize and that we've got our work cut out. In the past it was always brushed off as easy and I wondered why I couldn't do it. Now I know it's difficult for a lot of people, I can accept it and start working on it."

USA: Ollie, "Now that you've told us about visualization I can really see myself in all sorts of situations. It's great fun. I never used to fantasize because I thought it was dangerous."

England: Phil, "At school I was taught how to do everything except think."

USA: Chuck, "This is a tool I shall use for the next forty years. It's a shame that I haven't used it for the last forty. I might have something to show for them."

USA: John, "When I thought I was visualizing

before, I was definitely confused. What I was really doing was closing my eyes and relaxing and talking about the future in words. Now I know the difference. You really do have to create pictures, but you have to be told."

USA: Ted, "I used to think human beings were left brain dominant that's why they were so intelligent. I now see the error of my ways. If we want to attain our goals we must see them in pictures. That's where the teleological aspect comes into play."

USA: Isabelle, "I can see that by creating pictures, you can see something that would take ten million words to describe."

USA: Nancy, "By using this method of programming I have actually been able to pinpoint my self-destruct mechanism. I always thought I was self-destructing because I thought other people would be jealous of my success. I always thought I was self-destructing because I thought I'd leave my friends behind and not have any. The real reason why I self destruct every time is because I could not see myself as a success or living in luxury. Now I can! I think you have to be very careful about what other people say about their programs because they may or may not apply to you. It's very easy to say 'Wow! yes, that's why I self-destruct' and really it isn't. Do you know what I mean?"

USA: Paul, "The inner projection gives you the outer reality!"

ZOOM SECRETS!

1. Reprogramming the right computer is a major aspect of the complete philosophy, because it has been the most overlooked and for most people is the hardest to do.

2. When you make up the audio cassette tape to reprogram your right computer it is essential to have a five to ten minute induction at the beginning of the tape to deactivate the RAS.

3. After each goal on the tape it is essential to leave a forty-five seconds blank, to allow you time to visualize your goals.

4. At the end of the tape you can put a final cue, to remind you to visualize six of your past successes, to give you a success feedback loop.

5. At the end of the tape is is imperative to snap yourself out of the altered state of consciousness.

6. The human biocomputer runs very efficiently on one tenth of a volt of electricity. You will need all of that electrical energy to create mental images with. Make sure you visualize when your energy level is high.

7. The right computer tape will be programmed like this: Five or ten minute relaxation induction, first verbal goal, forty-five seconds blank, second verbal goal, forty-five seconds blank, third verbal goal, forty-five seconds blank, forth verbal goal, forty-five seconds blank, fifth verbal goal, forty-five seconds blank, sixth verbal goal, forty-five seconds blank. List of six past successes, forty-five seconds blank.ONE, TWO, THREE, FOUR, SNAP OUT NOW!!!

8. The program for the right computer must be used once in the morning and once in the evening.

11

Reprogramming the Left Computer

WARNING: The format of this work-book changes considerably over the next three chapters. You have probably formed a biocomputer program telling you that each page of the work-book is written in a certain format, that you have now got used to. Most readers, when the format changes, they change, they switch off, skim or jump a chapter. (Because they fail to insert a new program into their biocomputer!)

Don't do that! Recognize the format has changed and insert a new program into your biocomputer. Visualize right now, that you are reading and studying chapter eleven through fourteen in the new format. Visualize that you are reading each word and not jumping and skimming and fooling yourself that because the format has changed, the words don't apply to you! They do! (They apply to you more than anyone else, especially if you have tried to accomplish goals and read a lot, and still not achieved success, your program has not allowed in the pertinent information to allow you to become successful, but all that's behind you.)

The words are only example goals. What does apply to you, is the fact that there are many clues about how you can go about making up your own programs for success. **END OF WARNING!!!**

The next audio cassette tape that you should make up is for reprogramming your left computer only. This is a program that consists of words only and you can play it over and over again while you are driving your auto. Literally hundreds of hours of repetition is the key to success here. Remember the little Chinese boy? (How could you forget him!!!) How he got a sophisticated program into his biocomputer, repetition, repetition, repetition!

This is a program for the language center only. It will help you tremendously when you come to play your right computer tape if your biocomputer language program is deeply imbedded in the electro-chemicals of the left computer.

The left computer program comes in a number of menus. Basically to give you a 'quick start.' I think the most important aspect is that you get programming immediately and start developing more sophisticated programs as you go. This is not a ten minute project, done properly it will be a lifetime project.

Let me give you MENU ONE of the program so that you can make up your own cassette tape that you can play in your auto, as you drive.

I am a great believer in writing down one's goals and you are well advised to do so before undertaking the making of your audio tape. When writing your goals you can actually see whether you have got them written in their present tense, in biocomputer language, that will not bring about your own demise. Make sure you write them in a way that will create the output you desire. You should study them for a while, maybe they will need beefing up a little or expanding or rewording.

On this tape you can put as many goals as you like including the six that you already have on the right computer program. List all the goals in the present tense. On this tape you can also put any of the ideas and highlights that you have taken from this work-book. Anything that can give you a better appreciation of what it is that you are trying to accomplish.

MENU ONE: It is very important to start making up tapes and using them as soon as possible, whether you completely understand biocomputer language or not. You can start using MENU ONE, working with your ideas and goals. All the time look out for clues to see if you are putting the biocomputer into Mission Accomplished or Self-Destruct mode.

There are many blanks in the following goals. Write in any ideas that you get, as they come to you, about modes that will bring about your demise. It is imperative that you fully understand the wording of your own programs. It is vitally important to your wealth!

Obviously you will put your own goals on the tape, but MENU ONE should sound something like this:

I own a Rolls Royce. It is a Silver Spirit and I paid $20,000 cash deposit for it and I can easily afford the monthly payments.

(Remember, sometimes it pays not to put in too much detail.)

Repeat three times.

Mission Accomplished/Self-Destruct Signals to look out for: *Have you taken into account running costs? Have you any idea how long you would like to keep the auto for? Will you suffer financially because you have drained cash from somewhere else? Will you be able to garage the auto? Are you going to suffer a financial shortage in the near future that will cause you to sell the auto?*

I own a dream house and I can easily afford the mortgage repayments.

Repeat three times.

Mission Accomplished/Self-Destruct Signals to look out for: *Will you be able to afford to furnish the house? Will you be able to sustain the upkeep of the house?*

I feel healthy. I feel happy. I feel terrific.

Repeat three times.

Mission Accomplished/Self-Destruct Signals to watch out for:

I am prosperous and my wealth increases daily.

Repeat three times.

Mission Accomplished/Self-Destruct Signals to look out for:

I own a Harley Davidson Motorcycle.

Repeat three times.

Mission Accomplished/Self-Destruct Signals to look out for:

My book is selling in over forty countries around the world.

Repeat three times.

Mission Accomplished/Self-Destruct Signals to look out for: *What if the book sells only ten copies in each country, will you have attained your goal? Say if you get offers from other countries, will you turn them down? What if you get a distributor that only distributes in thirty nine countries will you turn them down?*

I am married to a beautiful woman and we are very happy.

Repeat three times.

Mission Accomplished/Self-Destruct Signals to look out for: *How long will you be married for, do you see yourself being together a long time?*

I am married to a wonderful man and we are very happy.
Repeat three times.
Mission Accomplished/Self-Destruct Signals to look out for:

I have one million dollars in the bank.
Repeat three times.
Mission Accomplished/Self-Destruct Signals to look for: *How did the million dollars get there, is it a high interest loan that has to be paid back? Did your business burn down? Did you have to sell some assets?*

I increase my customer base by over twelve percent every year.
Repeat three times.
Mission Accomplished/Self-Destruct Signals to look out for: *Say if you get that increase in the first month of the year, will you not try to get a further increase in the next twelve months? Say if you get a twenty five percent increase will you destroy part of the business to bring it back to twelve percent?*

I realize that success demands high degrees of relaxation. Firstly, when I visualize I know I must relax to deactivate my RAS, and secondly I know I must have other periods of relaxation to allow my two computers to communicate with one another. Relaxation is part of my daily program.
Repeat three times.
Mission Accomplished/Self-Destruct Signals to look out for: *When you start achieving great success are*

you programming to keep using the principles as you have just laid down?

I keep studying the biocomputer work-book and I completely understand the principles.
Repeat three times.
Mission Accomplished/Self-Destruct Signals to look out for:

I make up new tapes for the right and left computers as and when I need them. I continually improve the quality of my biocomputer programs.
Repeat three times.
Mission Accomplished/Self-Destruct Signals to look out for: *You will always be needing new tapes. Other than just making them up, will you be listening to them?*

I come up with a continuous supply of solutions to problems as a result of reprogramming my bio-computer.
Repeat three times.
Mission Accomplished/Self-Destruct Signals to look out for: *Will you put the ideas into practice immediately?*

I am always coming up with creative ideas as a result of reprogramming my biocomputer.
Repeat three times.
Mission Accomplished/Self-Destruct Signals to look out for:

I reprogram my biocomputer daily.
Repeat three times.
Mission Accomplished/Self-Destruct Signals to look out for:

I fully realize my two hemispheres are like two separate computers that go about their problem solving in two totally different ways. I also understand that the most marvellous thing is that they communicate with each other when I relax.

Repeat three times.

Mission Accomplished/Self-Destruct Signals to look out for:

I play this tape over and over again while I am driving my auto and I realize that it is hundreds of hours of programming that does the trick. I never give up on reprogramming my biocomputer.

Repeat three times.

Mission Accomplished/Self Destruct Signals to look out for:

Yes, I fully realize that Ron Holland has finally got through to me. I have to think very clearly in pictures when I am relaxed so my right computer gets programmed in pictures. I also realize I have to listen to the words over and over again to program my left computer. I know that the pictures must match the words.

(This last one is my joke. You don't really have to include it on your tape!) Oh, all right, you can if you must!

I suggest that on the tape for your left computer you put a number of different things. I'd like you to include all the material possessions that you would like to own. I would like you to include all the goals you would like to accomplish. You may even want to include some behavior modifications, particularly if you are shy or uncomfortable with people. You may want to include that you are a happy person or a successful person. Maybe you want to be more aggressive or less aggressive. Take care with the wording of your program to insure the exact output that you desire.

In the past you have berated yourself for mistakes that you've made, you've talked yourself out of all sorts of good things, you may have constantly affirmed how stupid you've been, how fat you are, how ugly you are, how poor you are, that you don't have two pennies to rub together, that you're only just scraping through, in effect what you have been doing is negatively self-programming yourself from within and that input has come to express itself in the person that you are right now. By playing your left computer tape as often as you can you'll soon overtake the old programs and very soon you'll be running on the new.

Many of the programs that I used on myself were much more than just one liners. I also used to make up new tapes on a regular basis. For example the goal I used for being happy, I put a lot of thought into. I was determined to be happy all the time, not just when things were going well. I have discovered this is the real key to positive thinking. Anyone can be happy when things are going well, but that isn't the secret. The secret is to be happy all the time. It took me a long time to realize that success is not a destination, it's a journey. In actual fact it took me about twenty years to learn that. (Looking back, it's taken me a long time to learn most things, things that most of mankind never learn at all.)

I sustained happiness by learning to enjoy the moment for what it is, not what it will bring in the future. The Chinese have a saying, 'Live happily by living today' and Alcoholics Anonymous have a saying, 'One day at a time.'

When I put my program into my biocomputer I spend quite a time getting the wording right. You may want to use the following wording or make up your own program: "I keep myself happy all the time. I do not let outside influences disturb me. I realize that many things happen in business. The things that happen in business happen in business and they do not make me unhappy. I enjoy everything that happens to me. Success is not a destination it's a journey, a journey that I have chosen to be very happy on."

I remember someone asking me how I could be so happy doing some gardening, when I knew the house was going to be repossessed the next day. The secret is that I loved the gardening for what it was right there and then, not what pleasure it was going to bring me in the future. If things that I do give me pleasure in the future, that's a bonus as far as I'm concerned, I have to be happy in the present. Unfortunately most people affirm to themselves, "I'll be happy when I make my million" or "My happiness equates with the money I have in the bank" consequently they're never happy.

It took me many years to realize that debts, employees not turning up to work, sales not coming in, trucks breaking down, fires, employees embezzling, partners not coming in with their funds, computers breaking, mail not arriving on time, checks bouncing, loans getting refused, partners blowing out deals, people being negative, general mistakes, bad decisions, are all part of business. Not just my business. They happen all the time. I recall discussing a few of my problems with old Seamus, thinking I had the weight of the world on my shoulders, with problems that I thought only happened to me, and all he could say was that "It sounds to me like business as usual!" If you're in business you'd do well to appreciate that there are many things that can and will make you unhappy, very unhappy, if you let them.

Old Seamus told me time over, the only reason he ever went into his business every day was to solve the problems. Solve the problems and you move ahead!

It took me a long time to discover that you need to play these tapes for hundreds of hours before the program forms in the electrochemicals. I've often wondered to myself how many people say their affirmations once or twice a day and wonder why they never get any appreciable results.

When I made my first reprogramming tapes my life was a real disaster. My biocomputer was a Tangled Loop. I was a Chocolate Mess! Everything was a screwed up. Finances, emotions, relationships the lot. I played my tape in the auto for literally hundreds of hours and I also played the tape for the right computer twice a day. I also played the left computer tape in my home, just for background noise. I left it on all the time. An old Jesuit saying: 'Repetition is the mother of learning!' I received literally thousands of hours of reprogramming.

Believe me, I was pleasantly surprised, when one day, I was driving down the road, when I suddenly realized that I had accomplished three of the goals on the tape. Making exciting new tapes very quickly became part of my routine. Needless to say my life turned around, which was fantastic, at last I'd found something that worked!

You will obviously want to progress and you will understand more and more of the biocomputer language and understand more ways in which you can bring about your own success or your own demise all according to how you create your programs. MENU TWO shows how you can progress even further:

MENU TWO: Obviously you will put your own goals on the tape but it will sound something like this:

I have completely overcome my resistance to working on computers. I practice every day and with practice my skill improves. Nothing disturbs me and I learn from my mistakes. I earn over twenty-five thousand dollars a year from my first word processing job and I am developing my skills beyond that level.

Repeat three times.

Mission Accomplished/Self-Destruct Signals to look out for: *Will you go on to learn other skills other than word processing? Will you ever earn more than twenty-five thousand a year?*

I have my weight problem completely under control. I control my food shopping habits and I am directed to buy only food conducive to my health and diet. Even when food is free, I am able to say "No" very easily. I only place half the amount of food on my plate that I normally eat and I have lost the desire to keep eating. I understand my desire to keep eating is tied to my emotions. Everyday I listen to my emotions tape. I am driven every day to look at my self honestly with regards to my eating habits and I write down ideas as they come to me. I know that if I cheat, I am only cheating myself. I have lost the desire to eat. Once I have lost weight I keep it off. I 'see' myself being the right weight twice a day with my RAS deactivated.

Repeat three times.

Mission Accomplished/Self-Destruct Signals to look out for:

Every day I get more enthusiastic about selling insurance. My enthusiasm comes across in my voice

and my behavior. I never hesitate to pick up the phone to call a client. I always visualize before I make my phone call so I can actually 'see' my prospect in my minds eye. My closure rate increases all the time. I sell financial products that my client has a need for and as a result of the good service that I give, my clients always give me referrals. My clients always phone the referrals and let them know I will be making contact. I constantly set and achieve goals. As I attain my goals I keep setting higher goals.

Repeat three times.

Mission Accomplished/Self-Destruct Signals to look out for:

I am the sales manager at the New York branch. I earned seventy thousand dollars in my first year. I am very popular with the sales force and as a result we increase the team by twenty percent and the sales by one hundred percent. My sales team respect my leadership. I am motivated all the time. I bring in new motivational speakers once a month for the sales meeting.

Repeat three times.

Mission Accomplished/Self-Destruct Signals to look out for:

I am always persistent. I never give up on my goals. I have very clearly defined goals and I know that makes the job easier. Because I can actually 'see' what it is that I am trying to accomplish, it is easier for me to keep heading toward that vision. I am very resilient. I use rejection as a spur to further creative effort. I know that being persistent is not enough on its own. I have combined my persistence with other things including offering a good product and service and doing more than one is paid for.

Repeat three times.

Mission Accomplished/Self-Destruct Signals to look out for:

I save ten percent of my gross revenue every month. I use my imagination to help me purchase the things that I need for everyday living. I know that I need capital to help start my future business. I no longer live hand to mouth. I 'see' many ways extra income can come to me and I have found a source of income that enables me to sustain the lifestyle that I am visualizing.

Repeat three times.

Mission Accomplished/Self-Destruct Signals to look out for:

I am a man of action. Because I have programmed my biocomputer correctly I do not have any incongruities between the pictures and the words. My goals are very clearly defined. Because my words and my pictures match, I have two very powerful computers working for me, not against me. I spend my time acting on the ideas and developing my plan. I employ my biocomputer to do my problem solving for me. By doing that I am free to implement my ideas. I have lost my inhibitions. If there is a place to go or someone to see that is relevant to the project, I do it.

Repeat three times.

Mission Accomplished/Self-Destruct Signals to look out for:

I am a deal closer. I never forget the reason for meetings, meetings, meetings is for closing, closing, closing! I stop talking and I listen. I listen for clues that my prospect gives when he is ready to close. I close professionally and quickly. I always give the full sales pitch but then I stop and listen. I do not talk myself out of deals. I actually ask for the orders and the check. I 'see' myself twice a day, when my RAS is deactivated, actually closing deals and getting people to sign contracts and hand over checks.

Repeat three times.

Mission Accomplished/Self-Destruct Signals to look out for:

I am a money magnet. I am always attracting money to me. I am drawn to people and opportunities that increase my wealth. I am drawn to various magazines and meetings and seminars that put me in contact with similar money conscious people. I am never short of money. I visualize, twice a day with my RAS deactivated, that money and checks keep coming to me in all denominations. I literally attract to me the forces of success through my visualizations.

Repeat three times.

Mission Accomplished/Self-Destruct Signals to look out for:

I always get referrals. Everyday people give me referrals. I know that contacts, contacts, contacts equal contracts, contracts, contracts! All the time my contact base increases. People like me because I always help them and go beyond the call of duty. People are genuinely pleased with my service and they have no hesitation in giving me referrals. I ask every client for five referrals. In return I always reciprocate by doing something special for my client, to help him in his business. This could be giving him a book, giving him a newspaper cutting that will help or just giving him an extra few moments of inspirational time.

Repeat three times.

Mission Accomplished/Self-Destruct Signals to look out for:

Nothing holds me back from success. I realize that my biocomputer programs have been holding me back in the past. I also know that a lot of these are still not obvious. I stop to think every time I find myself being nervous about moving forward. I look at my old biocomputer programs and I try to analyze what is holding me back. Even if I cannot discover exactly what is holding me back I make up a new program that will allow me to move forward. I study biocomputer language more and more every day.

Repeat three times.

Mission Accomplished/Self-Destruct Signals to look out for:

MENU THREE: In menu three you will be making up programs that will increase your use and knowledge of biocomputer principles.

You don't want to make hard work of success. (You've been doing that for years, and where has it got you?) You can use the actual biocomputer principles to help you use the principles more and more. The sooner you can make up and use this tape the better.

I fully understand biocomputer principles. I know that the biocomputer book is not just a book to be read once. It is a work-book. It is a tool. I know that every time I read it I learn something new. I get other people to read the book and I have discussions with these people and further my knowledge even more. I know that reading the book is just the instruction for actually visualizing in the right computer. I actually devote fifteen minutes in the

morning and fifteen minutes in the evening to creating pictures in my right computer. I am never too busy to create pictures in my right computer.

Repeat three times.

Mission Accomplished/Self-Destruct Signals to be look out for:

I use my right computer daily. I find myself pulling my auto to the side of the road in safe areas, where I stop and I start thinking things out in pictures. I practice using my right computer more and more every day. I work out ideas and concepts in pictures. I see deals before they happen in pictures. Every day I work with biocomputer principles. I read and study the biocomputer work-book and I spend more and more time thinking in pictures.

Repeat three times.

Mission Accomplished/Self-Destruct Signals to look out for:

I have both my computers working in harmony. I spend time looking at my goals and working out a plan of action for the future. When my biocomputer gets me to a goal, I know I have to immediately program in the next goal. If I can I work out a strategy in advance so I am always ahead of the game. I fully realize the biocomputer must never be left without a goal.

Repeat three times.

Mission Accomplished/Self-Destruct Signals to look out for:

I use the biocomputer tapes on an ongoing basis. I know that if I stop programming the biocomputer, I will immediately run on old self-defeating behavior programs. I have discovered the secret of sustained success. I have to keep programming for the future. I always have goals that I want to accomplish. I now know that because I can achieve anything I want in life I can choose goals that I desire, not just goals that I think I can attain.

Repeat three times.

Mission Accomplished/Self-Destruct programs to look out for:

I actually create pictures in my imagination. I know that reading about visualization is not doing it. Everyday I stop reading and stop working with my left computer and deliberately work with my right computer no matter how hard it may be. I know that I must keep exercising the faculty to get its potency back. I work hard on creating pictures in my imagination. I never give up trying to create pictures in my right computer.

Repeat three times.

Mission Accomplished/Self-Destruct Signals to look out for:

Relaxation is part of my daily routine. I find the more relaxed I am the easier it is to visualize. As well as deactivating the RAS twice a day for reprogramming, I also take time out to swim. (Or play golf or ride my bike or go jogging or play football or walk in the countryside) During my relaxation periods I get so caught up in them I completely forget about my projects and my burning desires. I give my biocomputer time to assimilate all the input. I know that when the output is ready to come it will. Therefore I let go completely and enjoy my relaxation periods for what they are. I am never so busy that I put off my relaxation program. Relaxation is one of the keys to making the biocomputer work efficiently.

Repeat three times.

Mission Accomplished/Self-Destruct Signals to look out for:

I can actually 'see' myself looking successful in my imagination. Everyday I create a picture of myself having accomplished my goals. I can 'see' myself being confident and successful. Everyday I 'see' myself having the behaviors that I need to accomplish success. I don't just tell myself that I am confident or assertive or a good salesman, I can actually 'see' it in my right computer as well.

Repeat three times.

Mission Accomplished/Self-Destruct Signals to look out for:

MENU FOUR: Menu four is specifically designed to program good habits so you automatically do the right thing all the time. This is an extremely important part of the program. Be careful to select programs that you need and hone them up to your own certain needs and temperament.

You can make up a separate tape or you can include these on a master tape, like making up a combination pizza! Don't forget that your success will depend largely on having a mixture of various programs. Have fun with it! Work with it. Look at the principles. Study them. Above all start making programs up for your own use.

I am extremely persistent in everything that I do. I never give up. I keep on keeping on. I use rejection as a spur to further effort. I look at rejection to see if there is any reason at all whether I should alter my product or service or behavior. I look at rejection as feedback and I use it accordingly. If I can use it I

will, if I can't I reject it. I know that persistence is only part of the success formula. I have to persist with something that is worthwhile attaining. To this end I have various other goals I am actually persisting with.

Repeat three times.

Mission Accomplished/Self-Destruct Programs to look out for:

I am very positive at all times. I keep myself positive by making sure that I have ruled out all incongruities between the words and pictures in my two computers. I make sure that I keep positive by attaining goals. I break large goals down into small goals and I keep attaining the smaller goals that get me closer to my main objective. In this manner I keep positive all the time. I take time out to celebrate goals when I accomplish them.

Repeat three times.

Mission Accomplished/Self-Destruct Signals to look out for:

I am very enthusiastic. My enthusiasm shows in many different ways. I always have a smile on my face and my clients and friends are always pleased to see me. I am always welcome at people's homes and businesses because of my enthusiasm. My enthusiasm is contagious and people like being around me.

Repeat three times.

Mission Accomplished/Self-Destruct Signals to look out for:

I am very creative and very productive. My creative powers are always available because I spend time thinking in pictures. This stimulates my creativity. I use my creativity in constructive ways. I always have time to write (or sew or cook or garden or work on the auto or whatever it is that you do when you are creative.) or develop creative ideas for selling and marketing. I am productive every day. I do not let the grass grow under my feet. I always get my work done everyday.

Repeat three times.

Mission Accomplished/Self-Destruct Signals to look out for:

I do not suffer from call reluctance. I make my telephone calls to clients on a day-to-day basis and I enjoy every call that I make. Before each call I actually visualize getting the response from the prospect that I desire. I clearly 'see' that response in my imagination. I make my door to door calls without any hesitation. I always visualize the call in advance. I ensure I keep my closing rate consistently high.

Repeat three times.

Mission Accomplished/Self-Destruct Signals to look out for:

I discipline myself on a daily basis. Because I am the master of my own destiny I keep my self disciplined. I work very hard. I play very hard. I practise the biocomputer principles daily. I listen to my right computer tape twice a day. I listen to my left computer tape as often as I can.

Repeat three times.

Mission Accomplished/Self-Destruct Signals to look out for:

I am self-reliant. I rely more and more on my own resources. I find everyday I am able to do more

because my skills and confidence increase. I get tremendous joy out of being self-reliant. Out of self-reliance comes self-esteem. If I discover that I cannot do a thing, I look at it and then I make up a program that allows me to overcome my resistance.

Repeat three times.

Mission Accomplished/Self-Destruct Signals to look out for:

I am a leader. People follow me because I have a mission. Because my goals are very clearly defined I know exactly what has to be done next. I encourage my followers to study biocomputer principles, in that way we all speak the same language.

Repeat three times.

Mission Accomplished/Self-Destruct Signals to look out for:

I am extremely confident at all times. My confidence is based on the fact that I can actually 'see' myself doing all the things that I try. My confidence builds each and every time I apply myself to a certain task.

Repeat three times.

Mission Accomplished/Self-Destruct Signals to look out for:

I have extremely good concentration. I spend time concentrating on the wording of my goals. I spend time concentrating on the visual images of my goals. Every day my concentration increases. I am not distracted by the thousand and one minor irritations that there are in life. I concentrate on the goals I have set myself. I use my concentration to help me create mental images of the things I want to happen in the future.

Repeat three times.

Mission Accomplished/Self-Destruct Signals to look out for:

When making up tapes you can take various parts from each menu and make up a tape suitable to your needs. The main thing is to get started.

LIVE AT THE BIOCOMPUTER SEMINAR:

USA: Michael, "I have been using Ron's Program for some time now and there are a few contributions I would like to make. I found it beneficial to start making up programs but to change them very quickly if I felt something was not quite right. I have come to realize that biocomputer language needs some thought. I agree that for many goals you need a lot of flexibility to allow various elements to come into the equation. On the other hand one has to make sure that you set your goal within certain parameters otherwise the biocomputer will set its own. Balance is the key word."

USA: Carter, "What I have found marvellous about playing my tapes is that they affect you in such wonderfully subtle ways. I had played a certain goal over and over again, in the auto, at home, on my Walkman, while I was at work, without really thinking about it, just playing it. I did my twice daily visualization as well. About two months later I found myself embarking on this major project that was going to lead me directly to my goal, so simply and effortlessly. In actual fact I opened up my own business and I had it up and running and profitable from day one."

Singapore: Chung, "For years I used to have a list of goals under my pillow. I was under the impression if I left them there I would accomplish them. I used to

168

read them out aloud every night and every morning. Nothing ever happened that convinced me it was working. By using this method, it is obvious to me that I will create proper programs in my biocomputer."

Australia: Zack, "I have had a very close look at my programs that I have been running on. At parties I have always ended up with the first woman that would talk to me. I have always ended up with the first women that would make love to me. That has been my program and I have run on it constantly for years. I'd never thought about it before but I was being driven biologically. I was never happy in any aspects of these relationships. Now I realize I can say 'No' and choose to be with whoever I want."

England: Sally, "For years I've been very confused. I always thought I was accomplishing my goals, but I've always been unhappy and dissatisfied. I've only just come to terms with the fact that I have accomplished all the things that I had set in my biocomputer but not a single one of those things was what I really wanted. Does that make sense?"

USA: Kevin, "I set many goals for all the things that I wanted. A guitar, some airline tickets to Aruba, a new Datsun Turbo, some new clothes, there was quite a lot more. Basically my program was to get me these things regardless. Within a very short space of time I had all of them. I found various ways of getting all those things on credit or with various loans. For a time I was very happy with my purchases, then the bills started to come in and the pressure was unbearable. I lost everything and as Ron says, I slipped down a snake. I now know that with careful programming it doesn't have to be like that at all. I can and I will get everything I want, paid for in cash by putting the correct program into the biocomputer. In actual fact, now I come to think of it, I actually used to program my biocomputer to help me attain credit cards and bank loans. It worked on the program that I gave it."

USA: Bob, "I have made up my tape to get me a million dollars and I have included on it all the ways that I will sell and market my product. In the past my goal was to have my product always available for distribution, which it has been for the last ten years. Now I realize that I have to get out there and sell it all over the world in huge numbers. This never dawned on me before, but I can see you have to put some exact detail in the program."

USA: Bernie, "I think the major thing that's come home to me this weekend is that the moment the biocomputer gets to the end of the program it just stops. The times that's happened to me! I hate to tell you just how many times! I always forget to ask the biocomputer to move me onto the next point and therefore I keep slipping back to square one."

USA: Lee, "Because of the phenomena of the biocomputer stopping when it reaches a goal I am going to devise a small chart so I can actually chart my progress. The moment I think the biocomputer is going to stop I will insert the next goal. In actual fact what I will do is even before the biocomputer stops I will insert my next goal. This is the turning point for me. At my age I ain't going backwards no more!"

USA: Trevor, "It never dawned on me before but I've been going around for years saying to myself that I hate my job. I can't think of a day that goes past when I don't say it. The penny has dropped. I can see that everything we do is just a habit. Those habits are a result of our self-programming, talking to ourselves all the time. That in turn transmutes itself into the output of bad habits. If you program positive all the time that will result in good output. My point is that I never realized any of this, because you're too close to your own thoughts all the time."

Australia: Lenny, "I had heard all this before. I heard the words but I hadn't understood the meaning of the words. Ron Holland has taught me the meaning of the words. He really is a brilliant teacher. Amen to that. What I have come to realize is that for some unknown reason I keep setting my sights far too low. I suppose I must have an inferiority complex or something. My biocomputer keeps getting me what I ask it for and no more. It also lets me just survive and skim through at the eleventh hour, because that's been my program. In future I'm going to get it to work overtime to make up for the easy time it's had in the past!"

Australia: Rodney, "For years I've been telling myself that the business has to turnover three thousand a week to break even. I've told myself that a thousand times. The business always does three thousand a week, I make sure it does! That's my program. As of now I shall be using different programs."

England: Stephen, "For years I've been telling myself all I want is my family and my home and my job. Which already I've got. But that's just a program. I didn't realize until today that I could add to those programs and have a business of my own and money as well."

England: Harvey, "All my mates are just right. They all think like I do, we have a great time together. All the women that seen attracted to me I don't really like at all, but I keep ending up with them. There must be a program that I can insert that will get me the woman of my choice."

England: Francis, "Oh boy I've made some classic blunders. I've taken lots of notes this weekend. Going back over them I can see I've made all the classic mistakes. Mostly, I have always got the output that came as a result of my input. But my input was always wrong. I keep programming with the things that I think I can attain, not the things I really want to attain. The next mistake is that the biocomputer stops working the minute it gets me there and leaves me hanging in the lurch."

USA: Meg, "Let a tree be known by its fruit. You can see looking at me I'm grossly overweight, I don't have the confidence, I keep telling myself I don't have the confidence. I keep telling myself I'm grossly overweight. I chatter to myself all the time negatively non-stop. I know I have to stop it. I have three wonderful grandchildren and if I don't put some new programs in I'm going to die."

USA: Herb, "I have left a trail of devastation all across the States because of my programs. I have always said 'Whatever it takes.' So it took it. I've always said 'Whatever the price.' So I paid it. Looking back on it now, I know I've hurt a lot of people, but at the time I didn't even notice. I kept forging ahead. It hasn't got me anywhere because all the other programs have been negative too."

Australia: Paddy, "What I've come to realize is that if we keep talking negatively to ourselves, that is programming from within, that will create a permanent track for us to run on. I know, I've been doing it for years."

USA: Jack, "One of the main aspects of the biocomputer is that it can run many programs, all at the same time. It can and will come up with ideas for products and businesses, marketing methods, loans for your business, missing links, people to help you and complete Eurekas! But you have to program for what you want."

Australia: Wayne, "We really do have to be aware that good things and large offers do come into our lives, when we're not expecting them. If we haven't 'seen' ourselves accepting a large offer we'll blow it when the time comes."

USA: Dick, "We should drink to Ron Holland's genius. He has pulled together four disciplines, physiology, psychology, business acumen and computer programming. Not only that, I think he's done a brilliant job of it."

USA: Barney, "So many of us have read all the self-help books and listened to all the tapes but at the end of the day haven't accomplished anything. Ron's program is very clever in two ways. He actually tells you that you have to do something other than reading with your left computer. You have to stop reading and start creating pictures with your right computer. The other thing is that many of the goals that are on the tape for the left computer are worded in such a way as to guide and direct you to using the right computer more and more."

England: Craig, "I've been using Ron's program for over three years. I first met him at the Rubens Hotel in London. Since then I've made literally hundreds of tapes. I now spend quite a bit of time wording each goal because I am acutely aware that I can bring about my own demise as well as my own success. You want to start taking this thing seriously as well as having a lot of fun with it. I'm living proof you can go from rags to riches. One final tip, get to see this man perform wherever you can, however you can! Seeing him once is not enough!"

Ireland: Duane, "A little knowledge is a dangerous thing. Don't get paranoid about making a start because you don't fully understand the principles or biocomputer language. Start making two tapes now and hone them up as you go. Spend time on the project!"

USA: Jerome, "There was a time when I was accused of something that I didn't do. The problem was the accusations affected me emotionally, just as much as though I had really done it. Now that I have put in a completely new program, I feel fine."

USA: Bertha, "I used to have a bad program. I could never say "No" to anyone. I was always lending money to my brother-in-law, and saying "Yes" to every business opportunity that came my way. I got burnt every time. You have to learn to say "No" until your tongue bleeds. It took me a long time to change my program, but now that I have, I feel in control."

USA: Angela, "My father was an alcoholic, but he was also very successful. He was a millionaire, and controlled a very substantial engineering business in Ohio. He was a terrible father and husband. I have programs that say, success is getting home drunk at 2am, and leaving at 6am with a couple of bananas for another round of the same. I've been telling myself for years, that this is what you have to do to become successful, and of course I've cut myself off from many things. I am now programming for what I want, in the way that I want it to happen."

USA: Otello, "I'm in the insurance industry. I have no problem making initial contact with my clients. I had a major problem doing any follow up or follow through, but I've cracked it now. I'll tell you what I did. I simulated making phone calls. I'd pick up the peanut butter jar and pretend to punch in phone numbers, then I'd put it to my ear and make a phone call. I'd go through the whole routine. I'd pick up a candle and do the same thing, I'd punch in those numbers and make a phone call. It didn't matter where I was in the house I'd pick up whatever object was available and punch in numbers and make a phone call. I'd punch in the numbers on a cornflake packet and then I'd say "This is Otello, just phoning to see if we can progress things." I've made pretend phone calls on cartons of milk, mustard jars, a plastic Buddha, a coffee mug, a toilet roll and a pair of scissors. One day I picked up the phone and did the real thing! This programming is magic!"

ZOOM SECRETS!

1. The tape for the left computer is in words only.

2. The tape for the left computer is played in your auto, in your home and on your Walkman for literally hundreds of hours.

3. On the tape you can include material possessions you wish to acquire as well as behavior modifications you require.

4. It is essential to word goals semantically correct in their present tense.

5. Repetition, repetition, repetition is the key to reprogramming the left computer.

6. It is important to repeat each goal on the tape three times.

7. Word each program very carefully to ensure that you do not put the biocomputer on standby.

8. Word each program carefully to ensure that you do not activate the self-destruct mode.

9. The more emotion you can put in your voice the quicker you will program your biocomputer.

10. The left computer tape will look like this: Verbal goal, repeat three times. Verbal goal, repeat three times. Verbal goal, repeat three times. Verbal goal, repeat three times, for as many goals as you have, on both sides of a sixty or ninety minute tape.

12

Quantum Leaps

Quantum means abrupt transition from one discrete energy state to another, with particular reference to atoms, electrons and molecules. A quantum leap is a sudden increase or a dramatic advance or dramatic change.

The tiny neurons that make up your biocomputer programs are full of chemicals and electricity. At the moment they are probably full of negative images, of the things that you don't want to happen in your life. They are probably full of images that have not gone far enough into the future. The whole secret of course is to change what's inside those neurons from negative pictures and words to positive pictures and words. This is where you have to make your own quantum leaps.

When you consider the tiny size of those individual neurons and consider the power that they have over your destiny it allows you to concentrate your effort on making the quantum leap required. With a little practise you will find you can do it easily and regularly. This chapter is about various aids that will bring about the quantum leap that you need in your biocomputer.

Since I started out on the long pilgrimage, striving to find the 'secrets of success', I have made many discoveries and have come across many of the factors that allow one to attain success. I can honestly say, from my own personal viewpoint, the application and proper use of the RAS was the turning point in my life. The fact that you can actually bypass the intellect and get below the threshold of consciousness and insert programs without any resistance, is what made it all come together for me. Since then there have been other quantum leaps that I'd like to share with you. Although they are not in any particular order, I think they all add up to making quantum leaps with your biocomputer.

Quantum Two, audio cassette recorders: These are common place, so are tape decks in autos. Everyone should have easy access to equipment to be able to make up the two tapes you need for your right and left computer. I really got serious about this method once I discovered how quickly it really worked. (I don't consider a period of a month or two, or sometimes a little longer on major goals, to be too long a period of time for inserting input to start getting appreciable output.) I had tapes in both autos, I played tapes continually at home, morning, noon and night for 'background noise' I never stopped programming. I really did put hundreds of hours of input into my biocomputer. No, correction, I put thousands of hours of input into my biocomputer! I have had fabulous results using this method, I mean what could be easier than just listening to a cassette tape while you are driving your auto, this is your university on wheels, this is your command center on wheels, this is your biocomputer programming center on wheels. This is your action base where you are going to start making major things happen in your life. (If you don't have an auto, or have an auto without a tape deck, play your tapes at home, and make sure you program for an auto with a tape deck as priority one!)

There was one period of time, when I did not have access to tapes and I still managed to reprogram my biocomputer. I did it the old fashioned way. I repeated my affirmations over and over again. Not just once or twice, I really did spend hundreds of hours putting in a program, saying the words out aloud to myself. The results were fantastic. I really got the outcome that I had wanted, the effort had proved worthwhile!

This work-book, incidentally is part of that output. This work-book will probably gross me over three million dollars over the next three years. Not bad for a few hundred hours programming? eh!

Quantum Three, the Eureka! Factor: The main output you will derive from your biocomputer will be correct habits. Instead of being tardy you will be punctual, instead of being boring you will be a brilliant conversationalist, instead of blowing out deals you'll close deals, instead of being lazy you'll be productive, automatically, once you have inserted appropriate programs.

The other output you will receive from time to time will be brilliant flashes of inspiration, hunches or what I prefer to call Eurekas! You will find the more clearly you visualize your goals the more Eurekas! and hunches and guidance you will receive from your biocomputer. Eurekas! I love 'em. Input equals output! The reason why Edison got the solution to the electric light bulb was that he was working on the problem. He was feeding his biocomputer all the input it needed. He was visualizing the end result. If you are not getting sufficient output from your biocomputer you are doing something wrong. Are you programming the biocomputer with specific goals in words and pictures that match? Are you properly deactivating the RAS when you visualize? Are you getting periods of relaxation to allow the two computers to communicate with one another?

Quantum Four, Understanding the Mistakes of Others: I have had the privilege of working with biocomputer students in many countries around the world. I have learnt a lot from my students which I want to pass on to you.

The most common failure people have in reprogramming their biocomputers is the fact they are just paying lip service to visualization. Many biocomputer students wanted success in their lives but didn't realize what dedication and concentration and discipline is needed to actually create pictures in one's biocomputer, especially if you are an auditory or kinesthetic person. Visuals don't have too much of a problem, once they know the correct way in which to visualize.

Only the results make it all worth while; convince yourself and make the start and move into the world of awesome unparalleled opportunity!

Quantum Five, Emotion Puts the Programs in the Quickest: One of the hardest things for many people to access at will is their emotions. However, it is when you are emotional about something you can put a program into the biocomputer in literally fractions of a second, a permanent program that you will run on for the rest of your life.

At my biocomputer seminars I always have a trash-can lid with me up on the stage. I know my biocomputer students are always puzzled and I can tell by their expressions they just can't wait to see where this particular prop comes into play. It is my favorite part of the seminar, and it never fails to give me a hearty chuckle.

I start talking about phobic responses. I ask my audience if there is anyone who has had a phobia of one sort or another. I explain that we get phobias when we access a visual experience at the same time we access our emotions. I say, " It's like when you lift up a trash can lid, like this!" With that I jerk the trash can lid from the floor and to my glee a huge snake hurtles out. Of course the snake is only made of plastic and it's attached to the trash can lid with a length of wire. I have to say the effect is awesome and I'm sure I've probably given quite a few people the snake phobia! However, the point really comes home. People scream! I'm shouting, "Its a snake! It's a snake!" People really get the message. Everyone knows that once you have a phobia, you have it for life, it goes in with emotion and it stays there as a permanent track for you to run on. The way to cure phobias is to go to a hypnotherapist, who will deactivate your RAS and insert a new program into your biocomputer.

Many self-help books talk about burning desire and that you must emotionalize your goals but fail to make the point. When you read about emotions and burning desire in a book, all that is, is ink on paper. Before you know where you are the reader has turned the page and the last thing he has done or is ever likely to do is to become emotional about his goals.

It is difficult to emotionalize one's goals. If you're laying on the floor, visualizing, it is best to do just that and concentrate on the quality of your mental images. You can, however, add emotion to your voice when you make up your program for your left computer.

What I prefer to do, above all else, is single out one goal at a time and work on it. I really do go around shouting and screaming and getting emotional about the goal of the moment. It's what I call supercharging.

All of these things are worth doing, they are the small price one has to pay for success.

Quantum Six, How to Emotionalize Goals: Have you ever watched a Frenchman or an Italian gesticulate? He gets all emotional just conversing with someone. He waves his hands, points his fingers and smacks his thigh. If you get angry with someone you wag your finger or shake your fist at them. If you're really pleased to see someone you throw your arms outward to express your joy. You shake peoples hands firmly and you slap their backs. The way you can access your emotions in the biocomputer is through physical movement! So when you go around supercharging the one particular goal you have selected for the treatment, you should shout and scream as well as punch the air and slap your thighs and grip your hands. The more movement you can add, the more emotional you become, the quicker the biocomputer will take in the program.

Quantum Seven, Recognize the Two Different Computers: You made a breakthrough when you realized that we had two separate computers, the left one processing in words and the right one processing in pictures.

Many times we are firing on the wrong computer for the job. Paul, a biocomputer student, came to me, he is an artist. He sustains himself by working in the local supermarket, stocking shelves. He came to me because he was in fear of losing his job. I asked him how could he lose such a simple job. He then told me the complete tale. He found he was putting the baked beans on the wrong shelf, he was putting the corned beef upside down and the wrong prices on the tins of peas. He explained that stacks of cornflakes would fall over in the aisles and all sorts of simple things kept going wrong and breaking. A living horror show! I asked Paul what he thought about, as he worked. Would you believe he thinks about his paintings and his sculptures as he tries to stack the supermarket shelves. I pointed out to him, although his job was a simple one, it was an analytical one, a job for the left computer, processing in words, not a job for the right computer processing in pictures.

As soon as he changed his thoughts and started to concentrate on what he was doing he was able to keep firing on his left computer and consequently he kept his job.

I know my own thought patterns very well. As a writer I know that when I awake in the mornings I am firing on my right computer, processing in pictures. I sit at the typewriter and write as fast as I can to get all the ideas down. Of course, because I'm firing on the right computer, (Wrong computer for the job of typing.) the words come out all jumbled up and misspelled. I do not let that concern me. My main concern is to capture the creativity. Later, during the course of the day, I start firing on the left computer, processing in words, analytical, it's then and only then, that I go back to my work and try to edit it and make some sense out of it.

Another one of my biocomputer students is an organ builder. He does all the designing and wood work and creativity while he is firing on the right computer, however when the organ is completely finished he makes sure he tunes it when he is firing on the left computer!

If you can recognize the computer firing on each different mode you will be able to use this to tremendous advantage. All too often I have noticed people doing tasks in totally the wrong computer mode. You will become so much more efficient once you appreciate and respect the two different modes. You will find that you can work with the two computers, not against them!

Quantum Eight, The Firewalk: We started to do the firewalk because we wanted to do something a little different, particularly to round off weekend seminars. The Firewalk proves to be a good highlight for many people, especially when we stand around the fire at the end, shouting "If I can walk across red-hot coals I can do anything!"

People do get burnt on firewalks make no mistake about it. It isn't something to be taken lightly. I have seen many mistakes made and I would like to enlighten you.

I have seen seminar leaders build huge fires piled high with railway sleepers, that took all afternoon to burn through. By the time the evening came around the fire had burned down and left an enormous pile of glowing red hot embers. These were raked out and spread into a bed about twenty feet long and nine inches deep. I'm talking about incredible heat emanating from this massive pile of ashes and I saw many people walk through this and everyone of them got burnt. Sheer stupidity. Nothing to do with mind programming.

First, the fire was far too hot, particularly for a first firewalk.

Secondly, the program inserted into these peoples' biocomputers was far from correct. No wonder so many people went away hobbling! I hope you never have the misfortune of experiencing such a seminar!

Make sure you do the fire walk with someone who knows what they are doing. In my experience the fire should be made of barbecue coals and the bed should not be all that long or all that deep. I have walked very hot fires and very long fires, but I really don't advise it first time around. You get exactly the same 'high' no matter what fire you walk.

The program you should insert into your biocomputer should be one where you have actually 'seen' yourself walk across red hot coals. It helps if you can give yourself a visual reference of having done it before. If you can 'see' it, you can do it! Input equals output!

It also helps if you put yourself into the success mode. You do that by accessing the feelings and emotions that you had when you did things that you felt particularly successful about. If you can put yourself in this 'resourceful state' it will help you tremendously when it's your turn to walk across the hot coals.

You can practice getting yourself into the success mode, 'resourceful state', for other times in your life as well, particularly when you need to draw on reserves of power.

The final recommendation that I would make is that you don't all line up in single file and walk the hot coals in turn. What you should do is gather around in a semi circle and let people walk, when they feel they are ready. In my experience many people can actually 'feel' when they have got themselves into a 'resourceful state', if that feeling comes over them they should walk the hot coals right there and then. They should not wait until it is their turn in the line to go, when the feeling of resourcefulness has probably disappeared.

Quantum Nine, Visualize the Worst Scenario: The first time I ever did the firewalk it was quite a feat. In my mind I had always assumed the coals would be charred or grey or smouldering or black or something. I had imagined they would be anything but actually glowing red hot! (Where I got my erroneous program from I'll never know!) Everyone walked across the red hot coals with absolute ease because they had been programmed to the fact they would be walking across red hot coals. I stood at the edge of the pit absolutely mortified. I had something before me that I just had not visualized.

Once I realized what I had done I very quickly changed the program in my biocomputer and I imagined that I had already walked across red hot coals, not just blackened coals. Then I did the real thing! Now, as you know, I teach the firewalk to other people.

This was a valuable experience. Many people practice the art of visualization and in doing so insert a track into their biocomputers that they will run on.

However, it also pays to visualize the worst

scenario as well. Not to put the program into the biocomputer to give you a permanent track to run on, but to give you a glimpse of the future, should things go wrong. Many times in business the strangest things happen; many times people in business do what you least expect them to do. (You realize of course, that all the players you deal with have biocomputer programs of their own. Many of these programs are self-destruct programs and self-defeating behavior programs) Many times people don't make the right decisions or choose the right option for themselves. Many times they take options that are obviously wrong. When people do this, they often have a habit of upsetting your own goals and plans. If you visualize the worst scenario, you will at least have had a glimpse of the future and should be able to make alternative plans and create yourself some options.

Many times we go into deals expecting far too much out of them in the way of sales or cash or performance from people. If you had used your biocomputer to run a few negative programs, you would have, at the very least, been able to come up with some alternatives and some ways of salvaging the deal. This is a biocomputer program that I would call looking at the negative with a view to extracting the positive.

Quantum Ten, Two Powerful Computers: We have made a lot of fuss about the pictures dominating the words. The pictures win every time! A picture is worth a thousand words! Visualize! Visualize! Visualize!

Does this mean we can ignore our left computer? Of course it doesn't. Our extraordinary power comes from the very fact that we do have two computers, one processing in words and the other processing in pictures and both going about their problem solving in two totally different ways.

Many races are predominantly right brained, such

as the Aborigines in Australia and the Maoris in New Zealand. Many artists are predominantly right brained. Many artists who create beautiful paintings and sculptures often have great difficulty in selling their work. I have worked with many artists and many of them have the same trait in the fact they hate selling their own work. It's not until they affirm (verbally, left computer) that they will sell their work, as well as actually visualize themselves selling their work, that things start to happen for them. The only time you, or they, will ever accomplish your goals is when the words and the pictures match!

Quantum Eleven, Corpus Callosum: We have mentioned the corpus callosum a number of times. This is the substantial band of transmission fibres that joins the two computers together and allows the words and the pictures to communicate with one another. It allows the two computers to get whizzing and whirring together on your problems. A number of years ago surgeons used to cut the corpus callosum with a scalpel to divide the two hemispheres, on certain patients, to prevent disease or tumors spreading from one hemisphere to another. The most amazing thing about the operation was that on the surface the patient seemed to have changed very little. There was no loss of speech or learning ability, no loss of co-ordination, or disruption to the individuals personality. To the outside observer the patient seemed to function normally. However, what did change was the patients PROBLEM SOLVING ABILITY, because the two computers couldn't communicate with one another they had no way of cross-referencing or coming up with creative ideas using both words and pictures. I must admit I find it quite fascinating to think, that when I relax, the words and pictures communicate with each other. (I often think to myself what a shock it must be to my system when some of my visual fantasies clash with some of my verbal reasonings!)

Quantum Twelve, Simulation and Role Playing is Essential: The idea is to program your biocomputer with the things you want out of life to give you a track to run on. For many, visualization is very hard. For those people to act and to role play is absolutely essential. More and more sales teams role play various sales pitches and deals at the beginning of every selling day. I know another guy who actually built a model of his dream house and he pushes a wee model of a BMW up the drive every night. Use your imagination!

Develop a team of people who are well versed in biocomputer principles, who you can role play various exercises with. You can take it in turns role playing various situations that you both would like to accomplish.

Quantum Thirteen, The End of Survival, the Beginning of Living!: What I have shown you in this instruction manual, can and will create permanent change in your life. Take care that you make programs up of things you really want and outcomes that you really desire. Do not undertake the reprogramming of your biocomputer lightly. The biocomputer is tremendously powerful, it will take you wherever you want to go. It will never let you down. Never! It will take you right up to the point that you program into it. If you fail to insert the programs or fail to use correct programs, you will have no one to blame but yourself.

We can completely control the material that reaches our biocomputers. All we have to do is exercise that control. We also have the ability to override anyone else's programs, that we no longer have use for. Again, we must decide what it is that we want for ourselves. Once you have made that decision you end survival and start living!

LIVE AT THE BIOCOMPUTER SEMINAR:

USA: Grace, "Ron Holland is a quantum leap! For years I used to struggle. The last eighteen months have been an absolute revelation!

For those of you here for the first time I should give you a little warning. When you first start playing your tapes don't expect results the same day. Concentrate on getting as many tape listening hours in as you can. Visualize as clearly as you can. I found it practically impossible to visualize when I first started, but I persevered.

The output comes in the strangest, most gentle ways you could imagine. Without any conscious effort or thought you become driven and motivated, what's more, driven in the direction of your goal. Don't quit with those tapes."

USA: Bart, "Don't underestimate listening to those tapes. It undoes all the negative self talk that you have done to yourself over the years. I often think you have to listen for a long period, that is just overcoming the negative program, then after a while the program you really want begins to take."

Poland: Lidia, "I think one has to be aware not so much of the biocomputer language but to immediately set the next goal as you arrive at your goal."

USA: Edwin, "I have a terrible program that tells me not to be a success because I'll leave all my friends behind and then I won't have any. I've put a new program in now, that will allow me both friends and success, together. I will even make new friends, if necessary."

USA: Charlie, "You have to keep programming, especially when you reach your goals, that's why they say there's plenty of room at the top of the ladder, but there's no room for sitting down!"

Australia: Richard, "With a properly programmed biocomputer combined with properly activating and deactivating the RAS you won't be able to stop yourself!"

USA: Maud, "I have the program I will make a million in five years time, but my real program is that I don't have two nickles to rub together!"

Spain: Catherine, "I'm a good starter but a bad finisher. I thought it was just me. Now I can see lots of people who have programs like that."

USA: Lipson, "Ron Holland, you're a wizard! Don't worry whether you think you're being too repetitive or not, you've got through to me! For years I've read about visualization but I haven't done it. All the books say the same thing, but they just don't get through. You're a magician!"

ZOOM SECRETS!

1. Audio cassette tapes can reprogram your biocomputer very quickly. Make sure you have a cassette player everywhere you go!

2. By correctly inserting programs you will get brilliant flashes of inspiration known as Eurekas!

3. Understand the greatest mistake that many people make, it is just paying lip service to visualization.

4. Emotion is the key to inserting programs into the biocomputer quickly, that's how people get phobic responses.

5. Recognize the way in which the two computers operate. Use the correct computer for the job.

6. Visualize the worst scenario. Get a glimpse of the future, of what could go wrong, so you can organize counter moves before mistakes are actually made.

13

Questions Asked at Biocomputer Seminars

You have now come to the most important material in the work-book. Here you will actually learn how to integrate everything that we have discussed so far. Here you will find practical applications for re-programming your own personal biocomputer.

My seminar audiences are a vast mix of people, all nationalities and from all walks of life. If there was a common denominator it is that these individuals want to get ahead in life. They want to excel. Even if they are not goal oriented already many of them know they should be, but just don't know how to go about it.

Many of the attendees are from the Life Assurance industry. Others come from various Multi Level Marketing and direct selling companies. I have worked with thousands of individuals in sales and thousands who own their own businesses or aspire to own their own business.

The youngest student of mine was nine. (I taught him how to win at martial arts using his biocomputer) and the oldest was seventy two, who I taught how to relax for the first time in her life, take control of her RAS and cure her insomnia.

During the biocomputer seminars there is always a lot of humor and exchange between myself and the audience. I have always made a point of teaching in a relaxed and informal atmosphere, and indeed I deliberately create an atmosphere that is conducive to learning.

During my ten year period teaching biocomputer principles it has never ceased to amaze me that business people all over the world are making the same mistakes over and over again. It is also interesting for me to observe, that for many, the biocomputer seminar is the turning point of their lives. I have met many of my students over the years, many come to refresher courses, and we talk. Many take the principles on board and attain sustained success.

We are now ready to start our next session, I hope you are relaxed and learn more about how to put the biocomputer to good use! Back to the auditorium:

"Well I hope everyone had a good lunch, not too much too eat I hope, I don't want you drowsy this afternoon, I want to see those biocomputers like steel traps! You all look refreshed and raring to go, that means I've got my work cut out, you're going to make me start thinking on my feet. Well before we start I thought I'd better tell you a story. 'The super powers got together to pool resources to build the largest, most powerful, most sophisticated and most expensive computer in the world. They had unlimited resources to create this device. They pulled in experts from all over the world to help them, every country was represented. After spending four years and hundreds of billions of dollars they had created the latest neural computer that was more like a human biocomputer than a human biocomputer, there was nothing it didn't know or couldn't do. It was programmed with all the knowledge of the universe! The computer was voice activated and could think in words, pictures and feelings and could speak every language in the world."

"There were scientists and computer experts and experts from every field imaginable to put the super duper super computer to the test. It was quizzed and tried and tested and attacked from every angle, but every question that was raised it answered perfectly in a matter of milliseconds. During the coffee break some young wag programmed into the computer the ultimate question: IS THERE A GOD? to which it instantaneously boomed back in a very loud voice, "THERE IS NOW!"

Auditorium fills with spontaneous laughter and the mood is set for a cracking session of questions and answers.

"Right let's be having some questions, next!"

Can blind people visualize?

The answer is yes they can. The degree that they can visualize depends on when they went blind. If they went blind some time after they were able to see enough of the world to know what it's all about, they can create better internal pictures than people who have been blind from birth. I know a number of eminently successful handicapable people and they use their biocomputers in the exact same way we have discussed here.

Does it matter if I'm left handed?

No, it makes no difference at all. It means that in all probability your left computer would process in pictures and your right computer would process in words. It wouldn't make any difference to how you reprogrammed your biocomputer or to your performance.

Can this program help me lose weight?

Yes it can, without a doubt. In fact I would say it would be very difficult to lose weight without putting a program into your biocomputer, because you would always be governed by your imagination. We talk about weight problems in the chapter on failure programs. It is imperative to 'see' yourself slim and 'see' yourself eating the correct food and 'see' yourself taking the correct exercise.

What would be a good time frame to make a million dollars in?

Good question. Before I could answer it, I would want to know a number of things. How adept are you already in the practise of visualization? Are you really putting programs into your biocomputer through the art of visualization or are you just paying lip service to it? Is the million dollars something you really want?

I would want to know if you already had some success with programming your biocomputer and attracting to yourself some of the smaller things that you had wanted to acquire.

There are many factors involved here. I think the person who is already goal oriented and already using biocomputer techniques would be able to make a million in a reasonably short period of time. I think more than anything you have to be aware of allowing too long a time frame for any goal, because it has the affect of putting the biocomputer on 'stand-by.'

I have read your brilliant 'Talk and Grow Rich'. Do you still meditate?

Yes I do. I take time out everyday to meditate and allow the two computers to communicate with each other. Since I wrote 'Talk and Grow Rich' I have discovered many people 'meditate' in many different ways. I think they are all beneficial. As long as you stop that internal dialogue that goes on, the brain chatter, that's what counts. Many people find gardening useful, others take long walks in the countryside. I prefer to be driving fast! Some people find they stop the internal dialogue by doing the washing up or scraping the wall paper off the wall. Others take long baths or showers, many find jogging or working out is the best activity for stopping their internal dialogue.

Are you married?

No I'm not. I was, but I'm now divorced, without children. Just in case you're interested, I've recently been programming the following into my biocomputer, 'I am dating a beautiful woman, with a view to marriage and starting a family. She has long legs and a voluptuous figure and a vivacious personality. She probably has long blonde hair but I'm very flexible. She has some tremendous programs herself. She is highly creative, loves entertaining and is extremely feminine. She is used to living an unconventional and sometimes alternative lifestyle. She adores travelling and is probably between twenty eight and thirty years old. She is more than likely English but could well be American or Australian.'

I am also visualizing the scenario, so I do practice what I preach. I think when it comes down to relationships one should be particularly flexible as long as you set certain parameters, because there are so many people out there that could fulfill all your worldly desires and make you very happy!

Will this program help me increase my insurance sales?

Yes, without a doubt and very quickly too, if you take time out to insert correct programs. I have worked extensively with the Life Assurance Industry and have had some incredible results. Not only have we been able to increase sales but also increase the recruitment rate and reduce the drop out rate. The industry has appalling figures for people dropping out of it. If the industry were to adopt biocomputer principles it would save billions of dollars.

Does belief come into it at all?

No it doesn't. Once you have a program in your biocomputer that is the track you run on, permanently. Getting back to my favorite subject, the little Chinese boy. Did he have to believe Chinese before that program took hold? Of course he didn't. The fact that he heard Chinese over and over again was enough to create a permanent program for him to run on. If you hear your programs over and over again and visualize your programs over and over again, things will happen for you, whether you like it or not, whether you believe it or not!

When you didn't take the money in New York, I thought you were mad. What is the main reason that you put that down to?

I told you the story in detail. My biocomputer got me right up to the point that I had visualized over and over again, when the man offered me the money for the deal. After that there simply wasn't a program in my biocomputer. I hadn't visualized signing a contract or getting a check. So what I did automatically was run on the biocomputer program that was the strongest. My strongest program at that time was one of survival only, not one of money, it was a program of not doing what was best for me, it was one of doing what I always did, keeping in my comfort zone. I didn't know anything about having a $125,000 in my pocket, my program was one of scrimping and scraping, my program was one of never having two pennies to rub together.

Your biocomputer will get you exactly to the point that you visualize. At the end of your program you will come to a GRINDING HALT!

Baroque music, do you think it can help?

Yes I do. I think many people can benefit by using baroque music on their visualization tape. I do think one also has to be careful that you don't fall asleep, because if you do you obviously can't visualize. I would suggest baroque music be used by people who find it very difficult to relax and, therefore, find it difficult to deactivate their RAS. Try Handel or Bach. What you need is sixty beats a minute, although some of my biocomputer students inform me their biocomputers respond better to loud pop music!

When I awake in the mornings I feel as though my RAS is deactivated for quite a period of time. Is this a problem?

It could be, let me give you an example. A colleague of mine had the same problem and to him it really was a problem. He would get up in the morning and put the coffee on. He knew something was wrong, but he couldn't quite put his finger on exactly what. He was unfortunate in the fact that he didn't realize that his RAS was deactivated for maybe an hour or two in the mornings. It just so happened that for eleven years his wife verbally attacked him and abused him every morning while his RAS was deactivated. Now you know, that when your RAS is down, you are particularly susceptible to any kind of suggestion. In fact suggestions go straight into the biocomputer completely bypassing the intellect. So for eleven years my friend had all this negative input going into his biocomputer without him even realizing it. All he did know was that he never got ahead in life, despite the fact that he wanted to. All his wife's negative input became his output, which was pretty grim. The good news is, that once he got away from her and started to put programs into his biocomputer that were compatible with his dreams and aspirations, he saw a remarkable improvement in a very short space of time.

You failed on your first business trip to the States, what do you do different now?

Good question. Let me give you an example. When I did my recent tour of Australia I spent a few weeks beforehand, visualizing all the things I was going to do. I 'saw' major seminars, I 'saw' many TV and Radio interviews, I 'saw' successful travel, I 'saw' the success of the tour many times over before it actually happened. I 'saw' the successful outcomes of many business meetings. I did this from my base in London. The outcome of the Australian tour was that it turned out to be so successful that I overstayed my Visa by three months, but that's another story! I take great pains to visualize trips, business deals, meetings, all before they happen. I really do practice what I preach!

How does all this figure in the education of our children?

It all figures pretty heavily. I think the school educational system is pretty abysmal. The authorities still insist on gearing most education toward the left computer, relying heavily on words. At least most schools do. Another big blunder is that many schools have stopped teaching by rote. That is the one major way the biocomputer operates. In the very near future I shall be putting a series of videos together to enable caring parents to teach their children how to access both computers.

Did you suffer at school as a result of teachers not knowing about the two computers?

I most certainly did! I distinctly recall that I had problems with my handwriting. The teacher used to shout and scream and try to tell me how to write properly. Obviously writing is a visual task (right computer, pictures) but this teacher insisted on trying to teach me a visual task, verbally. The worse my handwriting got the more verbal she got.

What she should have done is told me to close my eyes and 'see' in my imagination the beautiful loops and curves of the letters, then open my eyes and follow those loops and curves with my pencil on the paper.

Furthermore, I mentioned this before, I recall being told not to visualize and daydream. Instead of being encouraged, I was chastised, for using the greatest tool that I possess!

How can I reprogram my biocomputer to come up with a good product or service to sell?

Good question. I know lots of people out there are trying very hard to make money and they keep falling into the same old trap. They keep getting tied up with MLM schemes that last a few months, make a few people at the top a little money and then collapse. (Don't get me wrong, there are a few

MLM's around that are good, but it really is only a handful)

What I suggest you do, is first list out all the things that you like doing. In my experience, people who make a lot of money love their work. In actual fact many of them could hardly distinguish between their work and a hobby; they attack it with that much gusto and enthusiasm.

Once you have decided what it is that you love doing, then look around and see how other people are making money, out of what it is that you love. I am a great believer in not re-inventing the wheel. Use your eyes, look around, read magazines, ask people, get feedback.

Put a program into your biocomputer that 'sees' you actually earning money doing whatever it is that you really like. The more detail you program into the biocomputer the sooner you will get the desired output.

Many years ago I got out of the building industry (that I hated, it was really hard, dirty and heavy work) and got myself into the motorcycle industry, which I loved with a passion. Since then I have switched careers many times, always doing what I love. At the moment it's travelling the world, writing and promoting human biocomputer technology.

Why do you drink so much water when giving seminars?

Because I've got a leaky head gasket! Next!

What are the best types of relaxation that allow the two computers to communicate with one another?

It all depends on the individual's likes and dislikes. I don't think anyone could relax properly if they were doing something they didn't like. I know many people who love horse riding. I have turned a great number of people onto two of my great passions, gardening and walking in the country. I also love driving fast. On very long motorcycle rides I get some fantastic output from my biocomputer. If you have ever read Robert Pursig's, Zen in the Art of Motorcycle Maintenance, you will realize that he did the same thing and some of his biocomputer output was pure genius.

One of my partners loves watching TV and videos at four or five in the morning, when his house is very quiet and he knows he won't be disturbed. He just spaces out and glazes over as the video plays. He finds that it relaxes him enough to start getting the output from his biocomputer. (At about six in the morning he usually phones me up and leaves messages on my answering machine about all the ideas he's had, so I know it works for him!)

More than anything, I'm glad that you've taken it on board, that high performance human behavior demands high levels of relaxation. Now it's up to you to take time out doing something that is pleasurable and relaxing to you. It is imperative to relax! The biocomputer demands it!

You mentioned that we use the wrong computer for the job. Would you care to expand on that?

Seeing as you put it so elegantly, yes! All auditory tasks should be carried out while you are firing on the left computer (words, sounds, auditory, left computer). Things like piano tuning, telephone sales, any selling in fact, seminars. However, when you want to be creative you should switch onto the right computer (visual, pictures, creativity, visualization) If you are trying to design something, or trying to understand how your auto engine works or your lawn mower works you'd be far better off trying to visualize what was wrong with it.

I remember being stuck way up in the Scottish highlands at about four o'clock one freezing cold morning. My partner was verbalizing the problem (I can't even repeat what he said, for fear of being struck down, but it was definitely something to do with brass monkeys!) What I did was sit in the auto (freezing cold, wouldn't start, no heater) and I visualized all the components that could have possibly gone wrong or broken. I came up with the idea that it was a loose ignition wire. I also knew it was freezing cold outside and we didn't have a flash light. I visualized getting a spare length of wire and a bulb and connecting this to the battery and making myself up a little extension light.

I got out of the auto, proceeded to get my length of wire and bulb, made up my extension light (all in the pitch black), lit up the engine, found the loose wire, reconnected it, slammed down the hood and drove off. My colleague called me a genius, which pleased me no end, he happened to be a leading figure in MENSA.

What do you call "Going through hoops of fire!"

I'm glad you picked up on that one! This is the term that I use for getting past the point where we normally self-destruct. Now that you know all about your failure programs I hope you will be on the look-out for the 'failure mode.'

In future you should be very aware that when it comes up to deal closing time, you are going to do the 'right thing' not the 'wrong thing.' The 'hoop of fire' is when you can sense the point where you would normally blow the deal or self-destruct and keep right on going and say "Yes!" instead of no or "No!" instead of yes.

Even now I get twinges when I think I should cancel a meeting or not do a deal or say "No" not "Yes" or vice-versa. I am now very careful. I make sure I am overriding any negative programs that I may have about that particular topic or deal. Many times I recognize them in time, and put a program in that is very positive. In all cases I program my biocomputer to get me beyond the point where I would have automatically failed in the old days. Yes! Every day I go through 'hoops of fire.' Does that answer your question?

Can you give us a few more clues about loosely writing our goals? I have come from the discipline that says everything must be in fine detail, although I agree with you it hasn't worked too good!

Yes. There was one time when I had the goal, 'Talk and Grow Rich is a #1 Bestseller in the USA.' I looked at the goal (I often appraise goals to make sure they are right, semantically correct, what I really want and not in conflict with other goals that I have set) and decided I would alter it. I altered it to 'Talk and Grow Rich is a bestseller in the USA.' I figured that the difference in the money one makes between a book being a bestseller and a number one bestseller is not all that much. When I next re-evaluated the goal I altered it completely. I changed the goal to : My book is a bestseller in the USA. This is the goal that I stuck with and I think it's accomplished everything I wanted to happen. The reasoning was simple, if any of my books became a bestseller in the USA that would open up many doors for my other books to become bestsellers. Why should I cut myself off from letting many good things happen by creating such a tight window of opportunity, when a very flexible picture would do?

I have been visualizing for a long time now. I am fairly successful, but I love your program and would like to do more. I have a problem. Every time I try to visualize certain things, terribly negative pictures come up in my biocomputer and it distracts me from concentrating on what I'm really trying to visualize. Can you make some suggestions?

Yes, this is far more common than you could possibly realize. The first thing I would suggest is that I wouldn't push the negative pictures away too quickly. First have a good look at them. Try to learn from them. Your biocomputer is very clever and very powerful. It may be trying to show you something or tell you something.

Have a good look even if it's painful. If you decide there is nothing that can be learnt, that is the time to get rid of any negative images. You can do this simply by pretending the image is painted on a huge sheet of glass. You then get a large hammer and smash the whole picture into smithereens. You keep smashing up all the slithers of the glass until the image is destroyed. Alternatively you can have the negative image on a canvass and burn the thing on a bonfire or wrap the images up in snowballs and throw them in a fast flowing river. I've personally used all the techniques with great success. Yes, you do want to get rid of negative pictures, sooner rather than later! It also helps if you have some very good, clear and positive pictures to insert into the biocomputer. If you don't make up your own programs, the biocomputer has a habit of making its own. You've heard the expression, control your own mind or it'll control you? Same goes for the biocomputer, control it or it'll control you. Your choice! Next!

Do successful people keep at one level because of their programs?

Yes! I could tell you numerous stories but I'll only tell you one! I used to work with a reasonably successful accountant. He had three offices and about twenty partners. The three offices and the twenty partners were always busy, the business was thriving. However, every time this guy tried to expand further, disaster would appear. He tried time and time again to open a fourth office, but every time he did he was forced to shut it down and retrench. Once he'd consolidated he'd try to expand again. Everything was crying out for expansion, the business was there, he opened offices in thriving business communities. What was wrong of course, was that he only 'saw' himself as a three office, twenty partner accountancy practice.

From the outside looking in, it was really quite amusing watching this guy keep self-destructing. Time and time again he used to ball out his subordinates in front of other people in board meetings, other times he'd roll up late for meetings with new partners or potential investors, sometimes he'd be suffering from jet lag and make stupid board-room decisions, other times he'd tell people to take it or leave it (I was one of those who left it, thanks, but no thanks!) All of this accountant's habits (as a result of the negative programs in his biocomputer) had the result of keeping the firm the same size, three offices and twenty partners.

Obviously something went wrong with this guy's programming, because in the end, instead of cracking it and getting the fourth office open, all his partners left him and he slid back down the snakes, back to zero, he didn't even collect $200 as he passed GO!

Do you believe in Role Models?

Yes I certainly do. I think one of the quickest ways to put a correct program into your biocomputer, is to research someone who has already accomplished what it is you are trying to do and model them. Once you have come up with a role model you should read all about them and study in great detail, find out what it is they have done to achieve success. There is nothing wrong with actually trying to get to meet people who you intend to use as role models, most successful people are flattered. 'Emulate the Great' is probably one of the most underestimated statements of our time. I have used many role models. I copy their facial expressions, the way they speak and smile and move. I try to find out how they think and process information, I try to find out what their daily habits are. (Their biocomputer programs!) I try to find out what it is that makes them tick. I try to find out what motivates them. I try to find out what strategies, if any, they use to attain success. When I've found out as much as I can, I program my biocomputer to become like that person. I create a picture in my biocomputer of what they look like doing a certain task and then I step into the picture myself and become that person.

I have modelled motorcycle racers, salesmen, firewalkers, entrepreneurs, public speakers and writers. Make sure you choose a role model that is suitable for the task and don't model any bad habits. I saw a beautiful young girl singer destroy herself, (true story, very sad) because she modelled herself on Janice Joplin. She had a beautiful singing voice, and boy could she dance, but the drink and drugs got to her, she died at the tender age of nineteen, before she had a chance to get her singing career off the ground.

In your bestseller 'Talk and Grow Rich' you talk about creating wealth without capital, what's the program we should insert in our biocomputer for that? Do you think anyone can do it?

Of course I think anyone can do it. Not only that, I can assure you most people will have to do it, because most people really do have to start out with nothing, they really do have to create wealth without capital. High achievers are literally driven to create something out of nothing.

I tell the story in great detail in 'Talk and Grow Rich' (which, incidentally, is subtitled 'How to Create Wealth Without Capital') of how, many years ago I owned seven motorcycle shops. I nearly went bust and I got cleaned out. I ended up with seven empty shops, no money, no stock, no nothing. I went around the merchant banks, the clearing banks, the vulture capitalists, everyone. No one would lend me stocking finance to fill my showrooms with motorcycles. I literally knocked on every door in the city. I was not about to give up. I intuitively visualized what I wanted the outcome to be. I didn't visualize money, I visualized my seven shops bulging with motorcycles. In fact in my imagination we had so many motorcycles we couldn't close the doors at night-time. I 'saw' motorcycles every where. I 'saw' hundreds of them. I remember this as though it was yesterday. I visualized this goal clearly in every spare moment that I had, for about three days. On the third day, Wham! Bingo! Eureka! I got the output from my biocomputer! It was clear! It was concise! It was marvellous! My biocomputer told me, "You don't need capital! All you have to do is phone all the motorcyclists who are trying to sell their bikes in the classified advertisements in the motorcycle press. Ask them if they'll bring their motorcycles in for me to sell on consignment!" Eurekas! I love 'em!

That was the Eureka! I had been waiting for. I didn't really understand how the biocomputer worked in those days, but I certainly knew good ideas when they came. I got on the phone. I made literally hundreds of phone calls. The rest is history. I filled those seven showrooms with bikes, within seven days of coming up with the idea! We couldn't close the doors at the end of the business day. It was fantastic. It was better than fantastic. We went from strength to strength, because, as those motorcycles sold, I didn't have to reinvest any money into more stock. All I did was pay the owners their cut of the money, keep my commission, and make more phone calls to get more motorcycle stock! I was laughing all the way to the bank. Ooh la la!

You can put similar programs into your bio-computer right now. There are literally hundreds of opportunities out there right now just waiting to be milked. You put in the appropriate program, then go to harvest!

I am in the insurance industry, I am always busy in meetings but I don't make a lot of money. What programs can I insert into my bio-computer?

As you know I have done a tremendous amount of work within your industry and yours is a very common problem. You obviously know all about prospecting, because you manage to keep yourself busy. You obviously don't suffer from call reluctance because you are managing to get in front of people all the time. You seem a personable and intelligent enough guy to me and I can only assume your product knowledge is up to speed. What I suggest you look at is your programs for closing the deal, or in your case not closing the deal.

Without a doubt you should be closing your eyes and actually 'seeing' your prospects writing out the checks and signing agreements. You can, and should also role play this scenario out with a colleague of yours who doesn't have any problems with closing. You may even ask your sales manager, if he can line you up with someone who's a good closer but a bad prospector. I'm very pleased that you have recognized the fact that all you are short of is a little software. Now that you have overcome that hurdle, creating the software for your biocomputer is the simple part.

Do you believe in drawing up a list of goals?

Yes I do. Many people draw up lists of goals and end up very disappointed with the things they actually end up accomplishing. Most people write down that they own a Rolls Royce, they are millionaires, they earn $10,000 a week. These are all verbal goals. (Words, left computer) unfortunately what they visualize (pictures, right computer) is the exact opposite of the words. The secret is to visualize the things on your list exactly as you want them. Most people imagine living a Dallas lifestyle in their left computers , but all the time they're visualizing Coronation Street or Archie Bunker's Place in their right computers. Unfortunately it's the pictures that win every time, without exception! Input equals output!

What do you think of the Doom and Gloomers?

Not a lot. I think people who spread Doom and Gloom are a real problem to society and to themselves. If you keep reading Doom and Gloom and talking Doom and Gloom and watching Doom and Gloom on the television, it obviously programs the biocomputer and becomes a self-fulfilling prophecy. If you think about it, Doom and Gloom is a multi-billion dollar campaign fuelled by the media. Doom and Gloom has now become a multi-billion dollar industry and what worries me more than anything, is they've started to import it! If only the media would spend the same amount of the prime time TV and radio hours and column inches in the press promoting positive material you would really begin to notice the changes in the economy. I very rarely watch the television, listen to the radio or read newspapers (I read the barest minimum that allows me to keep abreast of current affairs and what is pertinent to my business in hand) other than that I am very particular as to what I will allow to become a program in my biocomputer.

Will you tell us more about the difference between subjective and objective visualization?

Yes I will! The way to visualize properly is to visualize subjectively. Many people don't, they visualize objectively. Let me give you examples of both. If you were to visualize your dream house objectively all you would 'see' is a picture of the house. You would see the object. If you were to visualize your dream auto objectively you would 'see' a picture of the auto, in your imagination.

To visualize subjectively, and this is the program you want in your biocomputer, you would actually become part of the experience. You would 'see' yourself in the pictures, you would walk around the dream house, you would take a shower in the bathroom, you would swim in the indoor pool, you would play table tennis in the games room. You would become part of the subject. Further, you would smell the lime tree in the garden, you would listen to the stereo playing in the living room, you would water the plants in the hall. You would access feelings, emotions, smells, sounds, tastes as well as the visual experience.

You would subjectively visualize two ways. You would 'see' through some one else's eyes yourself in the picture, doing all these things in your dream house. The other way that you will visualize subjectively is to actually be doing the things we talked about. If you are actually doing the thing, you may not be able to 'see' yourself, but you will be able to 'feel' as though you are part of the picture. In fact, many times, to prove you are really doing the things, you can step back and have a 'look' at yourself. It helps to put the program into the biocomputer, if you use both methods of subjective visualization.

A friend of mine wanted a particular job in a specialized music store. He knew there would be many applicants. He took time out to visualize the interview in great detail. He went over the whole interview, he 'saw' himself being interviewed. He 'saw' himself being asked lots of questions about various music, records and tapes. He put a perfect program into his biocomputer. The interview went exactly as he had visualized it. The interviewer also asked him some trick questions, as it happened my friend had visualized these as well, (You always visualize the worst scenarios don't you?) and he answered them perfectly too. He won the job, hands down.

Sometimes I'm brilliant on the telephone at others I'm a disaster. What am I doing wrong? I'd like to be brilliant all the time. I know you can help me!

I know I can help you too! And help you I will!

I'm brilliant on the phone too! (I used to be big headed, but now I'm perfect!) You'll have to read my book, 'The Golden Phone', when I get time to write it, the program's in the biocomputer, I'm expecting the output any day now!

Quite a few things I'll tell you about selling on the phone. The first thing of course is to be on the correct computer when you make your phone calls. Many people make their phone calls when they are firing on the wrong computer. The correct computer to make phone calls on, is your left computer, right! No I'm not trying to confuse you. Let me give you an example of why so many people get their wires crossed when making phone calls.

My partner Neil, he does this all the time and we get a great buzz out of it. We're in a brainstorming session, trying to solve some problem or another, or just trying to make something happen. Neil gets creative and starts processing in pictures. (Right computer, pictures, creativity.) Suddenly the phone goes and it's for Neil. He's in completely the wrong mode for taking a phone call and trying to talk sensibly with someone. He talks a lot of gibberish, then he tells the caller that he'll call back and we all get a great belly laugh! He's in the creating, dreaming, pictures mode of his right computer and he's trying to talk sense to someone on the phone about a deal. In other words, on the wrong computer for the job of talking to someone on the telephone. So there's the first tip. Even when you make sure that you're firing on the left computer (logical, words, analytical, rational, calculative) so you can talk logically to your prospect, you have no guarantee that the prospect is firing on his left computer and will be talking logically, in my experience, chances are he won't!

The other thing of course is that the left side of your body is connected to the right computer and the right side of the body is connected to the left computer. Therefore if you put the phone to your left ear you'll be processing with your right computer (pictures, visual, ideas, creativity, non verbal, artistic, right computer) and if you put the phone to your right ear you'll be processing on the left computer (words, logical, sequential, rational, calculative) so you can see, we are just scratching the surface of the complications of telephone sales.

Of course we haven't even started on the programs we should have in our biocomputer to make ourselves brilliant telephone sales people. I'll give you a few of the programs that I've got. I realize how delicate things can get on the telephone. I also realize how complicated the whole thing can become when you understand biocomputers and programs. Try to sell on the phone? In a word I don't. What I do is use the phone as a tool to make things happen, introduce myself, fix up meetings and appointments and lunches. I know exactly what outcome I want from a phone call. I will not risk blowing a deal by making a phone call that I don't think will work. I know how easy it is to blow out deals and in many cases you only get one bite at the cherry.

Do you believe in levitation?
Yes, I've been living without visible means of support for years! Next?

Were you born with a silver spoon in your mouth?
No! In actual fact I was brought up in extreme poverty. Looking back on it now, I realize I was programmed with some diabolical programs during my upbringing. To balance that, both my mother and

father inserted some very good programs into me as well. The good programs were, Leos are leaders, you know best, the world is your oyster, never give up, try, try, try again. My father also encouraged me to be self-reliant, he had me chopping down huge trees, on my own from a very young age. I also had to ensure that there was always enough firewood for the fires and I had to help in the garden, all things that I loved doing, which turned out to be good programs for my biocomputer.

The bad programs included, 'Don't make money your God, (not that I'm saying you should make money your God!) You'll never be as clever as your sister, you never finish anything you start, you're always scruffy, why don't you get a nine to five job like everyone else? You don't care.' All these things I heard over and over again. There are others that I picked up from our very existence and environment, and everyday I have to remind myself to be careful not to slip back into the old ways and start sliding down those snakes. I know I have already overcome many of my negative programs, but believe me, I know I mustn't become complacent!

Can you highlight the various types of output we will get from a properly programmed biocomputer?

Yes I can, there are three main categories. The first will be in the way of correct habits. I hope you will make up tapes to program yourself with habits like:

Every day I feel more and more confident. You would visualize yourself talking to people that you wouldn't normally, you would visualize yourself being with people and being in situations at the same time feeling comfortable. A program like: Everyday I move on my tasks, I stop procrastinating and I get the job done, I stop stewing and I start doing. You would visualize yourself writing letters and doing the things that you would normally push to one side. A program for resourcefulness would be good. I am more and more resourceful every day. I rely on my own resources, I become less reliant on other people all the time. You would visualize yourself doing the tasks with the tools that you have at hand, knowing that as you start projects, better tools come along. As a result of inserting positive programs, the output from your biocomputer will be automatic. You will find yourself being punctual, industrious, creative, confident, enthusiastic, diligent, harmonious, flexible, all in accordance with what you have programmed yourself with.

The second type of output is extremely important and it is the behavior that will allow you to go beyond the point where you normally fail or self-destruct. You intentionally get that output by deliberately 'seeing' over and over again, in your imagination (role playing and simulation too) that you are actually going beyond the point where you normally fail. For arguments sake, in selling, say you have a lot of meetings, but few or no closings. You would visualize intently that your prospects were signing the contracts and handing over the checks. You would then 'see' yourself going to the bank and paying the checks in. You would visualize your weekly statement. (All business people have weekly bank statements, don't they?) You would then visualize yourself spending the money and living the kind of lifestyle that you will be enjoying when you have attained your goal.

You may be a businessman that gets involved with business after business and never makes a success out of any of them because you always quit three feet from the gold. You must visualize yourself over and over again sticking with the project and actually 'see' yourself selling out for a lot of money.

The main point, of course, is to recognize your self-destruct modes and take great pains to program in well beyond that point. It is also important to realize that when you do finally reach 'that point' you will very quickly have to visualize where it is you want to go next, or you'll find yourself sliding down one of those snakes!

The third type of output you'll experience from a properly programmed biocomputer is the Eureka! experience. This comes in the form of creative ideas and hunches. For the best results, know what it is you want to achieve, program the end result in words and pictures. Increase the input to the biocomputer by feeding in research, detail and information pertaining to the project. (Read magazine articles, go to the library, send off for information, subscribe to specialist magazines, clip articles, find out how others made money in your field) Help the biocomputer by brainstorming and crossing out any particular options that don't really appeal, wait patiently for the results. You don't have to be thinking of the problem once you have put the program in. The output comes in flashes of inspiration and it helps to capture these on paper when they come. Unlike a conventional computer, our biocomputers don't have printers attached to them to turn the output into hard copy! I've made it a rule to have pen and paper available in the auto, at the bedside, in the bathroom, in my pocket, everywhere. However, I still get caught out from time to time, because the output from the biocomputer often comes at inconvenient times and more often that not, while you are doing the strangest things! (My output usually comes just as I'm about to nod off to sleep, or just when I'm negotiating a rotary, or just when I'm about to board a plane, or just when I'm about to sit down at a dinner party or just when I'm making . . . , anyway that's another story!)

What is the most important aspect of the whole biocomputer program?

The most important aspects of the program are the twice daily programming of the right computer in pictures and the constant programming of the left computer, while you are driving your auto. More important than that is to keep up the practise on a daily, weekly, monthly and yearly basis. The programming should never stop, unless you like sliding down snakes!

What is one of the worst programs you have ever seen?

I have seen hundreds of bad outputs from people's biocomputers. I once had a guy come to meet me because he had a board game he wanted to finance. I saw the game (I think it was called Millionaire, or something like that), and I immediately liked it. In actual fact a colleague of mine, was chairman of one of the largest board game manufacturers in the world. I knew I would be able to convince him to do a deal with me. I told this guy I thought we could do a deal and he went on talking and talking and talking. I told him about five times, I thought we could do a deal. He kept telling me that he nearly got the finance once, but the deal never came off. He told me he'd been hawking the game around for about ten years. I told him another ten times how I thought we could do a deal. He kept talking and talking and talking until he talked himself out of a deal. This guy never heard a single word I said! I am sure he walked out of that meeting thinking he couldn't get a deal with anyone. His biocomputer program made it a self-fulfilling prophecy.

What do you think of subliminal tapes?

They can be OK, but only to a point. First, it is imperative that you know what the messages on the tape actually say. Most of the messages are far too general. Many of the messages are worded in such a way that they could not possibly govern your biocomputer output in anyway whatsoever. Many of the messages are just single words, I would suggest that the biocomputer would need to know exactly what you wanted to happen. A single word like 'truth' or 'creativity' or 'harmony' could mean one of a million things to the biocomputer. Are you sure you want all those inputs for your own biocomputer? Why not make up specific messages that will give you the precise outputs that you desire and need? You have seen how crucial biocomputer language is!

The second thing is, don't forget they program the left computer only. It's the right computer that governs everything we do. The pictures win every time!

In the very near future we will be producing absolutely specific subliminal tapes that have been put together with a tremendous amount of forethought to give you very specific outputs from your biocomputer; these are still being developed and will not be released until they are one hundred percent.

What do you think of listening to tapes while you are asleep?

OK! The Russians are tremendously advanced in this area. Don't forget you would be programming the left computer only. I think this is an ideal way of learning a language, although if you want to learn a language really quickly you should be programming in pictures as well! But don't forget the left computer relies on hundreds of hours of programming and if you had tapes playing while you were asleep your RAS would be deactivated as well. You may very well want to experiment in this area.

Do you listen to your own tapes everyday?
Is the Pope Catholic? Next!

I have never had a single success in my life. I would very much like to have success, what can I do?
I don't believe you? You can't get to be your age without ever having a success! Have you passed your driving test? Yes! I thought so! Are you married? Yes! I thought so! Do you have a job? Yes! I thought so. Do you have children? Yes! I thought you would have! You have had many successes and you've never realized it. Nobody told you that you have had successes. You've had lots! I want everyone in the room to stand up and give Daniel a round of applause. Good. How does that feel? Good eh?

What you've got to do is start recognizing some of your successes. I'm a great believer in little celebrations to mark success. I may have dinner out (steak, medium rare and bottle of Burgundy for me! P.S. Throw in a couple of lobsters as well!) or I may buy myself a book or a special gift, (Last time I did that I bought a three and a half carat diamond ring!) but I always take note of my successes and my accomplishments. I continually re-enforce that I'm a success.

I suggest you start programming that you are a success. Visualize over and over your past successes.

Visualize some successes that you haven't even had yet. It will be impossible for you to become successful, if you don't 'feel' and 'see' yourself as successful. I hope that has helped you. Next!

Do you use your biocomputer to find things that you've lost?

Yes and I drive my partners nuts! I remember one day, everyone was in a real panic, trying to find some replacement ribbons for a printer we had. Employees were looking high and low and no one could find the package of replacement ribbons. It was getting late and soon all the stores would be closed. One of my partners said he would dash out and try to see if he could locate a stationers with the correct ribbon. I put my feet up on the desk and visualized all the likely spots in the office where the ribbons were likely to be. I knew my partners had searched high and low, in every nook and cranny, shelf and cupboard. I then got a blinding flash of inspiration. I felt toward the back of one of the cupboards, sure enough, the shelf was loose and the package of ribbons had slipped down the back of the cupboard, out of sight.

When my partner finally returned, all the shops had closed and he had failed to purchase any ribbons. I handed him the package, I let him install them!

I have made up a list of goals, I would like you to check them for me. I have purposely kept them loose, without specific time frames and I have a burning desire to get these things right now. I will have my masters degree. I will get my pilots license. I will be the owner of a fast-food franchise.

No you won't! You won't accomplish any of your goals, all the time you say I will. You have put your biocomputer on permanent stand-by. To word your goals, semantically correctly, you should say: I have attained my masters degree. I have, not I will! I have earned and attained my pilots license. I am the owner of a fast-food franchise.

You really must take biocomputer language seriously, otherwise you will be doing a lot of programming, but will not be receiving beneficial results.

I read that, if you visualize that your goals are already accomplished, the mind will not deliver for you, because it becomes convinced that you have already arrived. Is this true?

I read that as well and I also did extensive research to find out if there was any truth behind the concept. I can assure you, there isn't. Over the years I have asked literally hundreds of biocomputer students if they have failed to reach their goals because they had previously vividly imagined them. Not one of them reported that 'seeing' the goals, before they had happened, had stopped or impeded their progress. On the contrary, hundreds of them confirmed that the only times they had accomplished their goals, was when they had visualized them beforehand.

Everything I tell you, you should be able to confirm with your own experience. If you cannot verify things with your own experience you should search deeper and deeper until you find a successful philosophy that works for you.

What happens when we don't have goals?

The biocomputer literally demands that we DO have goals. When we don't we really suffer. We immediately slide back down all the snakes without even collecting $200 at GO. We become unhappy, miserable and depressed. The biocomputer is teleological, it is goal seeking.

Giving your biocomputer a simple task like 'Jog a mile each day' would make it happy. The exercise would do you good as well. But it's having goals that's important!

I was talking to a group of elderly ladies the other day. They confirmed that they were bored most of the time. However, every time there was a community project to get stuck into, their spirits rose and they became contented and happy. I remember my mother. (Definitely the most negative person in the whole world.) Her cat became ill and demanded constant attention. Trips to the vet, pills to be popped, cat to be fed, cat to be walked. All of a sudden she had goals in her life. A definiteness of purpose. She became vibrant and happy, the change in her was remarkable. The cat got better and lived another two or three years.

People need goals. A definiteness of purpose is absolutely essential. The biocomputer is teleological, it is goal seeking. Reprogram it today or slide down a snake!

I have a terrible memory and I think it is probably holding me back. What can you suggest?

On the contrary you don't have a terrible memory. You remember just about everything that happens to you. In fact we all have brilliant memories. Congratulations!

What I think you probably suffer from is bad recall, which is something totally different. It's your recall I can probably help you with. I suggest that you start thinking in pictures more and more. The visual side of our biocomputer is the key to recall.

Ask any one who specializes in mnemonics (memory expert) and they will tell you they always attach a picture to a word or a name, that they would like to be able to recall. Let me give you an example. If you were to try and remember the name Mr Treadwell, you would visualize a man with a huge pair of boots on, treading into a huge wishing well. Next time you saw him you'd bring back the image of the guy with the huge boots, standing by a wishing well and you'd say, "Ah! Mr Treadwell, how are you?"

If you enlarge the parts of the picture that are relevant, that also can help you bring back certain details and names. What I also suggest you do is to move your eyes around your head to access certain information. If you want to recall visual information raise your eyes towards the top of your head. We have talked about this before; the eye movements are connected to the neuronal patterns in the biocomputer. To access verbal information slant your eyes down and to the left and to access feeling and emotions slant your eyes down and to the right.

By far the most important tool to help you with your recall is to think in pictures. I would suggest too, that you start reprogramming your biocomputer with appropriate input: Every day my recall gets better and better. I observe things more and I take mental notes, in pictures, of certain events and names that I know I may need to recall. I hope this answers your question. Next!

Although I have had many successes, I can now see the error of my ways. Time and time again I've built up businesses and just walked away and left them. Quite literally left them to whom ever was there at the time and never returned or just walked away

and let them collapse after they had sustained me for years!

Yep! Join the club. I know all about that one! What you have to do of course, very early on in the enterprise, is to set up an exit route for yourself. You know now, that you love starting businesses, but very soon get bored with them. You are a true starter of businesses (That's the real forté of many entrepreneurs) and I suggest that you keep doing that. Only this time, I suggest you play over and over again, into your biocomputer that you will sell out, all, or part of the business, in one, two or three years from when you start it, or alternatively you will get a management team in, to run the business for you. You see what you have been doing is running on your program and coming to a GRINDING HALT at the end of it. That's what we all do. Unfortunately you haven't been capitalizing on what could have been the real reward for you, the actual equity that you have built up in the businesses that you walked out of. Good luck, and don't forget to send me ten percent! Next!

In 'Talk and Grow Rich' you advocate the use of a scrap book to paste in pictures of all your goals. Do you still recommend the use of them?

I do, but not as much as I used to, once I realized that the pictures actually have to be created in the electrochemicals in the biocomputer. I also realized how easy it was to look at all of your goals in a scrap book and not accomplish what you really have to do, which is creating the pictures in the electrochemicals in your biocomputers. Looking at goals is passive and doesn't actually create the pictures in the neurons. Visualizing is active and that is what really puts the program in. If you use the scrap book as a cue for creating the pictures in the electrochemicals,

I'd say that was fine! Yes, all in all I think scrap books are good!

We've all enjoyed ourselves this weekend and I know my family and I have learnt a tremendous amount from you, we can't thank you enough. What will be the single biggest cause of our failures when we leave here?

First let me thank you, that was very nice. The major cause of failure will be, if you rush out and buy more self-help books (don't get me wrong, I'd like you to buy 'Talk and Grow Rich') and not put into practise what you've heard here. You see, coming to the seminar or reading the biocomputer book doesn't count for anything. No Brownie points at all! The only thing that counts for anything is actually carrying out the instructions. The instructions are to make up two tapes, listen to the right computer tape twice a day and the left computer tape for as many hundreds of hours, as you possibly can. All that takes time, discipline and effort. The only thing that makes it worthwhile, are the rewards. The biggest cause of your failures will be not creating pictures in the electrochemicals of the biocomputer, of what you want to happen for your future! Comprende!

Do rapists use their biocomputers? If so how?

They do use their biocomputers, unwittingly, and I'll tell you how. Rapists and sex offenders have the habit of lying on their beds for long periods of time, fantasizing. This is what they do. Of course, without realizing it, they are relaxed and they deactivate their Reticular Activating Systems. They fantasize over and over again and because they are in the relaxed state and the RAS is down, the programs go straight into the biocomputer.

Many serial killers are highly organized individuals and they do a lot of mental planning; what psychologists call "rehearsal fantasies" One study concluded that vivid fantasies are a major driving force in serial homicide. "A fantasy is a script, these people are sort of choreographing a script." says Robert Prentky, a forensic psychologist at the Boston University School of Medicine.

If you recall, the main function of the RAS is to actually ACTIVATE the mechanisms of the willpower (left computer), and ACTIVATE the mechanism of the imagination, (the right computer). So, unwittingly, the potential rapist has used the biocomputer perfectly and of course he is now actually strongly motivated to carry out the deed.

You can and should use the exact same method and in doing so you activate the exact same mechanisms that are tremendously powerful.

Obviously you should be fantasizing businesses and deals and selling and the exciting things that you would like to happen in your life. Only the method is the same, the pictures that you insert into your biocomputer will be different, your output will be different, but nevertheless, if you visualize properly, you too, will be highly motivated into action.

If a person has difficulty visualizing one particular thing, (He can visualize most things OK) does that mean he has a hidden program in his biocomputer, that either goes against what he is trying to visualize, or against the effects of what he is trying to visualize.

Yes, there could well be a hidden program, but it really doesn't matter. Many times you will never get to the bottom of programs that are stopping you accomplishing your goals. Many people can visualize

OK, but have great difficulty 'seeing' themselves as slim or with a lot of money or with a beautiful woman. If you like it's a foreign language to that person. In actual fact it is a foreign, visual language. Of course what you have to do is know exactly what you want and work hard on creating those mental images, in exactly the same way as you would persevere with a foreign language. It's important to know you can overcome all negative programs, by relaxing and visualizing the future as you desire it, albeit with discipline and perseverance.

The main thing is to keep dreaming, as it says in the old song, "If you don't have a dream, you're never gonna have a dream come true!"

Can we get back to the million dollars in five years. That's one I've been after for a long time. I have had a certain degree of success, I've always made a good living. I've always had the goal, 'A million dollars in five years' although you're right it doesn't work. What can I do to ensure success and how long a time frame should I give?

Yes, we keep coming back to this one, don't we? There are two types of knowledge that we should concern ourselves with. The first type is business acumen. You have been in business a considerable number of years. You know there's no free lunch. You know that you have to market a product or service, get customers, sell to them and keep them happy. Business acumen is the least of our worries. The second type of knowledge is psychological knowledge, or more to the point, knowledge about how to reprogram the human biocomputer.

Let's assume you want a million dollars. The first thing I would do is start at Z and visualize the million dollars in the bank. Then you can visualize spending it on a home and auto and start living the life-style you will acquire when you have the million dollars. Then work back towards A, 'seeing' yourself in your office or warehouse selling the product or service in sufficient quantities to make you a millionaire. 'See' also that you have a very low overhead, so the money you make doesn't get frittered away on paying rent, salaries and fixed overheads.

My real concern is that you can actually 'see' these things happening in your mind's eye. Repetition of mental images is the key to success. The more visual detail that you can actually create in the electro-chemicals, the more material your biocomputer has to work with. If you can 'see' it you can have it! If you can 'see' it you can do it! If you can 'see' it you can be it!

That is the real secret, inserting those pictures in the biocomputer in clear, concise terms. A real biocomputer program, a track for you to run on, input equals output.

If you really do all this, the making of a million dollars may only take you fifteen or five months, and at the end of it, you may have made much more than a million, but the mental pictures must come first. I hope this answers your question.

What's the program for writing a bestseller? I've been toying with the idea for ages, but I keep putting it off!

When I decided to write 'Talk and Grow Rich' I wanted a bestseller and I deliberately programmed my biocomputer. I had an idea for a book on selling. It was called The Psychology Behind Success and Selling. All the time I kept writing the book, I kept visualizing its success. I could 'see' it selling all over the world. I could 'see' myself doing tours in many countries to promote it. I could 'see' offers from publishers coming in. The more I visualized the more material came my way, to help me write the book. The more I visualized the more ideas came to me, to make the book tighter, sexier and more readable. The more I visualized, the more exciting the book became, and I became more and more motivated to finish it. The more I visualized the success of the book, the easier it was to overcome writers block. In the end my mind yielded the output, the Eureka! "Call the book 'Talk and Grow Rich'!" The rest is history! (I love it when a new light flashes on in my biocomputer, Eurekas! I love 'em!)

Any goal you set yourself should be visualized over and over again, from every angle until the project takes off, even then you don't stop visualizing, you just alter your visualizations to take you to the next step, the next goal!

Do you get impatient waiting for output from your biocomputer?

The answer is no, but I do understand your question. When you're at rock bottom and only have yourself and your biocomputer as your main resources, yes it's very easy to get impatient waiting for output.

I learned two very valuable lessons when I was at rock bottom. The first lesson was to use my valuable time to program. The second lesson was don't give up, just keep programming. When you're without, program within!

Once you're up and running with your projects, and have successes all over the world, all you have to do is keep programming for future successes, by that time there usually isn't time to be impatient!

Do you insert different programs when dealing with successful people and millionaires and people who are at the top?

I do now! You'd think that a millionaire would be a sound person to deal with, straightforward and rational, and not likely to make silly mistakes. Don't you believe it! You can never tell when any particular person is at the end of their biocomputer program. For all you know, their program may have just come to an end and they are about to slide down a snake. If they are, you must make sure they don't take you with them.

Time and time again I've got involved with people who had reached the end of their vision and a few times these people took me down their snakes with them. This is something you must learn to recognize. A lot of it comes with experience. The more successful the person is, that you are dealing with, the easier it is to get lulled into a false sense of security.

I know that you must be inundated with enquires from all over the world by people who are interested in biocomputer technology. What can the serious investor of either time, resources or money do to ensure that his or her request is answered promptly?

Good question. It helps to send a professionally typewritten letter, on letterhead. State precisely what your interest is. Whether you are interested in promoting books, tapes and seminars, whether you can help in audio and video tape production, or whether you think you can help with writing programs, or whatever your particular interest is. We need all the help we can get! It also helps if you give some detail about resources that you may have at your disposal. Biocomputer technology is in its infancy. The major advances, breakthroughs and rewards are still to come!

I'm a writer, but I have to sustain myself by doing cleaning jobs and working in the local store. I keep telling myself that I've got to do whatever it takes, but I still find it very distracting. I feel that I should be concentrating on my writing, full time. Any ideas?

You are running on a very strong program that tells you that you should be working to earn money, to make everything go round. What you should be doing of course, is putting a program in about what you really should be doing and what you really want to do. You should vividly imagine that you are writing full time. Make up some dummies of some books with your own titles and name on, so that everytime you start typing you can actually 'see' that your books are already in print. Put a program into your biocomputer that 'sees' yourself sustaining yourself as a writer. Also visualize in great detail, grants and checks coming in to help support you while you are writing. Money comes from very mysterious sources once you have begun to visualize.

I am a very creative person, but I find everywhere I go I get driven mad by noise. I keep telling myself that I'm driven mad by noise. I think I must have such a very strong program, that I'm now attracting noisy environments to me. Any suggestions?

Of course you're right. If you keep telling yourself something, anything, so be it! Start programming immediately that you can work with noise, not against it, let it stimulate your creativity.

Learn to enjoy it for what it is. You can also start to program that you have created your own noise free environment, maybe out in the country. Also program that you have bought your own white noise machine, that will even out any of the noises that drive you mad.

You will also find that once you get your RAS under proper control, it too, will filter out any noises that are not important to you. Also, as you learn to control your biocomputer, you will be able to actually turn the noise level down inside your biocomputer so that it doesn't distract you.

I have started looking at the failure programs of people around me, and it's so true that you can see in everyone else, why they come to a grinding halt. It is because their programs run out. I find myself talking to people about their programs and trying to help them onto the next stage. Is there anything wrong with this?

No, not at all. I would also recommend that you get these people to read and study the biocomputer work-book. In this way they'll have much more of an idea of what you're talking about. They will also be in a better position to give you feedback about your own programs and goals.

I heard that negative commands actually make you respond to them. For example, 'I don't smoke' would be translated by the biocomputer to 'I do smoke'. What are your thoughts on this?

Yes, we come back to biocomputer language. If I was to tell you not to think of the monkey, you'd be able to think of nothing but the monkey! You'd be much better off wording your goals without any negative commands at all.

From everything that you have told us, I would deduce that the biocomputer is far more efficient at solving short term goals than long term goals. Am I correct?

Yes! Very much so. As from now you should be running your life and your biocomputer in terms of minutes, hours, days and weeks instead of months and years. The biocomputer is a very precise instrument.

If you have long term goals you would be far better off breaking them down and letting the biocomputer solve immediate problems for you. I have found that if you have a real burn on for a short term goal, with your pictures matching your words, you'll accomplish it very quickly. Then you immediately set the next goal, get a burn on for it, and keep at it until you accomplish it, all the time enlisting the aid of your biocomputer. I hope that answers your question.

I have a slight speech impediment. I always go for girls who have something wrong with them. Either a limp, or zits or buck teeth or they're overweight. I can't seem to stop myself, it's like I'm compensating for my own handicap. I can never ask out a girl that I would consider beautiful?

You know the answer. You have already recognized the problem. Mind you it is a very common problem, in the old days we'd have called it an inferiority complex.

Start now and insert a program that tells you that you feel good about yourself all the time. You may even want to insert a program that tells you your speech impediment has disappeared, because that too, is just a program! Next!

I'm an entrepreneur. Like most of us, I've had a lot of ups and downs. I have a bad program. I keep thinking to myself and telling myself that everyone else is better than I am. If we have a deal going down, I will always revere the accountants and lawyers. I marvel at them. I let my partners do the talking at deal-closing time, and time and time again all these guys goof-up. I know I am just as good as they are, if not better. I keep getting suckered. Any ideas?

Yes lots! As an entrepreneur you must start controlling situations, deals, your life and your biocomputer. As far as I am concerned lawyers and accountants are just there to assist you to bring a deal together legally and make sure the deal is done professionally. The professionals are just there to carry out your instructions. (All too often they screw deals up by trying to justify their own existences. You have been warned!) You can start inserting programs right now, that everything revolves around you, and that you know what you are doing. (If you don't know what you are doing you should do. You should program your biocomputer so that you do know what you are doing. I would suggest that if you don't know what you are doing, you will find it very difficult to make the money that you think you're going to make!) Program that you are the leader. Program that you can take deals to closing and beyond, if that is what you want.

Getting back to my heroes; Getty, Onassis, Hughes, Armand Hammer, all these people were deal makers and everything revolved around them, they ran their own programs in their biocomputers, and that is the track they ran on!

I do a lot of consultancy work and I started charging a standard fee of $150. One day I decided that I wasn't charging enough and I started practising inside my biocomputer, that I was asking for $1500. Very quickly I signed up my next client at that new fee of $1500 and I've never looked back. Everything you do is just a program. I'm now practising and visualizing getting $15,000 per client. Any comments?

Yes! You've just given me a brilliant idea! Next!

I have made a great discovery this weekend that I would like to share with you. I have been to the top. I had a dream house in Beverly Hills, a Porsche and a Rolls Royce and a dream lover. I had the lot. Life was grand. I was living on a grand scale and I got it all by relaxing and programming.

Then, just as quickly, things started to go down hill and I lost the lot. Looking back on it, I can see where I went wrong. Before I had all those things, I'd take long walks in the country alone, visualize a lot, meditate a lot, in actual fact I'd indulge myself in all the principles of programming.

When the house and the autos and the lady came along, I got involved in a lifestyle. A lifestyle of parties and conversation and having house guests. In actual fact all my programming time was used up in entertaining time. I never want to go through losing it all again. What can I do next time around?

It's a question of discipline. A very tough question I hasten to add! I've been there, done that! I can relate!

Start programming for the things you want right now. Start over. This time also add to your program that you will continue to use biocomputer principles. Build a very strong program into your biocomputer that you will never stop using the principles even when you succeed. We have already been over many of the ideas that you can put into your programs about developing and continuing the use of biocomputer principles.

Earlier you were saying that when you get up in the morning you are firing on your right computer, but still write to capture the creativity. Are there any people around who have both computers firing away simultaneously?

Yes, but they are few and far between. These people are either lucky or well developed. It is exactly what we are all aiming for, or should be. To be able to use both computers equally as and when you want, spells genius!

I deliberately try to go through 'hoops of fire' every day. By pushing myself like this, I know I'm making progress. I'm now very aware of the areas where I normally self-destruct. Any comments?

Yes a few. I think having awareness is essential. Of course most people don't even know what's hit them or what's about to hit them, until they find themselves all alone, sitting at the bottom of a snake.

The other point is that you should continue visualizing success all the time until you have actually been through the 'hoop of fire'. Then as soon as you have accomplished that goal, set the next.

During coffee break you were talking to about five of us about our individual programs and after a few moments you told each and every one of us what our programs were. When you left us to talk to someone else, we talked amongst ourselves and

were all equally surprised about how perceptive you were and your accuracy in deducing our programs. What is the secret about recognizing our programs?

No secret. A tree shall be known by its fruit. If you are a certain person, doing certain things it's solely because of your programs. By looking at where and how you live right now, you must have had certain programs to get there. To get up the ladder to the next step you will need certain programs to get there also.

I always maintain, it's not where you've been that's important, it's where you're going that counts. As long as you have a very clear picture of what you want to accomplish, old programs don't matter.

Why do they say ignorance is bliss?

It's a good question, lucky I know the answer. When I was a young entrepreneur, just starting out, I didn't know anything about profit margins, overheads, marketing, or business in general. All I did know was that I wanted to make money, and I started out in business. Of course problems came up and many times I was able to overcome them, because I had a very clear vision of where I wanted to go. Usually I got there. All the time I kept my vision, I did get there, without a doubt. To all intents and purposes I was ignorant and I learnt as I went.

Now what happens as you grow older, you learn, absorb and assimilate. You begin to understand profit margins and overheads and marketing and selling and locating products and everything else there is to know about business.

The problem is, many times you can know too much because all too often you will be able to see that the figures don't work and you won't go ahead with the project, whereas years ago, in your ignorance, you would have gone ahead with the project, solved the problems as you went and made a success out of it.

The biocomputer is brilliant at solving problems as you go. It loves working hard and the solutions it comes up with are not normally text book material.

This is the problem that so many 'wet behind the ears' accountants have. They look at figures on a spreadsheet and with a flick of the wrist and with unbelievable conviction, announce that the project won't work! It always amazes me because they always miss two vital factors, before they issue their death warrant. The first factor is pretty obvious, the figures on the spreadsheet can be what ever you want them to be. That's how they got there in the first place! You made them up. The second point they miss, and it's not so obvious, it only comes with the experience of actually starting projects, is the biocomputer will solve all your problems on a daily basis, providing you instruct it to and visualize the outcome you desire!

You keep telling us input equals output. I would like to say something even more than that. If input equals output then we'd only just balance out all the time, we'd never get ahead of the game. The output must always be far in advance of the input. Any ideas?

Of course you're right! You could compare the biocomputer to baking a loaf of bread. You put in the oven a mixture of wet inedible dough and the output is a lovely crusty loaf that smells and tastes delicious.

If you program your biocomputer properly, output should well exceed your input. For example, you may input a lot of research and the output may be a bestselling book, that nets you millions of dollars. You may input a lot of ideas and material about a certain application or a device and the output may very well be a patent that makes you a small fortune, or leads to an invention that makes you a large fortune. You may input lots of pop music and go to a lot of discos and the output may be that you write a smash-hit single. (I personally know people in every one of these categories, people just like you and me, who all made more than a million dollars each, by doing just that and they never complained once!)

I would say the formula should be: Output Equals Input^2. How's that! Next!

I really do feel a worthless, useless individual. Any ideas?

Yes lots! A lot of people have this problem, you'd be surprised. The problem is of course, the more you keep affirming these thoughts and feelings to yourself, the more powerful the program you build against yourself. The more you impregnate those electrochemicals, the stronger the negative output from the biocomputer.

You must start to program that you love all the skills that you have, whether they be cooking skills, or driving skills or social skills. Start to feel good about the programs that you already have, and with a little inner searching you'll discover that you have lots of valuable programs, you can't get to your age in life without accumulating lots of decent programs, it's just that you've never recognized them before.

Then start adding some programs about the things you want for yourself and where you want to go. Believe me you can overcome any amount of negative programming. I'm living proof that it works!

I don't want to slide down anymore snakes. I've had enough! I've also witnessed it in other people, many who attained major success. What is the one thing that we must do to ensure that we keep moving onward and upward?

You already know the answer to this one, you just like to hear it coming from me!

You must keep visualizing into the future and never stop. You must program the next goal, the one after that and the one after that and never stop. The programming never ever stops. If you stop for a single moment you slide down a snake! Have vacations by all means, but don't retire the biocomputer!

I can see the error in my ways. I've read all the books, done all the seminars and looked at my wish book every night and every morning. The one thing I haven't done is to actually create pictures in the electrochemicals in the neurons in the biocomputer. Is this a common mistake?

Yes it is! Now you know what to do, you have some catching up to do! Next!

What do you think about sophisticated dream building activities, such as going into jewellers and trying on diamond rings, test driving exotic autos and looking at expensive homes?

OK to a point. It all helps, but the most important thing to remember is to create the program in the electrochemicals in the biocomputer.

If you think about it, Rolls Royce mechanics don't end up owning Rolls Royces. Butlers don't end up owning million dollar homes and assistants who serve in jewellers don't end up with million dollar diamond rings and necklaces.

When dream building or role playing, to make it effective, you actually have to 'see' and 'feel' that you are really part of the reality that you are trying to create, not merely an outside observer.

Can we over do it, with the visualizations?

No, certainly not. You should spend equal time processing in words and pictures. For everything you discuss verbally inside your head you should also 'see' pictures for it as well.

The only time you spend forty-five seconds visualizing is in the early days when you are having to use a lot of concentration to get the imaginative faculty used to working properly. From that point on you must use the faculty for all you are worth. The more you use it, the more you will be worth!

Now you have explained in detail that for everything we do, we must have an appropriate program to see the task through to successful completion. I can now understand why there is so much frustration, failure and anxiety on such a grand scale, nationwide and worldwide. Other than starting to insert programs for our own benefit, what can we do to help on a much bigger scale?

Good question! We literally have to start spreading the word. That may not be as difficult as it seems. If each person who reads this book, tells two people, who read the book, and they tell two people, who tell two people to read the book, it's that kind of exponential growth that we need. I really do think that I have been a catalyst here. What is needed now is many people to get on the bandwagon and start coming up with all sorts of programs and tapes, similar to the kind of growth we have in the conventional computer industry.

I can see that to take us to any particular goal we will need a number of programs. How do we know which programs we'll need?

Good question. The first program that you'll need is the program that tells you the end result of that which you wish to accomplish. If you have tried this goal before and failed, you will know which areas of your programs need strengthening.

We all have weaknesses in particular areas. One may be deal closing. Someone else may talk too much. Someone else may quit too easily. Yet another may be too easily swayed by other people.

Weaknesses develop as a project develops. Should you see weaknesses develop or should you feel drawn to slide down a snake that is a sure sign that you will want to start visualizing exactly what it is you want to happen.

The other thing you should do is visualize all your deals in advance and your future in advance and then you will see any areas that you are particularly weak in. These will be the programs that you will want to insert.

I can hear my mother's voice telling me "You're useless" and a "SOB" and "a good for nothing". I can still hear my father telling me "You're a jerk and a bum". It doesn't matter where I am in the world I can still hear their voices.

Those voices are like programs to me and they keep making me feel bad and goof-up my life. Any ideas?

Yes. The biocomputer responds beautifully to being tuned like a radio. Next time you hear the voices you don't have to listen to them. What you should do is imagine a little volume control knob in your biocomputer. You can gradually turn the knob and in doing so turn down the volume until the voices disappear altogether.

If you like you can change stations altogether and listen to your favorite radio show. Failing that, have someone else come into the framework, in your imagination, so it's not you that your parents are talking to. You can even have them sing to you in stupid high pitched voices so they sound like opera singers and you can just laugh at it. I hope that answers your question. It really isn't a problem.

I have told myself that I can't get a woman until I have made myself financially secure. I know I've talked myself out of a lot of relationships. I'd like a female around right now!

Many people keep affirming to themselves that they can't have a woman until they become financially secure. Or they affirm they can't get a man until they become a certain weight. Of course all these things are totally unrelated to your real goal, as indeed many of our programs are.

What you have to do is to start realizing the marvellous scope of the biocomputer and let it get you all the things that you desire. But don't go and confuse it by saying one thing when you really mean another.

What happens if you are involved in very fast moving situations. For arguments sake, working with a business that's heavily in debt or on the other hand a business that's expanding rapidly?

Good question. Experience has taught me that in business, any business, you have to expect the unexpected. The unexpected will happen tomorrow. I guarantee it. Because the unexpected always happens you can program for it. You can program for total flexibility. You can program that you don't panic. You can program that you will always make the right decision, you can program that you will always take the right option. You can program awareness.

The other thing you must learn to do, is to program quickly. You do this by keeping your biocomputer off the thing you don't want to happen and concentrate fully on the thing that you do want to happen.

I'm always worried about my health. Any suggestions?

Yes, first I'd like to make a few comments. People who worry about their health build up a very negative program by affirming over and over again that they have health problems. (That's exactly what hypochondria is!) Of course, like all programs they become a self-fulfilling prophesy.

I have also noticed that it's the same people that buy all the health books, same as it's always the same people who buy all the diet books and the same people who buy all the wealth books. My point is, again, reading is a left computer exercise, without having matching pictures all is in vain.

Obviously you need two programs. The first one for your left computer affirming over and over again that you are in a very good state of mental and physical health. You can state on the tape any particular areas that you are concerned with. Maybe you want to include that your heart is very strong or that your liver and lungs are in perfect condition and function extremely well. You can also affirm that every day you are guided into a better way of living and that you respect your body and your health.

Include on the tape that you do correct and sufficient exercise and take a balanced diet.

On the tape for your right computer you will state that your heart is free of disease or that your lungs are free of disease. You will then leave the customary forty-five seconds blank on the tape. It is here that you will vividly imagine that your body is disease free. You will 'see' your heart pumping. Actually visualize your body being in tip-top condition. (Many patients have actually cured themselves of cancer by visualizing that strong blood cells are eating up all the cancerous growths. Others have visualized warriors eating up any bad areas that looked like bad hamburger. You have to use your imagination and find out what visualization works for you, that's why you have an imagination!)

Most diseases are caused by people being at dis-ease with themselves, so one of the most important things to put on your tapes is that you feel very happy, relaxed and comfortable about your life, your health and your biocomputer programs!

How do we know when to stop visualizing and stop listening to our tapes?

In short you don't stop. If you are carrying out the instructions to the letter, you should start accomplishing many of your goals very quickly. As you progress, I suggest you re-evaluate your goals all the time, to see if there are any conflicts or goals that can be broken down into smaller objectives. I suggest that if you are going for large, complex, out-of-reach goals and you just can't visualize them, try approaching them from another angle. I would suggest, that if you don't actually 'see' your goals, you won't actually accomplish them. If you do actually 'see' your goals, I think you'll accomplish them with astonishing rapidity.

You say we should emotionalize our goals and select one goal in particular that we should give the supercharge treatment to. What emotions should we use?

Gosh you don't miss a trick do you? Yes! The emotions you should use are positive ones. Positive emotions come under the following headings: desire, love, romance, sex, enthusiasm, hope and faith.

The negative emotions come under one of these headings: greed, hate, envy, jealousy, revenge, anger, superstition.

If you wrap up your goals with positive emotions, you won't go far wrong! Does that answer your question?

Do you believe in luck?

Yes, as it happens I do and the more I can get the better. Let me explain. It doesn't matter how much we know about reprogramming the biocomputer, all that can do is increase our chances of success. The point is you never know what negative programs the people you are dealing with have in their biocomputers. Their self-destruct modes may fire off just as you are about to close a major deal. In my experience they usually do. You need a certain amount of luck with you to ensure that not only have you got your programs right to close the deal, but to have the person you're closing the deal with, also have the right programs. If you can make that happen you're lucky. If you can make it happen all the time, you're extremely lucky.

Is it OK to keep zigzagging toward one's goals?

Yes, not only is it OK, I think it's probably the only way we reach our goals. The people who zig and then don't come back to zag are lost because they didn't have a clear picture of where they were heading. If you are continually playing your tapes and visualizing the future as you desire it, you will be amazed at the small amount of zigzagging you will do.

Don't forget the whole art of sailing an ocean racing yacht is to continually zigzag to get to the goal in the shortest space of time.

Do repeated attempts help us accomplish our goals?

Yes, absolutely. The more we try, the more feedback and input goes into the biocomputer. If you can temper these attempts, with honing-up the vision of what it is that you are trying to accomplish, that will give very strong input into your biocomputer. Most people who keep on failing, (and there are many) are those who do not have clearly defined goals or clearly defined plans. They just keep on doing and they just keep on failing. (They have only got the persistence part of the program right! For sustained success you will need many programs, not just one!) They have not taken great pains to insert proper programs into their biocomputer to give them proper tracks to run on. Consequently, they keep crashing and wondering why! Next!

Do you still try to solve your problems consciously?

No way! I have too many problems. I also take problems on from individuals and corporations, I am a professional problem solver, a hired biocomputer. I always use the same method, for my own problems or for my clients. I define the problem, I write it down. I try to define the end result. I don't necessarily try to find the solution for the problem, just the end result, that I would like to happen. I then list down as many possible options that I can think of consciously. Then I would go over that list and try to cross out as many of those options as I could, that I would find totally unacceptable. I help my biocomputer along as much as possible, although at this time I am still totally flexible, having no preconceived idea of what the final solution to the problem may be. I then visualize the end result of exactly what I want to happen. Input equals output. I come up with lots of Eurekas! for myself, businessmen, executives and corporations, and make lot's of money too. I visualize end results for people and get paid for it. Eurekas! I love 'em! It's better than working for a living!

14

There are More Questions Than Answers

One of the great things about the question and answer sessions is that a lot of material gets really aired.

I do everything I can to break down biocomputer student's inhibitions about asking questions so they really go away, having their own personal problems resolved.

Let's go back to the auditorium again and see what's on various students biocomputers, other than sex and making a million in under five years!

"Welcome back to session two! I hope you have all been discussing various aspects of biocomputer technology and have hundreds of questions lined up for a dynamic session this afternoon. You know I really like thinking on my feet. However, before we start I better tell you a little story. This story is about a man who invented a tiny little flying device, the size of a fly" (Before I get into my story I get interrupted) "Yes, Maxine, how can I help you?"

Will you Pleeeze tell us the story of Hissing Sid just one more time? Pleeeeeeze!

No, I can't, that's a story that has to be done spontaneously. Oh all right, if you insist!

This is the story of little old Johnny the Snake, I wish you'd stop calling him Sid!

One Saturday afternoon little old Johnny the Snake was playing around in his front yard and he got bored. He decided to go out the back and hiss in the pit. There he was hissing in the pit, making a lot of noise hissing in the pit, having a lot of fun hissing in the pit, when his Mom came out. "What are you doing there Johnny, hissing in the pit, that's my pit and you're not going to hiss in it." With that, little Johnny got out of the pit and his Mom went back inside to get on with the ironing.

Little Johnny got round to thinking "If you can't hiss in your own pit who's pit can you hiss in?" so he got back in the pit and started hissing. Johnny's Mom heard the noise and rushed to the back door. "You naughty little snake, Johnny, I told you only five minutes ago that you weren't allowed to hiss in the pit. That's my pit and you're not going to hiss in it. If you wanna hiss in a pit, you go up to Mrs Pots' pit 'n hiss." With that little Johnny the Snake said, "All right Mom," and off he went, tail between his legs, making his way to Mrs Pots' pit. On the way there he met his best friend Jimmy the Snake, "Where ya going?" says Jimmy. "My Mom says I'm not allowed to hiss in my own pit, I've got to go up to Mrs Pots' pit to hiss, do you wanna come with me?" "No I don't," said Jimmy. "All right I'll go on my own!" Says Johnny.

So off went little Johnny the Snake all on his own. He got to Mrs Pots' pit and started hissing and Mrs Pots came out and said to Johnny, "What are you doing there, hissing in my pit?" "Well Mrs Pots my Mom says that I'm not allowed to hiss in our pit Mrs Pots, my Mom told me to come over and hiss in your pit Mrs Pots so that's what I'm doing hissing in your pit Mrs Pots." "Well Johnny you can't do that because that's my pit and you're not going to hiss in it, you go right on back home now and hiss in your own pit!" With that little Johnny the Snake says "OK Mrs Pots, I'll go back to my own pit and hiss."

Little Johnny the Snake got back home and started hissing in the pit and his Mom came out, livid, " You naughty little snake, I just told you just ten minutes ago, that's my pit and you're not going to hiss in it, I told you if you want to hiss in a pit you go up to Mrs Pots' pit 'n hiss!" "Hold on Mom, I went up to Mrs Pots' pit and started hissing and Mrs Pots came out and told me I wasn't allowed to hiss in her pit, that I had to come back home and hiss in my own pit, so that's what I'm doing here, Mom, hissing in the pit."

"Let's get this straight Johnny, you mean to tell me Mrs Pots wouldn't let you hiss in her pit? Is that what you're telling me?" "That's right Mom, Mrs Pots wouldn't let me hiss in her pit," said Johnny. "The audacity!" said Johnny's Mom, "I knew the Pots before they even had a pit to hiss in!"

There are roars of laughter, everyone hopes that there will be a slip of the tongue, but I manage to squeeze through with out any major mistakes. (The only time I made a major mistake was in front of full auditorium at Birmingham University in England and I got all my mucking words fuddled!)

"OK so much for my story of the man who invented the tiny flying device, I'll save it for another time. Let's get on with some questions. Next!"

How can you tell when you experience a Eureka!

Good question! Eurekas! I love 'em. You'll know it all right because the flash of inspiration that you receive will be so 'right', many things will slot into place right there and then. Furthermore, because the idea is so right, you'll be motivated into action, because you'll have been programming the biocomputer correctly and as a result you will have been using the RAS properly. The RAS will activate the two individual computers and when you get the Eureka! you will also get the motivation to act it out. Many people tell me about good ideas they have had, but they weren't motivated to action. I doubt those ideas came about as a result of reprogramming the biocomputer properly, because when you get a Eureka! the output is strongly augmented, and of almost unbelievable power!

Why do people get divorced? My wife and I did. She used to think I was fooling around with another woman. I wasn't, I was working hard and late at the office. Every night, when I got home, she'd give me a really hard time. In the end I got out. She nearly drove me nuts!

Yes, I've heard this one before, I'm afraid. It's much more common than you could possibly realize. Your wife was visualizing over and over again that you were having an affair. She was not controlling her imagination. When you got home you experienced the result of her input, which was negative, because, in her pictures she saw you with another woman, so the output she gave you was hell.

Many people go through their lives not controlling their pictures or their words in their biocomputers at all. Often, others around them suffer as a result of their negative and uncontrolled thinking. The imagination is truly powerful. It can either make you or break you. Make sure you program into it, only the outcomes that you really want to appear in your life. Make sure your spouse does the same thing. Buy them a copy of this work-book.

Do people really collapse businesses and homes because their biocomputer programs run out?

Not only do they, but it happens all the time. I've talked to so many people, from many different countries, all who have done the same thing. They didn't recognize it at the time, but after one of my seminars, they realized what they had done.

I have talked to many people who have told me they built a business to a certain size, then collapsed it because they were getting divorced and they didn't want the partner to have part of the action. So they just collapsed the business. Nobody got anything. The thinking was that my spouse never helped me build the business, why should they have part of it. (Negative programs build up in peoples' biocomputers by constantly reinforcing negative thoughts!)

Many people told me they have collapsed homes to end a relationship, just sold up everything and moved to a new neighborhood. They figured if there was nothing in the home, there would be nothing for the partner to stay on for. If you have walked out of homes and businesses it may very well pay you to have a careful look at your biocomputer programs so you can 'see' for yourself the real cause behind the outward expression. You'd be surprised at the programs people have in their biocomputers.

The point of all this, is that if you want to move onward and upward, you have to end the self-defeating behavior and overcome the self-destruct mechanisms that we all have. The problem is that they are so insidious and so deeply imbedded that you cannot always be aware of them.

It pays dividends to program the biocomputer with outcomes that you really do want. If you program the biocomputer with the steps shown here, you will override any amount of deeply imbedded negative programs, even if you don't know what they are.

Where did you first come across the term 'human biocomputer' or is that a term you made up yourself?

I first came across the term in John Lilly's book, 'The Programming and Meta Programming in the Human Biocomputer', about twenty years ago. (Before you rush out and buy this book I should warn you that Lilly's way of reprogramming the biocomputer was through the use of LSD and various 'reprogramming substances') I've been studying the subject, or at least the teleological aspects of the biocomputer ever since then. Next!

Can this program help me overcome call-reluctance?

It sure can. I have helped thousands overcome call-reluctance; people in Amway, insurance sales people, business people, people from all walks of life.

Let me tell you what I used to do many years ago. I used to arrive in my office at about 9am. I'd look at the list of prospects that I should call. I'd look at my watch. 9am, too early for anyone to be in their office. So I'd make coffee. I like coffee so I'd have two cups. 9.30. Still too early to make phone calls, I'll go and fill the auto up with gas. I don't like to waste time. You understand? I'd meet my mate John and we'd go and have apple pie a-la-mode and more coffee, would you believe? I'd get back into the office, I'd look at my watch, 11.30, people will be going to lunch, so I'd say "I'll really get serious about getting on the phone this afternoon." That's what I did. That's call-reluctance. That phone got bigger and bigger, it turned into a monster. I could 'hear' the abuse and the rejection and the Noes!

What I do now and what I suggest you do, is to visualize very clearly that you are on the phone.

Visualize getting through to the person you want to talk to. Visualize eliciting the response that you require. Visualize over and over again that you get success after success after success. Door to door salespeople do the same thing. They visualize the rejection before it happens and then their imaginations begin to control them.

Call-reluctance is easy to overcome and it all begins by inserting pictures of acceptance not rejection into your biocomputer. Input equals output. Comprende! Next!

I've been here all weekend and I've come to realize I really do live from hand to mouth. I've been doing it for years, I'm now forty-three! Please help!

It comes down to your biocomputer programs. You obviously have very strong 'Just get by' or 'Just enough' or 'I'll survive' programs. You must begin to broaden your horizons and start to stretch. Start mixing with some positive go-getters who are not content to sit around and live from hand to mouth. Instead of pushing things away from yourself, start attracting things and people to you. At the age of forty three you have a tremendous amount of material in your biocomputer, you are just not using it, or accessing it. The reason is simple, you are not asking it to do anything for you. Therefore it doesn't. It will be a lot happier if you put it to work and give it some goals to accomplish. If you set yourself some goals in the field that you have been accustomed to working in, you won't have to go through a massive learning curve and you will be able to excel very quickly. Don't be shy, step up to the front and select what you want!

I'd really like a beautiful girlfriend. I've had lots of relationships but these have been girls who have just

come along at the right time. What I really long for is a beautiful woman. What's the program?

The program is so simple you'll kick yourself. You have to control your imagination instead of letting it control you. You have seen beautiful women, I'm sure, nearly asked them out, then at the last moment you've chickened out. You let your imagination win. Start putting some programs into your biocomputer, right now. You can start practising, by asking girls in shopping lines the time. You can progress by asking girls you like the look of, for directions. All the time actually visualize the type of girl that you would really like to be with. Don't just visualize her looks, but her personality as well and all the things you will be doing together, other than making love.

Most men just visualize themselves making love to beautiful women and then find themselves having a succession of meaningless, unrewarding relationships. All it takes is a little imagination to 'see' yourself dating the woman of your choice, 'see' yourself doing meaningful things, such as building a home and a family. The more you can actually add to your visualization the better.

The biocomputer is tremendously powerful. If you just keep having short term, sexual relationships with women, your biocomputer will translate that into a habit program. Neither your biocomputer or you, will know the difference between a girl that you just want to 'bed' or a beautiful girl that you want to settle down with and marry.

What are some of the best programs that you inserted into your own biocomputer?

Over the years there have been many and I haven't stopped yet! I'll give you three of the most noticeable one's and what they mean to me.

The program, 'I close deals all the time' made a tremendous difference to my life, as you can imagine. I beefed up the program with the following.'When I am in a deal I am always careful what I say, even when the other person says the most outrageous things. (Many times the other player says things either consciously or unconsciously that could be red rag to a bull) I am more inclined to listen and listen and listen and think very carefully before I talk. I realize there is many a slip between cup and lip. Over a period of time I beefed-up the statement even more to make sure I had a very strong program for closing deals. I continued on my tape program. I also go into deals well prepared and very flexible. I realize that the other player will also have ideas on how the deal can come together and he will also have things that he would like out of the deal. I am very keen to progress and I will do so by very carefully weighing up everything that is offered to me. My main objective is to close the deal and get some goodies for myself.

You can take it from me that fifty percent of something, is better that one hundred percent of nothing. Many times I took the fifty percent and lived to enjoy it. On the occasions when I turned it down I lived to regret it!

I also put in an action program and I suggest you do the same whether you think you need it or not. 'I am very quick to move on ideas and projects if I have made the decision they are projects for me. I realize that although I am my own man there is no one to make me work set hours, therefore I am the one who sets the discipline. I work very hard. I adopt the attitude of doing more that I am paid for because I know the rewards for my efforts equate to the law of the harvest. I do today what has to be done today. I don't procrastinate. I am a man of action.'

The other program I will mention is the one of persistence. This is my favorite program in the whole world and I now realize that I have become the most persistent, resilient, tenacious, stop at nothing, make it happen man in the whole universe. I think tenacity and resilience is above everything, if you want to accomplish the goals that you have set yourself.

'I will never give up because people tell me "No," I just keep going and going and going. I keep honing-up my plan to make sure my product, idea or service is suitable for those who I am selling to. I never quit. I know that if I get rejected, that is just one man's opinion. I know that no-one can stop me from accomplishing what I have set for myself. Everyday I become even more tenacious and drive my projects harder and harder. If I do get rejected I use that as a spur to drive me to greater tenacity. All the time I look at any rejections to see if they are founded in any way whatsoever and I use that as feedback to develop my product or service. I keep on keeping on. The word failure does not exist.'

That program has helped me above all others. Believe me, resilience, persistence and tenacity are to a man, what carbon is to steel.

Can you give us some more ideas for programs that we may like to make up for ourselves?

Certainly. Pick the ones you would like to use right now. Develop them and beef them up. Add to them, always using words in the present tense and make them suitable to your own needs.

Try key programs like, Diligence, Persistence, Empathy, Patience, Creativity, Energy, Confidence, Enthusiasm, Do it now!, Self-Reliance, Productivity, Punctuality, Concentration, Good Judgement. Does that answer your question. Next!

Can you give us tips on accomplishing really difficult goals?

Yes, I'll try. The problem I have with your question is the "really difficult" part. Why is the goal really difficult? Is it difficult because you are having trouble attaining it, say, like making a million in five years, or is it difficult because the task itself is difficult, like climbing a mountain on the north face, in winter, that no man has ever done before?

So to answer your question, if it is difficult because you are not attaining it, try to be creative, by breaking large goals down. Maybe you can't 'make a million' with the product or marketing method or sales team that you have currently. Look at every angle.

The key of course, is concentrated visualization, so you will actually be able to 'see' in your imagination, exactly how you will be able to accomplish the goal. Once you can actually 'see' how to accomplish the goal, you keep programming the biocomputer until you actually get the output you require.

For difficult goals that have never been accomplished before, you need even greater control over your imaginative skills. Houdini used to do this when 'visualizing' illusions that he had never used before. He used concentrated effort and eventually he would be able to 'see' how he could create a certain illusion. For climbing a mountain or some other task you'd have to visualize every possible hardship and danger. You'd have to do many 'dummy runs' in your biocomputer to ensure yourself of success.

You mentioned that you taught yourself welding, how in actual fact did you do that?

In my motorcycle days I used to have a number of workshops. I'd watch the welder and the mechanics. They never gave me any formal welding training but I watched and I observed. I 'saw' myself welding over and over again. I put the program into my biocomputer, that in actual fact I could weld. One weekend all the mechanics were out and I welded up a complete motorcycle racing frame that I went racing on. After that I went from strength to strength and over the years built many successful racing frames. I have taught myself to type by sitting in a chair visualizing myself typing. I had a seven minute lesson on a word processor then visualized the rest.

I know you have mentioned you love to drive fast. You talk about it quite a lot. Is there some analogy between driving fast and success in business?

I think there is. Yes, absolutely there is! I love driving fast, I've had Trans Ams, Aston Martins, Jaguars and all manner of very fast exotic sports cars, got some stories to tell too.

When you drive very fast you are not thinking consciously, you are running on your biocomputer program. When it all goes boss-eyed at a hundred and forty miles an hour, your biocomputer knows what to do. At that speed there is no way you can tell just how hard to brake, or just how hard to accelerate or just when to change gear or correct the drift. You run on the program. You do it all the time and you don't even notice it.

Success in business is very similar. If you have a success program inserted into your biocomputer, you will automatically, on a day-to-day basis, be making right moves and zig-zagging toward your goal. Remember most people don't have any programs at all in their biocomputers as far as the success of their business is concerned and that's why they fail. If you have a very clear picture of how you are going to attain success in your business you will be able to drive that business fast and hard, yes! like a racing car! Go for it!

I have had a bad back for a number of years. Is there a program that may possibly help me?

There sure is and this is one I've used myself. I used to suffer terrible back problems. I went to all sorts of specialists and none of them helped. (They relieved me of quite a bit of cash though, perhaps they thought it was weighing my hip pocket down, causing stress in the back!) The program you need is simple.

'My back is perfectly healed. Everyday I am directed to things that will help me with my back problem. As these things are drawn to me, I will immediately act upon them and implement them in my everyday life. I draw to me the right advice and I lead a life-style that incurs no undue stress on my back. I am completely free of pain because I have isolated the cause of my pain and it is medically cured.'

After I played this program for a number of weeks a lot of things happened. I met various people who introduced me to different aids. One was a 'Backswing' and I used this to invert myself for at least a few minutes everyday. I bought a special seat for my auto and I lost weight. I also got lots of other tips and advice that I quite literally drew to me as a result of the program. After years of pain, I couldn't understand why I didn't insert the program before. Next!

Is the story true, about you going into a Rolls Royce dealer in London to use the bathroom, only to be told that it was for patrons only, to which you replied "Well I'll have the green one!"

Something like that!

I just can't get motivated, although I know I should!

The reason why you can't get motivated is because you have a total incongruity between everything you 'say' you are going to do and everything you actually 'see' yourself doing.

I suggest that you take a very careful look at all your goals and the tasks that you have set for yourself. Maybe you are living your complete life through someone else. Maybe your wife or your employer want you to do many things that they want done. Have a look. There is something holding you back. I suggest that if you clearly set some goals of the things you really desire for yourself, regardless of what other people perceive to be best for you, then visualize the goals carefully so your pictures and the words match. The RAS will come into play and activate the mechanism of the will power (left computer) and it will also activate the mechanism of the imagination (right computer) and you will automatically be motivated!

I'm an auto salesman. I'd like to sell a lot more. A lot more than I already do and I already sell quite a lot. What's the key to success here!

Would you buy a used car from this man! No, quite seriously, this is a common problem in your industry. I'll tell you what happens over and over again. Auto salesmen 'see' themselves as fifty grand a year salesmen or hundred grand a year salesmen. You're probably in the two hundred grand a year bracket, right!

What they do is set themselves quotas. That is going to be the program they will run on. They may reach the quota in the first week of the month. If they do, they'll just lay back and take it easy for the next three weeks. Even if they don't lay back, something will stop them achieving more sales. However, if they happen to make no sales for the first three weeks of the month, somehow, it all comes good and they reach their quota in the last week of the month. It just happens that way. They are running on their biocomputer programs perfectly, what else, or what more could you want? By the time the year end arrives the fifty grand a year guy has made his fifty grand to the penny; the hundred grand a year guy has made his hundred grand and you've made your two hundred grand!

Input equals output. If you 'see' yourself as a fifty grand a year auto sales man that's what you will get, year after year after year. That's the program. Nothing else can or will happen. If you want to raise your sights and you can quite easily, all you have to do is take great pains to insert in pictures and words the outcome that you wish to achieve. Comprende?

Why do some people never finish projects? I really have created some good opportunities for myself but I have never reaped the rewards of a single project.

The reason why people fail to finish projects of course, is their programs, or more to the point, the lack of programs. When their program comes to an end, as you've seen before, they come to a GRINDING HALT!

I had a partner who bought a large piece of real estate that he wanted to use as an exhibition center. His whole program revolved around getting the building and then having it refurbished to make it suitable for his needs. This all could have been done in six months, but because he had such a powerful program to refurbish the place, the project has been going on for years. He blows out many opportunities that would allow him to get the project finished and the doors open but his program doesn't allow it.

As soon as he starts 'seeing vividly', in his imagination, that the doors to the exhibition center are open and the public is flooding in. That will happen, he'll find a way. He'll actually be motivated to make it happen, but the program has to go in first.

I was reading only recently about a group of people who decided to get together on a weekly basis to brainstorm a project for a new hospital wing. The group of nine met every week. Each week there would be a reason why a decision couldn't be reached. It could have been that more facts were needed, a little research on this or details to a business plan had to be added or altered. This went on for nine years. Years not months! One day the group was ready to meet to make the final decision, only to find that one of the group members was off sick. The woman in charge of the project said they'd have to put off the making of the decision until next week. Another member of the team suddenly stood up and said, "This debate has been going on nine years and I've just realized why. If we finally decide what it is that we're going to do, these weekly meetings will be no longer necessary. The end of the project will be over. The baby will have to be given to someone else. I say we make the decision today and let's get on with a new project." They voted right there and then and finally came to a decision, after nine years. Years not months!

I had dealings with a very creative woman. She came up with an idea that I'm convinced would have made her a small fortune. She designed her letterhead. It looked superb. She designed her products. They were eminently saleable. She put together a complete business plan. It was very comprehensive. The project 'worked', everything was in place. This thing was a flyer. I guarantee it. What did she do next. She stopped. She shelved the whole project. I came to realize later, she has done this, if not hundreds of times, certainly dozens of times, before. She cannot 'see' herself actually turning her dreams into reality.

She cannot 'see' herself with money. When I got down to it with her, it all came out that her childhood programs were those of failure, 'give up, you can't do that, you'll never be a success, you'll never have money'. It all became a self-fulfilling prophecy, over and over again in her adult life.

You have to take great pains to put the complete picture in, otherwise you come to, yes, you said it for me, a GRINDING HALT! when your program comes to an end.

When we insert programs into our biocomputers do we actually erase the old programs or just override them?

Good question. There are two trains of thought here. Mine is that I firmly believe that you just override the old programs. I have hypnotized people, who have been able to access old programs, but because the new program was put in with the RAS deactivated and the words were reinforced thousands of times, the output from the old program. It pays to test out programs. If you have correctly inserted a program you won't have any problems. If you do have problems with a specific program, use the supercharge method of using emotion. This will really reinforce programs and give you a permanent track to run on.

My name's Robert and I just wanted to thank you for the weekend. You've given me so much. I don't know how I've survived all these years with the programs that I've got. I do have one question. I want you to expand more on the 'Exit Routes' so I can actually get out with a million dollars. I see the importance of it, but I just don't know the options available.

Good question Robert, we've enjoyed having you here. The 'Exit Route' if possible should be part of your program that you are visualizing and playing on your tapes. A good business plan will always include a number of 'Exit Routes' so investors can see how they can get out, both with their capital back and a profit. There are a number of alternative 'Exit Routes' that you may want to program into your biocomputer. You may even want to program some alternatives just in case the first one doesn't come to fruition.

Obviously the kind of business that you're in will determine the 'Exit Route' for your million dollars, to a greater extent. You may want to consider some of the following: If you are building a retail business, can you build it so that you have a million dollars equity in it? Your 'Exit Route' would be when you sold out to another individual or made a trade sale to someone in the same industry. If you are building a business you may consider a management buy out. Will your managers be able to raise the money for the business? Is the business worth a million dollars? (Not just worth a million dollars, but does it have a million dollars equity in it?) You may want to consider going public. In that case you would need sufficient shares in a business, preferably lots of them, at very cheap prices, so when you get a chance to sell them, you may do so at a much higher price than you paid for them. You would need $50,000 worth of five cent shares to be able to make a million when the shares rose in value to a dollar each. All these things need thinking out in advance. You also may want to consider getting royalties for books, inventions, products, records and franchise agreements. You can also do some research to see for yourself how people in your field made a million out of their businesses and use that as a model.

Most people running businesses concentrate on getting wages and paying fixed overheads, not on cashing in a million dollars worth of chips. Put that in your biocomputer. Next!

I am very shy and would like a more outgoing personality. According to 'Talk and Grow Rich', I'm a wallflower, not a sunflower. I'd like to be a sunflower. What's the program?

'I meet people with ease and confidence. People enjoy what I have to say because I talk in a conversational manner, not about myself so much, but about the people I meet. Beautiful people often have troubles communicating with others and many times they are very pleased that I have made the effort to talk to them.'

Of course when you are visualizing this scenario, actually 'see' the smile on your own face and the smile on the person's face that you are talking to. People love to see a smile. Smiling is the language of breaking down barriers!

I am already intuitively practising a lot of what you are telling us. However, I know I keep stopping for long periods of time. What's the secret?

To be successful you have to keep on keeping on. Many people take their foot off the accelerator far too prematurely. What you should do is program into your biocomputer the diligence program.

'I work really hard towards my goals. I don't keep stopping and starting. I just keep on going even under adverse conditions should they arise. I work consistently and persistently. I do not take my foot off the accelerator until the deal is closed or the task is complete. When I succeed, I celebrate!' I hope that helps you!

I can very easily see how the biocomputer can operate as a computer, solve problems, come up with

ideas, especially the way you explain it. Fantastic! But what I want to know is something a little esoteric. Do you believe that the mind can act as a sending and receiving station? Can it contact minds all over the world? Do you believe in ESP? Can the mind bend metal?

Yes to all those things and many more besides! I'd rather not spin off at tangents right now, but I'd like to talk with you afterwards, if that's OK with you!

What can we do to hone-up the process of creating Eurekas!!

Lots. The main thing would be to have a very clear picture of what it is that you are trying to accomplish. Then make sure your picture programs match the words. Next you can supercharge the goal with a burning desire and add plenty of emotion. You can brainstorm the goal with members of a mastermind group in a spirit of harmony.

The normal steps to genius are conception/input then follows a period of gestation/incubation and finally you get your output which is illumination/ Eureka!

Sometimes you have to be patient. It pays to remember that farmers don't keep digging up seeds or bulbs at midnight, to see if they're sprouting!

I want to come back to beautiful women. Do you mean to tell me that if I go out with some women just for sex, then I meet someone that I really like and would like to marry, my biocomputer will not know the difference, and I'll end up treating her the same and I'll end up losing her?

Yes, I couldn't have put it clearer myself. If you keep going out with women for sex, that will be the program that you run on. The more often you do it, the deeper you insert the program into the electro-chemicals in your biocomputer. You'd be far better off programming your biocomputer properly from the outset, otherwise, sure as fate, you'll end up hurt. Don't forget your biocomputer programs direct you as a matter of habit. It's completely automatic. You'll do certain things without even realizing it, although the woman on the receiving end will.

Is there anything you don't know?
No! Next!

Does fight or flight come into play in our programs?
No I don't think it does, not in the world of business. Let me give you an example why. Years ago I rented a small office. Things were tough. This office was terrible. Everything was wrong with it. It was very noisy, despite having made many complaints. What was I to do? Fight? Go and punch up the guy's nose? Hardly. What was I going to do? Flight? I couldn't move at the time, (I was suffering from invisible entrapment) I couldn't afford to move. My business was well known where it was. Of course what I had to do was put in the appropriate program to get the desired output. I moved into a fantastic office in another city. The whole program came out exactly what I had visualized. Soundproof office too. Does that answer your question?

You say there are many ways people visualize. Tell us about them. And tell us the method you use yourself.
It always amazes even me to listen to people who can actually visualize. (Don't forget it is absolutely imperative for you to create the pictures in the electro-chemicals using one method or the other) Many

people can 'see' things clearly in their minds eye with their eyes actually open. In other words they see what is in front of them but they are also 'seeing' what they are visualizing. When I ask people where it is they are actually 'seeing' the thing they are visualizing, they normally point to a spot about four to six feet away. Many people can only visualize with their eyes closed. Many people can only 'see' still and not moving pictures. Others can 'see' only in black and white not color.

My preferred method of visualizing is this. I know the words, which I use as cues for the pictures. I relax myself, deactivate the RAS. Although I am lying down, I prop my head right up so I am not likely to fall asleep. Then I close my eyes and I concentrate very hard until I actually create the picture. (In case you haven't gathered, I find it very hard to visualize, although I know I absolutely have to).

I must have absolute silence as well, because I find that it takes lots of concentration to visualize and create the pictures that I need. If there are noises or interruptions I can't visualize and I will put off my session until it is quiet. Why waste my valuable energy, doing something that is extremely important to me, competing with the guy next door who's trying to cut out a massive root from his lawn with a blunt axe or trying to cut the grass when it's wet. (Yes, you've got a neighbor like that, you probably have one that plays drums as well, right!)

I find that when I have managed to actually create the image that I want, I can hold it there for quite a long period of time. I try to hold the image there as long as possible. The image is inside my head. Very clear, although the colors are not all that bright. I find that I can brighten up the picture and get the people and event to actually move, but I have to create a static picture first. I then add in the voices and sounds. That's the easy bit for me. I have to work hard on creating the pictures.

Is there any correlation between the amount of time you have the pictures held in your minds eye and the length of time it takes to accomplish a goal?

I was hoping nobody would ask me that one! This is something I have puzzled with over a long period of time. I am convinced there must be. I am sure it can even be put down to a law of physics. But I don't have a definite conclusion. Something I do know for certain, I never accomplish a goal until I have actually 'seen' it in my imagination. The other thing is the clearer I can 'see' it the quicker it happens. Sometimes things happen so quickly it literally frightens me!

Back to the old subject of failure. Is it true all successful people have failed? How many failures have you had?

In a way failure is my favorite subject because I feel I know so much about it. English novelist John Creasy got 753 rejection slips before he got his 564 books published. R.H. Macy failed seven times before his New York store caught on. Babe Ruth struck out 1,330 times, but he also hit 714 home runs. Heavy hitters who hit the most home runs always strike out a lot.

I got 137 rejection slips on one of my books. I have had numerous businesses collapse on me. (Really, knowing what I know now, I can see clearly that I came to the end of my program in each and every case) I have had various partners and I also have tried my hand at many different types of business. I have failed numerous times, that's why they now call me Mr Persistence. I just never, ever give up. Ever!

On the subject of hypnosis and deactivating the RAS how do we know when the RAS is deactivated and how do we know which is the level of ultra-consciousness that you talk about? If we don't reach a deep level are we wasting our time?

Good question. The most important thing is to relax prior to your visualizing. That state of 'ultra consciousness' would be felt by the fact that you were fully awake but feeling very relaxed. Your internal dialogue would have stopped. (You'd be wasting your time trying to reprogram, if you had the internal chatter still going on.) Milton Erickson, the world's greatest hypnotherapist discovered everyone would slip into the 'state' that suited them best. He also stated that some people would go into heavy trances and others preferred light trances, but he'd always be able to do good work, even with people in light trances. The main thing, was they relaxed in their own way.

Can one slip into the deactivated state by accident?

Yes and very simply too, under the right circumstances. It's happened to me on a number of occasions, luckily for me, on both I recognized them. The first time was when I was driving on a motorway on the way to Birmingham, in England. Luckily for me I noticed the altered state of consciousness. I read later that many motorway crashes were due to the fact the barrier posts in the middle of the road were a certain distance apart. At a certain speed, the lights of the autos coming in the opposite direction flash between the posts at just the right frequency to cause a hypnotic effect and deactivate the RAS. I'm convinced many people fall asleep on motorways and freeways, because of this phenomena.

The other time I was at a dinner party and I was

talking to a gentleman who had Parkinson's disease. He was talking to me in a very dreary monotone (although his conversation was interesting) and his right hand was shaking constantly because of the Parkinsons. This guy nearly put me right out, I only just managed to catch myself.

Is hypnosis dangerous? Is a deactivated RAS dangerous?

The answer to both questions is no, but I'd like to expand. What has been dangerous for you in the past, has been letting other people insert programs into your biocomputer, as and when they saw fit. If you take care to insert the exact programs into your biocomputer in accordance with the output you desire, it is far from dangerous. The most important aspect of the RAS is ensuring that you properly reactivate it after every visualization session.

Does deactivating the RAS get easier every time we do it?

You're just testing me, right?! Yes, of course it does. Like everything else you do, it becomes a program in your biocomputer. The more often you learn how to relax and deactivate the RAS, the biocomputer gets programmed to do it. Just like having lessons to drive a car or learning any other skill. In actual fact, many times, I just sit in my armchair and deactivate the RAS in literally a couple of seconds, I do this on many occasions, just before business meetings, to make sure I have the correct program in the biocomputer. I would certainly do it as well, if there was a task that I hadn't done before. I'd just drop the RAS, visualize myself doing the task, reactivate the RAS, then get on with it. What a tool! I hope that answers your question!

My name's Sandra; I've had an incredible weekend, I can't believe it! I want to know what words we can beef up our goals with?

That's a simple one and I often wonder why people don't beef up their goals instead of just accepting what they think they can get.

You can beef up your goals using words like, 'I accomplish my goal whilst having lots of fun', or 'I do it with ease', or 'I accomplish it with style and finesse', or 'I lead the good life while accomplishing this goal.'

You're absolutely right that most people program with the words: 'at whatever the cost' or 'regardless' and in the end they pay a higher price because that's what they programmed themselves with. Semantics are so important. You can also add, 'I remain being my own man' or in your case, 'woman'. You can add, 'and helping people at the same time' or whatever it is you would really like to happen. Does that answer your question?

Is your book 'Talk and Grow Rich' no longer valid now the biocomputer material is available?

No absolutely not! The 'Talk and Grow Rich' book is a complete philosophy in itself. The two books should be used to compliment one another. If you haven't already bought a copy, please do. I need the money! Next!

Getting back to persistence. I need help in that area. From what you've told us today I quit far to easily!

The secret of success is persistence. The secret of reprogramming the human biocomputer is persistence. If you don't keep putting the programs in you'll keep sliding down the snakes. No, you won't even collect $200 as you pass GO. Make a tape with this program on it. 'Press on. Nothing in the world can take the place of persistence. Talent will not; nothing is more common than unsuccessful individuals with talent. Genius will not; unrewarded genius is almost a proverb. Education will not; the world is full of educated derelicts. Persistence and determination alone are omnipotent. I will never give up. I will keep on keeping on. If it is to be, it is up to me. I use every rejection as a spur to further effort.'

As with all programs the secret is hundreds of hours listening in the auto as you drive. The rewards are living the lifestyle you desire, driving the auto of your choice, living where you want to live and doing what you want to do, when you want to do it. Make the program today. Today, not tomorrow!

Give us some examples of turning stumbling-blocks into stepping-stones!

You've just used one of my favorite expressions. Another one I like is turning lemons into lemonade.

Years ago I nearly went bust. I got inspired by Joe Karbo's, 'Lazy Mans Way to Riches' and I wanted a mail order product. I wrote a book called, 'Get out of Debt and into the Money' which sold over fifty thousand copies by mail order. (Soon that title's going to be re-released under the banner of 'Financial Kung Fu!') The book never made a lot of money, but it gave me a lot of credibility in the consultancy world, which did make me a lot of money! I am a great believer in programming the biocomputer to look for the seed of benefit in every disaster. Recently I was locked up in Australia for twelve days in the Immigration Detention Center, I'd overstayed my visa. I met a guy in there who had escaped from Vietnam with seventy-seven others. The outcome of that was that I wrote a very inspiring and motivating book entitled, 'Escape From Where I Am.' The point is that when I got locked up in the detention center, I deliberately programmed my biocomputer to make something happen. I was determined not to waste any time at all and that is all part of the story, I programmed my biocomputer to get the results. I maintain that there are opportunities everywhere, but you must program the biocomputer to let them come into your field of vision. That is one of the main functions of the RAS.

Will you tell us a few more of your funny verses, pleeeeze!

When you put it like that, how can I resist?

Bish Bosh, loads of dosh, get the deal, under the cosh!

He who climbs a tree and hollers, of wares he has to sell. Is bound to make more dollars, than he who whispers down a well!

Plod on, plod on, plod on! Plod ON, Plod ON, Plod ON!! PLOD ON, PLOD ON. PLOD ON!!!

There are many good reasons for living, and one's just entered my head. If a fellow can't live when he's living, how the hell can he live when he's dead! Next!

Can you give us another example of how the imagination can work for us?

I'd be delighted to. Let's imagine you were going on a very long trip in your Toyota Land Cruiser. Let's say that you'd never done such a long trip before and you'd be expecting all sorts of hazards because of all the varying terrains you'd be covering.

To put the program into the biocomputer for a successful trip you'd start visualizing the trip. As you started to visualize you 'saw' some snow falling, that would remind you to make sure you had a fully charged spare battery and a shovel to dig you out. You carried on visualizing and as you did you realized you'd got a flat tire. You'd check the spare to make sure that was OK and you'd also check the other tires.

You'd visualize crossing some pretty treacherous country so you'd make sure you had some flares, boxes of matches, survival rations, water and food supplies. You can do all this in your imagination before you leave the safety of your own home. So far we have only taken a few seconds. If we were doing this for real we'd spend considerable time visualizing every aspect of our trip to ensure our survival and our enjoyment.

In a business situation you can and must, do the same thing. You look at every aspect of your dealings and business building. That's what we have imaginations for. We are the only living creatures that can program our futures in advance. When you visualize, you really are getting a sneak preview of the future. Comprende!

Can you explain where the expression, "I saw it coming!" comes from?

Yes, indeed I can, in actual fact it's self-explanatory. Most people make the exclamation after they have had something nasty happen to themselves. They say, "I saw it coming!" and do you know what? They really did 'see' it coming. It was a complete visual picture in the biocomputer.

By using their imaginations they could have averted the catastrophe by creating mental images of the thing they really wanted to happen, but no one told them how.

If we keep inserting programs into our biocomputer, will we use up all the storage capacity and the biocomputer will not be able to process anything?

Don't you believe it! I doubt we have been using one percent of our capacity at the moment and I'm talking about people like Edison and Einstein and Margaret Thatcher! I have heard it said that in Russia they have programs and experiments going on whereby they teach children from an early age about twenty different languages; how to dance, sing, play the piano, as well as mathematics, computer skills and just about every other program you can think of, with no ill effect or side effects and no visible signs of using up the capacity in the biocomputer.

Quite honestly I don't think they have even started to scratch the surface yet. So keep programming for everything you specifically want. Do it now!

Does Emile Coue's formula still work?

I think you must be talking about, 'Every day in every way I get better and better.' It certainly does work and the sooner you get it down on tape and start inserting the program, the sooner it will work for you too. While you're at it, add another. 'I 'see' it, I am it: I 'see' it, I own it: I 'see' it , I do it,' I used to love playing around with lots of different programs, in actual fact I still do.

Can I use a Sony Walkman to listen to my goals on?

You mean you aren't already?

Can other people hold me back in my quest for wealth?

Yes, not only they can, they do. I love the story of the Mexican crabs. In Mexico, in the market place, there are huge baskets of crabs, to be seen everywhere. None of the crabs ever escape, despite the fact the baskets don't have lids. The reason why is simple. Everytime one of the crabs gets nearly to the top of the basket and starts to look around, his friends hang onto his legs and pull him back down again. People have the same habit of trying to, (either consciously or subconsciously or unconsciously) keep you at their level. The secret is to put programs into the biocomputer, without telling anyone, then leave them standing!

How can I hone-up my pictures?

One of the ways to hone-up your pictures is to treat your biocomputer like a TV screen. Turn knobs to adjust the brightness, push buttons to bring in close ups. Play around with dials to get the contrast. The biocomputer will do whatever you tell it to and you will find that it is very receptive to being treated in this manner. Does that answer your question?

Can we get back to dating beautiful women again? I want to know why I just can't ask the women that I really desire to date me? Many times I get right up close to the point of asking, then I change my mind.

Yes we can. I'm going to rename my biocomputer seminars 'How to Make a Million in Under Five Years, and Marry the Woman of Your Choice'!

You have a very strong program in your biocomputer that tells you that you can't date beautiful women. And you're wrong. It's your biocomputer program playing tricks on you. Let me tell you a story.

When I had my motorcycle shops I employed a secretary who was extremely beautiful. She was the cross between Elizabeth Taylor and Sophia Loren only younger. Everyone wanted to date her. At the same time I employed a truck driver, who was to say, at the very least, a rough diamond. I mean more rough, than diamond. (Male equivalent of the Pet Dragon!) He had goofy teeth, was overweight, he limped and he had zits. I mean he had zits! However, what this guy did have (And I know what you're thinking, but that's just your dirty biocomputer!) was a very good program in his biocomputer, he dated this girl for ages, he didn't marry her, but they did have a lot of fun together.

In all the time I knew this guy I never once saw him with anything else other than beautiful women. He didn't have a bad program in him, yet all the while, his friends were dating assorted Witches of the East, Pet Dragons and various versions of Battle Torn Sues.

You must not prejudge or pre-qualify who will or won't date you. You are a mere mortal. Your biocomputer, now you're really talking, will decide who and when and how, providing you put the right program in.

Most men program themselves for failure by saying, 'she'd never date me', over and over again, affirming something that is not true, but it will happen. They program in rejection before it even happens. They repel, instead of attracting the people, money and opportunities they really desire. Comprende!

I've got into the bad habit of telling people all my plans and goals before they come to fruition. They hardly ever do. I keep ending up with egg on my face. Any ideas?

Yes lots. You hit the nail on the head when you called it a bad habit. Bad habits are simply the results of bad programs. Input equals output. You really do have to stop telling people your goals and plans, because what you are doing is substituting talking, for actually doing it. I suggest the following program to be played over and over again, at least a mega zillion times!

'I show the world what I am going to do through

my actions. I tell no one of my plans unless they are actually helping me on a project. I tell them only on a need to know basis. I realize I have been dispensing my valuable energy and now I keep my lips sealed and start putting more energy into action and less into talking.'

If I go out to the bathroom, will you promise to stop talking until I get back? I don't want to miss a single thing!

"Yes, I think we'll break for coffee now anyway! Anyone want books, tapes or videos see Anita, Jody or Karen at the back."

During coffee breaks I always encourage people to talk to each other. As the day progresses I get them to talk to others they haven't spoken to before. I do everything I can to stimulate discussion between people who would not normally talk to each other. Many times, after coffee breaks, the atmosphere in the room is relaxed and the ideas start to flow again.

It is very important to realize that people learn from each other's questions. Many times one is too embarrassed to put their hand up and ask a question (Bad program) but someone else in the room broaches the subject. Many times questions have a habit of stimulating more questions about the same subject or spinning us all off on another tangent.

During the coffee breaks a lot of people confide in me, they ask all sorts of questions. Many times I am told how the questions and answers period has gelled it for many people. I find the questions always are very different from seminar to seminar but at the end of the day they always come back down to one thing, how can we make our biocomputers more and more effective and efficient, how can we reach our goals quicker and quicker?

I have noticed that quite a number of attendees never ask any questions within the auditorium but will always pull me to one side at the intervals. Many of the question sessions I have, go on for three or four, sometimes five hours, such is the thirst for knowledge.

"No jokes or stories now, time is catching up with us. Let's be having some questions!"

I think I must have a bad program, I am for ever trying to keep up with the Jones's, any ideas?

Yes lots. This is a very negative program, unfortunately millions of people have it and it gets them into all sorts of problems, like overdrafts, credit card problems and one, ultimately, the lack of self esteem. The program you need is: 'I do not spend beyond my means. If I require something or desire something I know the correct way to attain it, is make up a program for my biocomputer. I know that once I have correctly programmed my biocomputer I will receive the output that will lead me to my goals. I know with a correctly programmed biocomputer, the Jones's will be trying to keep up with me.' I hope that helps!

What are the main reasons why our new programs won't take?

There are only a very few reasons. I will list them in no special order, because they are all equally important.

1. You haven't deactivated the RAS when visualizing.
2. You are not really visualizing clearly or subjectively or both.
3. You are not listening to the left computer tape enough, literally hundreds of hours is required.
4. You haven't worded your goals semantically correct in the present tense.

5. You have a total incongruity between the two computers.

When can we expect output as a result of all our programming?

Good question. You have to keep going with the programming, most people give up far too prematurely. Everytime you play your tapes there is obviously an accumulative effect as the neurons all link together to form a program. I think you have to keep programming until you build a critical mass that overcomes the negative program, then you begin to feel the benefits of the new program.

I love the story of the old man in the railway station looking at a very old steam train that was trying to get up a head of steam. The boiler wasn't yet hot. He looked at his wife and said, "It'll never start!" The engineer kept stoking the boiler and all of a sudden the engine was belching out steam and smoke from everywhere, flywheels were whirring round, steam was hissing, pistons were belting back and forth. His wife looked at him and said with a smile, "What do you think now, honey?" to which he replied "It'll never stop!"

So it is with the biocomputer. Just get up a head of steam, keep putting the programs in, don't stop and very soon you'll be getting the output you need!

I know my problem is that I just keep stopping and I know I would be better off if I just kept going. What can I do?

Most people have a habit of taking the foot off the accelerator far to prematurely. The program you need is for diligence: 'I work really hard toward my goals. I work consistently and persistently and I don't keep stopping and starting. I keep going at my task because I can 'see' clearly in my minds eye what it is that I am trying to accomplish.'

You said that the minute we accomplish a goal the biocomputer says "Mission Accomplished". What does it do next?

Good question! It does exactly nothing. It sits around doing nothing, waiting for its next assignment. He puts his smoking jacket on, puts his feet up, has caramel cake and long refreshing glasses of iced coffee. This is the exact spot where most people slide down a snake back to zero, because they start running on old negative programs!

What you must do, every time you accomplish a goal, is set new ones. The moment you hand over new goals to the biocomputer he comes out of retirement and starts work immediately, you don't even have to pay him! This is the only way to move onward and upward! Next!

It almost embarrasses me to bring this up, but I feel I have to. Do you mean to tell us, that our relationships with women are affected by our biocomputer programs?

Absolutely. Are you sure we're not going over the same ground here. If you keep telling yourself, over and over again, 'She's too pretty for me,' or another favorite, 'I just can't 'see' her dating me,' or I bet you've run this program a few hundred times, 'I can hear her turning me down.' There are hundreds of programs that guys run over and over again in their biocomputers and that input has to become output. With programs like that in the biocomputer it would be an absolute impossibility to make an approach and ask the girl of your choice for a date. No way! That input has to be the output, the same as it is for any other behavior that you can think of.

I'd like some help with my kids. One of them in particular seems to give nothing but trouble. I even think he may be a little backward. Can you help?

I'll try, but having never met the kids I don't really know. A lot of kids seem like they're a problem, but really they're not.

Many times parents tell their kids not to do certain things. "Whatever you do don't kick the paint over," or another favorite is, "Whatever you do don't spill your milk on the clean tablecloth," or I'm sure you've used, "And whatever you do, don't come off your bike." When children hear statements like this, they have to actually do the thing in order to assimilate in their minds whatever it is that you've told them. Then you clip them around their ears and assume that it was their fault.

Lots of children don't feel good about themselves and there's quite a lot you can do to boost their self-confidence. I remember a story that Milton Erickson told. He was helping a little girl who lacked self-confidence. Erickson was in his eightieth year. The girl was nine. She was very shy and was not very competitive and lacked self-esteem. Milton suggested they play jacks together. Of course his hands were arthritic and he never managed to catch any jacks. The girl kept winning, but he kept trying to beat her. This was the first time in her life that she had ever won at anything. It boosted her confidence tremendously.

After a few weeks he suggested they go for a bicycle race. She was very reluctant but he persevered, in the end she agreed. Of course he was eighty years old and had great difficulty riding the bike. The nine year old won all the races, but Erickson kept trying to beat her. He had great fun! She won all the time, but again he tried very hard. This was the first time in the girls' life she had excelled at anything, she started to feel good about herself. Too many parents are too competitive with their children, what you have to do is encourage programs of self-esteem, competitiveness and self-reliance in the correct way.

How big do you think biocomputer technology can become?

Good question. I think we are just scratching the surface at present. What we really need is a substantial grant to enable us to do all the research that is required. We are so far behind the Russians currently, it isn't funny.

I'm hoping we can attract the attention of, maybe, a major computer company or an audio cassette tape company to come in with the dollars needed to get a research program up and running. We also need people, ideas, facilities, resources and guinea pigs to help with various projects. We know what has to be done, but it all costs time and money.

If the research dollars were available there is no telling where this could all end, or just how big it could be. What amazes me, is the amount of progress that we have actually made as a human-race with the diabolical programs that most of us have been running on.

Of course, as well as research and development, you have to actually manufacture books and tapes and videos, distribute products, put on seminars, disseminate the knowledge and attract favorable publicity. So we are also looking for help in these areas as well. I look forward to hearing from you!

I have heard that nothing succeeds like success!

I heard nothing sucks seeds like a budgerigar with no teeth! Next!

You mention many times that you have to actually create the pictures in the electrochemicals in the biocomputer, can you give us more detail on that!

Yes. Imagine when you take a photograph with a Polaroid camera, you can actually watch the film develop. First it's very blurred, then as the minutes go by it gradually develops and as the chemicals react the picture gets clearer and clearer. In the individual cells in the biocomputer you have electrochemicals. You actually have to implant proper pictures of what it is that you want to accomplish in those chemicals. If you just get blurred or fuzzy pictures all the time, when it comes time for your left computer to communicate with your right computer, it will have a difficult time trying to understand what those fuzzy pictures are. Your output will be negligible. On the other hand if you create concise and definitive pictures in those electrochemicals, when the two computers communicate with one another the left computer will understand exactly what those pictures are. Don't forget also that the right computer needs clear pictures to go about solving your problem anyway, in a totally different way to the left computer.

Is conventional computer technology leaving biocomputer technology behind?

Good question. I am afraid at the moment it is. But that will only be short lived. Most people who are using their biocomputers correctly at the moment are only doing so intuitively. The more this particular program is made available and people start to realize there is a very powerful way in which we can actually control the input into the biocomputer to ensure the output we desire, only then will things dramatically change for the better. People using biocomputer technology will make quantum leaps, daily!

Are people involved with computers likely to be able to pick up on this material quicker than the rest of us?

No, not really. I have noticed many computer programmers and people involved with computers do a tremendous amount of work with their left computers. I also have worked with many people in the computer field who have problems with relationships and attaining their goals. Many of them have great difficulty processing in pictures.

What would you like to see happen in the field of education with regards to biocomputer technology?

Education is a massive field. I would very much like to see schools teaching children more and more on how to think in pictures. Every lesson taught should be both verbal and visual. Schools should also be teaching children deep relaxation because this is the best method of learning quickly; below the threshold of consciousness and without the resistance of the intellect! There should be a lot taught on semantics as well as making sure children appreciate that input equals output. The old fashioned way of rote learning should be implemented all the time. It is exactly how the biocomputer operates. I seriously think this whole program should be taught in detail in every school throughout the world!

Would I be right in assuming that many times we inadvertently program an 'end' in quite the

inappropriate place. If so, can you give us some examples?

Yes, you are absolutely right. Many times we bring about our own demise, a little like the time I went to New York. I hadn't inserted the complete program, I came to the end of my program, before I had closed the deal.

You must take great pains to visualize beyond the point that you want to go. Otherwise you'll end up being disappointed. If you want to set up a retail shop it's no good just programming, 'I'll open my own retail business.' Many people open their own businesses, only to have them close down again two or three years later when the program runs out. You must program, 'Open the business, keep it expanding and profitable, keep the overheads low, get a wage out of it and then program in an EXIT route to allow you to be able to cash your chips in for your hard earned effort.(It pays to give considerable thought to what it is you want out of each and every business and deal that you get involved in, or you will find yourself continually sliding down snakes!) Most people end up going bust or walking away from their business. Only a small minority actually sell out or conclude a deal that is beneficial to themselves.

Back to visualization. I know how important it is, but try as I can I can't think in pictures. Pleeeeze help!

You can think in pictures, everyone can. Do you dream. Yes, you do right! In clear full color, right!

What I want you to do is this. In the morning just as you're waking, you're probably dreaming right then, this is when we dream most, not only that but your RAS is deactivated as well. At this moment switch your dreams into your visualizing, I guarantee that with a little practice you will be able to slip into your visualizations very comfortably. Everyone has to find what works for them, but visualize you can, and visualize you must!

Will it benefit my children if I read them bedside stories?

Yes and I think it is extremely beneficial if you read adventure stories and tales of self-reliance, winning and goal accomplishment. You may find your children love biographies of famous people.

Don't forget as the child drifts off, their RAS will become deactivated so they will become particularly susceptible to everything you tell them. You may even want to make up your own 'success' stories. You can read for a good ten or twenty minutes after the child is asleep, all to good effect.

All I think about, all the time, is buxom blondes, what should I do?

Take plenty of cold showers! Next!

I can see that we need to program when our energy level is high and when we can actually feel we have the tenth of a volt in our biocomputer and we are not drained. What can we do to recharge our batteries?

Good question! Many things will recharge your batteries and a lot depends on the individual. First let's have a look at the things that drain the batteries in the first place. Negativity is what drains you more than anything. I would do everything I could to cut myself off from the negative influences of other people, no matter who they were. Also make a point not to let negative emotions drain you from within. If you find that fear, jealousy, hatred, revenge, greed, superstition and anger are part of your programs you should make up tapes to eliminate them.

The positive emotions are desire, love, faith, sex, romance, enthusiasm and hope. You should make up tapes to encourage these.

You will also find that some energetic activity will recharge your batteries. You should try swimming, squash, jogging. Love-making works wonders for a lot of people! You should try it sometime! Find an activity that gets you associating with positive people, who can give you feedback and input and at the same time you can reciprocate. One of the greatest things to boost your power will be associating with people who have good programs in their biocomputers!

Who gave you the title, 'World Leader in Human Biocomputer Technology'?
I did! Next!

What is the difference between visualization and hallucination?
Good question! A visualization is a picture that we create inside our heads. An hallucination is a three dimensional image that we project outside our heads.

Many children can hallucinate very easily and many create playmates or men from outer-space. To them they appear very real. The problem has come about because teachers and parents try to get children to stop all this mental activity and in doing so curtail the activities of the right computer. Of course there is only a small danger that a child may hallucinate that they can fly or jump off buildings but this is small concern compared to trying to live a happy and successful life on only one computer. (Which I would say was practically impossible).

My name's Wayne, I'm a school teacher, I'm absolutely delighted with what I've learned this weekend. What else can you tell us about children at school especially with regards to spelling?

Nice to hear you talk like that! I have spoken to many teachers and most of them are very negative about changing their ways because of the powerful programs they have in their biocomputers. The problem with having powerful programs, is that it does not necessarily make them right. To answer your question; to many children spelling is a visual process. (Many children can actually 'see' the words up on their mental screens) To access the visual neurons in the biocomputer you have to look upwards. In many spelling tests at school, the children are told to keep their eyes down so they can't cheat. Unfortunately that stops them accessing visual material that is lodged in their biocomputers. One of the quickest ways to get children to learn how to spell, is to get them to write the words up on a black board that is a little out of reach. They are then forced to look upwards and they can access the visual mode easily.

This weekend has tied up so many loose ends for me all I wanted to say was thank you!

Thank you! Next!

Is it true people collapse businesses for the strangest reasons?

Yes I have seen people collapse businesses because their programs said, "There's no way my partner has earned his share of this business, I'll collapse it." Someone confided in me that he collapsed a business because his partner danced with his girl friend at a dance; this was his way of getting even. It was programmed. He was so upset by the experience he 'saw' it coming. Another eminently successful business man walked out on a business because it had already accomplished everything he had wanted it to and he didn't have any other goals. He slipped down a snake every quickly. As I mentioned before there are thousands of people out there who have attained success at one time or another but are now janitors, machine minders or mechanics. They've gone back to running on programs they had inserted years ago. You have to keep inserting new programs if you want to stay at the top!

If you were in Amway, what would you do to ensure you had the correct program in your biocomputer?

I would do lots. I would ensure that I played over and over again, a tape affirming that I am a Direct Distributor or a Diamond or whatever the particular level you are trying to attain. I would visualize very clearly that I was having meetings every day and actually sponsoring distributors as a result of those meetings. I would 'see' in detail prospects signing application forms, handing over their checks and accepting their starter kits. I would also visualize in detail, working in depth with those people to help them sponsor other distributors. I would visualize every aspect of growing my business. I would 'see' myself up on stage and actually hear the music playing that I wanted played when I became a Diamond. I would put a complete program into my biocomputer in pictures to give me an automatic track to run on. If you are at 12% it's only because that's exactly where you 'see' yourself. I have worked with lots of Diamonds who are stuck at Diamond level because they haven't put a Double Diamond program into their biocomputer. It sounds simple. It is!

I am thinking of switching careers, any suggestions?

Plenty. You should be visualizing right now, well in advance of any career change. You should actually 'see' yourself being a success in your new career. You can save yourself having to go through a massive learning curve by playing out all the roles and activities of your new post.

Quite a few successful entrepreneurs have made tremendous switches in their businesses; Howard Hughes and Aristotle Onassis to mention two. They did this by spending considerable time visualizing events before they happened.

You will considerably reduce the stress of a career change if you use your imagination. That's what it's for!

Does it matter if we are left brained or right brained?

It doesn't matter if you're left brained or right brained, so long as you're not hair-brained! The whole idea is to use both the left and right computer, the words and the pictures equally.

What are DT's?

Delirium Tremens are usually suffered by alcoholics who live rough on the street.

What happens is that because of the lack of sleep and because of interrupted sleep, the waking and dreaming states get out of phase. When you see someone suffering from DT's in the street, he probably is seeing Zulu Warriors and Bogey men, because he is in the dreaming state, with his eyes open. The cause of DT's has more to do with improper sleep than with alcohol, that's why it's the alcoholics who sleep on park benches, under railway arches and in shop doorways who suffer the problem more than alcoholics who are in full time employment and have homes to go to.

I had an experience when I worked a conference for four days at the Sydney Convention Centre and I hardly got any sleep. On the fourth day I nearly got run down by a bus in the auditorium, trouble was no one else saw it!

In your experience as a business consultant, what are the main problems business people are confronted with and why do so many businesses go down the tubes?

Good question, you obviously know I love consultancy work. One of the main reasons for going down the tubes is not getting into action quick enough when problems arise. In consultancy I would say nine times out of ten the consultants are called in too late. What we normally find, is a business that got into problems maybe twelve or eighteen months previously and the owners didn't recognize it or just plain had their heads in the sand.

One of the big problems is runaway overheads. This is an area that we always slash. We look at management and profit margins and ways of increasing turnover. We always find ways of pacing the creditors, make arrangements whereby they are paid off over a period of time.

One of your greatest assets is your biocomputer. You can visualize things in advance, before they actually happen. Remember Noah didn't wait for the rains, before he started to build the ark. I would suggest that every business-person, should, instead of rushing off to bed, spend a little time visualizing the business in advance, before problems arise. You can of course program the biocomputer to solve business problems. The problem most people have with that, is that because they leave it so late before they start to program their biocomputer, they are not in the right state of mind to be able to control their own input because they get into the habit of spending all their time worrying!

What has been your biggest disappointment with regards to biocomputer technology?

That's an easy one! Despite the tremendous advances in brain research made possible by the electron microscope and the discovery of the RAS, the fact that we really do know how to program our biocomputers for success, the discoveries have not been well promoted at all. My big disappointment is that many of these advances have been known for many years and are still not being taught in schools.

To keep teaching children as though they only have one computer is nothing short of a crime.

With every one of my goals I always have hundreds of little things stopping me actually doing them. Any ideas?

Yes! Only One! You have to develop a mind like a steel trap. We all have thousands of things going on in our lives, most of them problems. We use those thousands of excuses for not getting the job done. All we really need is only one reason to get the job done and that's the reason we relentlessly program into our biocomputers.

You really do have to blank your mind off to everything that is going on around you. I have found that particularly so, in the case of writing. I could write letters, make phone calls, drive here, run errands, go to the beach, and a million and one things, other than write. As I'm writing this, it's a beautiful day outside, I live on the beach, (There's a thousand distractions on the beach alone, most of them are little brown girls!) but stopping what I'm doing won't get the job done. I'm running on a program that allows me to work and feel good about it and complete the task. I'll worry about all the thousands of distractions when the book is finished. They'll still be there. (I sure hope they are, anyway!) Next!

Do you still believe in stopping the internal dialogue as much as you used to?

Very much so. I think it is practically impossible for someone to start reprogramming properly until they have learnt how to quieten the biocomputer.

My book 'Talk and Grow Rich' goes into great depth about how to stop the internal dialogue and I suggest anyone who has a problem with skull chatter, gets a copy or forever holds their peace!

What are your thoughts about the holographic brain? Some say that there is a comparison between a hologram and visualization?

Over the years, man has used many examples as models to try to show more clearly how the brain works. In the early days it was compared to a steam engine, then later a telephone switch board, after that came cybernetics and feedback, then the hologram.

Interestingly enough I have a massive investment in the hologram industry and my partner Bruce Snyder, founded the commercial side of the industry in the United Kingdom and made himself and quite a few others millionaires in the process.

The one point that I would make about holograms is they are exactly the way we should visualize, that is three dimensionally in color, just like the real thing.

What are the major problems associated with reprogramming the right computer?

There are a number of problem areas and I will list them in no particular order.

1. Through lack of use, the faculty has become dormant.
2. The individual is trying to reprogram the right computer when the left computer is firing.
3. Because it is difficult to concentrate, because of noise or some other outside stimuli.
4. Because the results don't come immediately, the individual may give up too quickly.
5. It wasn't realized the pictures actually had to be created in the electrochemicals.
6. Using objective not subjective visualization.
7. Not programming with the RAS deactivated.
8. Only visualizing the immediate goal and not going far enough into the future.

The biocomputer seminar has ended, your work has just begun. It begins with making up two tapes and playing those tapes over and over again.

Develop those tapes and programs over the days and the weeks and the years and you'll never look back.

If you find what I have shown you, makes you a lot of money, don't forget my ten percent to go to my numbered account in Zurich!

With that I'm going to leave, I have enjoyed talking with you immensely, who knows, we may meet again, in the very near future, maybe we'll even play a game of snakes and ladders together! Before I go I want to leave you with one final thought: **IF INPUT EQUALS OUTPUT, YOU HAVE NO ONE TO BLAME BUT YOURSELF!**

IF INPUT EQUALS OUTPUT, YOU HAVE NO ONE TO ACKNOWLEDGE BUT YOURSELF!

Afterwarning

One of the most amazing facts about Milton Erickson, is that throughout his very long career as a hypnotherapist, there wasn't a single person that he was unable to hypnotize.

Of course you realize that everyone has a RAS and it's only by relaxing someone that you deactivate the RAS and can insert programs into the subject's biocomputer. If someone wants to fight against you, of course it would be very difficult indeed for you to hypnotize them against their will.

A new patient of Milton Erickson's called to see him, he wanted to be cured of some ailment or the other. He emphatically told Milton that his problem was, of course, that he couldn't be hypnotized. Milton said he would do his very best anyway and started to work with the client. Of course Milton failed because of the clients' resistance, but Milton suggested that he stay for the rest of the day. During the course of the day he tried many times between other patients and of course the gentleman just could not be hypnotized. Milton tried every trick in the book, he really appeared to put himself out.

At the end of the day, fairly late in the evening, Milton advised the fellow that he was sorry that he'd failed but he really did give it his best shot. With that, he helped the client on with his coat, shook his hand heartily and walked him out the front door. Milton walked the client to the gate and shook his hand and apologized one more time and the client said that he understood. However, just as the client walked out of the front gate, Milton in a very slow monotone voice, told the client that he could now go into a deep trance and could come back inside the house for therapy, which the client dutifully did. What had happened of course was that all day long the client had been resisting Miltons attempts to hypnotize him. At the end of the day, just as he walked out the front gate he relaxed and dropped all his defense mechanisms.

The point of the story is this. I just want to give you one final reminder of what this program is all about!

It's imperative that you relax and visualize the future as you desire it. You must make up those tapes and listen to them. More important than just listening to your tapes, is that you actually create pictures in the electrochemicals in your biocomputer, create a permanent track for yourself to run on. Remember also, that we bring about our own demise by not visualizing far enough into the future. One final time, for good measure, input equals output!

I recall having one of my famous skull sessions, over two decades ago, with another entrepreneur. The subject, would you believe, was, what was the secret to becoming successful?

Both of us agreed to keep brainstorming the subject until we had conclusive proof that we had the correct answer. We came at the problem from every conceivable angle for literally hours on end until we had exhausted the subject.

We came up with such things as operating location, products, supply, demand, product awareness, distribution, so on and so forth. We went over marketing, money, manpower, margin, merchandising.

The final conclusion that we came up with was that it's all in the mind, and it's something I've never moved away from, from that day to this. Learn it sooner rather than later. Life is a do-it-yourself project! Stop doing it to yourself. Start putting some programs into your biocomputer that will take you exactly where you want to go. We are all ordinary people. Our mission is to do extraordinary things! If not you, who? If not now, when?

A PERSONAL MESSAGE FROM THE AUTHOR

Dear Reader,

I hope that you have enjoyed reading this book as much as I enjoyed writing it. However, as I always strive to be the best I possibly can be, I would appreciate your feedback on the information contained in this book.

In return I will keep you in touch with news of my seminars, new books and tapes and fabulous business opportunities which pass over my desk.

You can write to me at:

Apprentice Millionaires Club
BCM Box 8061
London WC1N 3XX

Positively and Profitably
Ron G. Holland

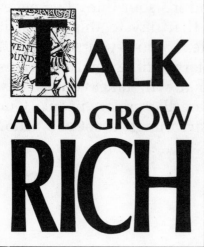